Romantic geographies

MANCHESTER
UNIVERSITY PRESS

Exploring Travel

Series editors: Sara Mills and Jill LeBihan

Exploring Travel is a publishing initiative which makes accessible travel writing which may be out of print or difficult to obtain. Travel literature currently has enormous popular appeal, and there is widespread academic interest from a number of fields, including anthropology, colonial and post-colonial discourse theory, literary theory, history, geography and women's studies.

The series has two main aims. The first is to make available a number of key, edited texts, which will be invaluable to both the academic and general reader. The texts will be edited by scholars from a range of disciplines, and a full introduction to each edition will aim to set it within its socio-cultural context, and explain its literary and historical importance. The second aim of the series is to make available monographs and collections of critical essays on the analysis of travel writing. In this way, the *Exploring Travel* series aims to broaden perspective on travel writing and the theoretical models used for its analysis.

Already published:

Tracey Jean Boisseau *Sultan to sultan: adventures among the Masai and other tribes of East Africa, by M. French-Sheldon, 'Bébé Bwana'*
Simon Gikandi *Uganda's Katikiro in England by Ham Mukasa*
Neil L. Whitehead *The discoverie of the large, rich and bewtiful empyre of Guiana, by Sir Walter Ralegh*

Forthcoming titles:

Sara Mills and Shirley Foster *Women's travel writing: an anthology*
Sara Mills and Indira Ghose *Wanderings of a pilgrim in search of the picturesque by Fanny Parks*

Romantic geographies

Discourses of travel 1775–1844

Edited by

Amanda Gilroy

Manchester University Press

Manchester and New York

distributed exclusively in the USA by St. Martin's Press

Published by Manchester University Press
Oxford Road, Manchester M13 9NR, UK
and Room 400, 175 Fifth Avenue, New York, NY 10010, USA
http://www.man.ac.uk/mup

Distributed exclusively in the USA by
St. Martin's Press, Inc., 175 Fifth Avenue, New York,
NY 10010, USA

Distributed exclusively in Canada by
UBC Press, University of British Columbia, 6344 Memorial Road,
Vancouver, BC, Canada V6T 1Z2

British Library Cataloguing-in-Publication Data
A catalogue record for this book is available from the British Library

Library of Congress Cataloging-in-Publication Data applied for

ISBN 0 7190 5576 8 *hardback*
      0 7190 5785 X *paperback*

First published 2000

06 05 04 03 02 01 00   10 9 8 7 6 5 4 3 2 1

Typeset in Adobe Garamond by Carnegie Publishing, Lancaster
Printed in Great Britain by Bell & Bain Ltd, Glasgow

Contents

Contents

Figures

Acknowledgements

I wish to thank the Rudolf Agricola Research Institute at the University of Groningen, which funded research and conference visits related to this project. I have benefited from the comments of the Press's readers, and thank editor Matthew Frost for his support and good humour. My greatest debt is to the contributors, who have stayed with this book on its long journey to publication and who have provided encouragement, friendship and intellectual insights. I especially thank series editor Sara Mills for her unstinting faith in this project, Clare Brant for her advice (and her postcards), and Wil Verhoeven for, amongst other things, his editorial expertise.

In memory of Gerry Gilroy (1921–1997)

Notes on contributors

Clare Brant is Lecturer in English at King's College London. She is the co-editor, with Diane Purkiss, of *Women, Texts and Histories 1575–1760* (1992). She has published various articles on eighteenth-century letters and is currently writing a major study of a wide range of epistolary writings entitled *Eighteenth-Century Letters and British Culture*.

Chloe Chard works on imaginative geography, the discourses of travel, and eighteenth-century aesthetic theory and art criticism, and she lectures at Wimbledon School of Art. She has co-edited, with Helen Langdon, *Transports: Travel, Pleasure and Imaginative Geography, 1600–1830* (1996), and is the author of *Pleasure and Guilt on the Grand Tour* (1999).

Amanda Gilroy teaches eighteenth-century and Romantic literature and feminist theory at the University of Groningen. She has published articles on women's writing of the Romantic period, and is co-editor, with Keith Hanley, of *Joanna Baillie: A Selection of Poems and Plays* (forthcoming). With W. M. Verhoeven, she has edited Gilbert Imlay's *The Emigrants* (1998), and *Epistolary Histories: Letters, Fiction, Culture* (forthcoming).

Keith Hanley is Senior Lecturer in English and Director of the Wordsworth Centre at Lancaster University. He has published many essays on nineteenth-century literature, edited critical editions of Meredith (1993) and Landor (1981), co-edited several collections of critical essays, including *Revolution and English Romanticism: Politics and Rhetoric* (1990) and *Romantic Revisions* (1992), and is the author of the *Annotated Critical Bibliography of William Wordsworth* (1995).

Chris Jones is Senior Lecturer in English at the University of Wales, Bangor. He is co-editor of two volumes of discursive prose, *The Romantic Age in Prose* (1980) and *The Victorian Age in Prose* (1988), and author of *Radical Sensibility: Literature and Ideas in the 1790s* (1993).

Beth Dolan Kautz is Professor of English at the University of Missouri, Kansas City. She has published on gender and medical discourses, and is working on a book-length study of health and travel in the nineteenth century.

Jacqueline M. Labbe is a lecturer in Romantic and Victorian literature at the University of Sheffield. Her articles have appeared in *Genre* and *The Wordsworth Circle*. Her most recent work is *Romantic Visualities: Landscape, Gender and Romanticism* (1998). She is currently working on the cultural significance of the romance, 1770–1830.

Nigel Leask is a lecturer at Cambridge University and Director of Studies in English at Queens' College. He is the author of two books, *The Politics of Imagination in Coleridge's Critical Thought* (1988) and *British Romantic Writers and the East: Anxieties of Empire* (1992), as well as numerous articles. He is working on a study of *Romantic Ethnographies*.

Dorothy McMillan (formerly Porter) lectures in English literature at the University of Glasgow. She has edited George Douglas Brown's *The House with the Green Shutters* and Elizabeth Barrett Browning's *Sonnets from the Portuguese*. She has published variously on Scottish and women's writing and is joint editor with Douglas Gifford of *A History of Scottish Women's Writing* (1997).

Saree Samir Makdisi is Professor of English and comparative literature at the University of Chicago. He has published essays on imperialism, and a book, *Romantic Imperialism: Universal Empire and the Culture of Modernity* (1998). He is currently preparing a study of Blake.

Sara Mills is Professor in the School of Cultural Studies at Sheffield Hallam University. She has published many articles on gender and linguistics and on women's travel writing. She is the author of *Discourses of Difference: An Analysis of Women's Travel Writing and Colonialism* (1991), *Feminist Stylistics* (1995), and co-author, with Lynne Pearce, Sue Spaull and Elaine Millard, of *Feminist Readings/Feminists Reading* (1989). She is currently editing, with Shirley Foster, an anthology of women's travel writing and is series editor for the *Exploring Travel* series, with Manchester University Press.

Jeanne Moskal is Professor of English at the University of North Carolina at Chapel Hill. She has published several articles on women travel writers of the Romantic period, and a book entitled *Blake, Ethics, and Forgiveness* (1994). She is currently completing a book-length study about women romantic travellers.

Jane Stabler has taught in the English departments of Glasgow and St Andrews Universities and is now Lecturer in English at the University of Dundee. She has published several articles on Byron and the Romantic period and is one of the editors of the journal *Romanticism*. She is working on a *Byron Critical Reader*, a study of transitions in English Romantic poetry, and a study of Byron's modernity.

W. M. Verhoeven is Reader in English and Chair of the American Studies Programme at the University of Groningen. He has edited several collections of critical essays, including *Rewriting the Dream: Reflections on the Changing American Literary Canon* (1992), *James Fenimore Cooper: New Historical and Literary Contexts* (1993), and, with A. Robert Lee, *Making America/Making American Literature* (1996). With Amanda Gilroy, he has edited two collections on epistolary writings as well as Gilbert Imlay's *The Emigrants* (1998). He is working on a study of transatlantic revolutionary writings of the Romantic period.

Introduction

Amanda Gilroy

In 1799 the conservative novelist Jane West warned against those trans-
gressions of gender, genre, and patriarchal privilege that were endemic to
the tales of the times:

> the title of a work no longer announces its intention: books of travels
> are converted into vehicles of politics and systems of legislation.
> Female letter-writers teach us the arcana of government, and
> obliquely vindicate ... manners and actions at which female delicacy
> should blush ... Tracts on education subvert every principle of filial
> reverence ... the novel ... is converted into an offensive weapon. [1]

Of the genres West mentions, travel writing in the Romantic period emerges
as perhaps the most capacious cultural holdall, a hybrid discourse that
traversed the disciplinary boundaries of politics, letter-writing, education,
medicine, aesthetics, and economics. The archaeological and anthropological research that was part of Britain's colonial project found its form in
travel writing; such genre crossings are acknowledged in the preface to
naturalist Anders Sparrman's account of Cook's second voyage: 'every
authentic and well-written book of voyages and travels is, in fact, a treatise
of experimental philosophy'. [2] Late eighteenth- and early nineteenth-century
travellers went to war zones and the imperial frontiers; they reported on
hotels and health spas; their concerns included ethnography and natural
history. Their journeys sometimes took them into the realm of the sublime,
provoking psychological and even physiological traumas. Whether undertaking the Grand Tour of Europe or travelling to the more remote 'contact
zones of America, North Africa, and the South Seas', [3] travellers often
sought to cross more than national boundaries. Sometimes the circulating
discourses of travel secured self-identity and reaffirmed existing convictions
of cultural superiority for the authors and readers of travel accounts, but
the experience of geographic displacement also helped Romantic-era writers
to renegotiate the cultural verities of 'home'. The disturbances of travel
could destabilise the boundaries of national, racial, gender and class affiliation, thus enacting the disciplinary miscegenation that defined the
mapping of geographical space. [4]

The period designated as 'Romantic' in this book, that is, the years between 1775 and 1844,[5] was a restless period in British cultural history, which witnessed the French Revolution, the Napoleonic and American wars, industrialisation, urbanisation, the growth of dissenting religions and the expansion of the British Empire. Men and women experienced a dislocation of traditional social roles at the same time as the parameters of travel began to shift. The period marked a particular phase in the history of travel, between the decline of the traditional Grand Tour, undertaken by British gentlemen 'for the purposes of self-cultivation and the reaffirmation of a common civilised heritage',[6] and the advent of rail travel in the 1840s, which made possible the growth of mass tourism in the modern sense of the word (the first recorded usage of the the word 'tourist' dates from the 1780s).[7] The rage for travel instigated by the reopening of the Continent in 1815 pursued an itinerary congruent with Romantic sensibilities rather than the classicist/masculinist agenda of the Grand Tour. Travel seemed to offer access to imaginary spaces of personal liberation and medicine for the troubled mind. Elizabeth Bohls points out that foreign destinations were rivalled by domestic sites, especially the Lake District and Scotland during the Napoleonic wars and as 'Travel within England became more practicable during the last decades of the [eighteenth] century with better carriage design, road-building, inns, and other services'.[8] Walking tours also gained popularity: walking emerged as a positive cultural practice at the end of the eighteenth century as a way of both moving through and knowing a world that was changing through enclosure and industrialisation.[9] Travel writers also registered ecological concerns, as in William Wordsworth's comment that the most celebrated sites in the Lake District had been quickly 'defaced' by the touristic 'intrusion'; ironically, travel texts promoted precisely the activity that contributed to land erosion and clearance.[10]

Various hot zones also captured the cultural imaginary, especially in the wake of Captain Cook's three great voyages of discovery (1768–80). The work of naturalists like Johann Forster and Anders Sparrman, and the writing and paintings of Sir William Hodges, are worth exploring for they expose the contours of the conflicting ethnological discourses that framed European fascination with the exotic topography and racial others of the South Seas. European travellers often used discourses of gender to organise their perceptions of race. As Harriet Guest has shown, in William Hodges's paintings of Tahiti the shifting boundaries of the exotic and the erotic place the non-European other in a complex relation of identity and difference to Western femininity.[11] Just as the late eighteenth-century growth in tourism focused on the collection of curiosities and mementoes, or souvenirs, so were representations of the exotic transported across the world, finding their way, for example, into William Thomson's account of northern European women dancers which, as Clare Brant notes in her chapter below, aligns them not only with Indian and Russian dancers but with the South Sea females who wiggle across 'the plates of Captain Cook's Voyage'. Dorothy Wordsworth invokes Cook's prints in her description of a pleasure-house at the falls of the Clyde in Scotland, and imports imperial imagery from Africa, America, and the Pacific to describe the 'savage' Highlanders of 'Britain's own internally colonized Celtic backyard'. [12] In other words, England's conflicted commerce with Scotland and with Ireland to some extent replicates the contours of economic and imaginative exploitation found in England's dealings with Asia, Africa, and the Caribbean. Postcolonial theories, especially Homi K. Bhabha's theory of colonial 'hybridity' and Mary Louise Pratt's cultural lexicon of the 'contact zone', 'transculturation' and 'anti-conquest', can help us to discern the complicated transports of imperial ideologies and discourses and the ways in which they shape exotic and domestic sites. [13]

The cultural specificity of travel literature invites an explicitly materialist criticism that reflects on the interactions of gender, class, national identity, and ethnicity. The chapters in this collection offer important contributions to the concern with cultural historicisation that is central to current Romantic studies; they explore issues of cultural power using the insights of feminist and postcolonial theories that are reshaping the map of Romanticism. They range far beyond the six male poets who have traditionally dominated Romantic studies, in favour of other previously occluded genres and voices, especially women writers such as Mariana Starke, Mary Shelley, Mary Wollstonecraft, Helen Maria Williams, Ann Radcliffe, and Priscilla Wakefield, to name only those most extensively discussed in the present volume. Most significantly, the collection engages in materialist terms with the desire to extend the boundaries of Romanticism, signalled by the recent critical favour extended to terms like boundary, margin, position, site, place, space, and by the spatial metaphors that have informed recent conferences entitled 'Placing and Displacing Romanticism' and 'Romantic Crossings', and books such as *At the Limits of Romanticism* and *Beyond Romanticism*. [14] As Favret and Watson put it,

> in the collective enterprise that constitutes Romanticism in general, and this anthology [*At the Limits of Romanticism*] in particular, we discover that, in Don Bialostosky's words, our 'development ... has taken us places we did not expect to go, put us in the company of people we did not expect to encounter, and confronted us with issues we did not expect to address'. [15]

This description of the current state of Romantic studies depends on the metaphor of travel. I hope that the present book will go some way towards specifying these metaphorical discourses, that is, giving them a material location in romantic culture, demonstrating that 'a place on the map ... is ... also a locatable place in history'.[16]

An emphasis on the situated nature of experience and of political critique, what Adrienne Rich calls 'the politics of location', is a defining feature of critical writing on Romantic travel, as well as of many of the primary texts themselves (as both explicit comment and as a site of occlusion). Though travel became more accessible and more affordable during the period – Romantic tourists were not quite so grand as their predecessors – nevertheless, the prerequisite of means, leisure, and education continued to limit the activities of travel and travel writing to a comparative elite. In other words, a social gap remained between the observing, travelling subjects and the inhabitants of the terrains through which they passed – those inhabitants, especially rural labourers, who are sometimes idealised and sometimes elided from written accounts (labourers are frequently not labouring, for example, but simply adorning the landscape). Those who worked on the land viewed it rather differently from those who contemplated the land(scape), a difference exposed in Fanny Burney's *The Wanderer*, in which we learn that 'the wide spreading beauties of the landscape ... charm only the enlightened rambler, or affluent possessor. Those who toil, heed them not'.[17] Burney's heroine, Juliet, for whom travel entails displacement and alienation, rather than the confirmation of identity, notes how much depends upon the place from which one is looking (and speaking):

> Juliet now, herself an inhabitant of the cottage, which, hitherto, she had only beheld in perspective, smiled, yet sighed at her mistake, in having considered shepherds and peasants as objects of envy. O ye, she cried, who view them through your imaginations! were ye to toil with them but one week! to rise as they rise, feed as they feed, and work as they work! like mine, then, your eyes would open; you would no longer judge of their pleasures and luxuries, by those of which they are the instruments for yourselves![18]

Aesthetic discourse was precisely calibrated in terms of class and gender and privileged the 'perspective' of 'the enlightened rambler, or affluent possessor'. An important category of late eighteenth-century aesthetics was the picturesque. The picturesque viewer's contemplation of nature was unhampered by specialised knowledge or attention to detail; in Sir Joshua Reynolds's formulation, the painter – and, by extension, the contemplator of natural scenes – corrects nature and deletes disruptive contingent details. As John Barrell observes, the subject surveyed 'the natural' with 'pure unmediated vision' and this natural picturesque was 'devoid of ethical, political, or sentimental meanings'; the picturesque viewer is thus aligned with the 'transcendent viewing-position which had through the eighteenth century been regarded as the perquisite of the gentleman'. [19] The paradigm of disinterested contemplation masked the idea of appropriation which linked the discourses of gardening, painting, and looking at landscape. Moreover, the claims of the autonomous subject 'can be converted from fantasy into reality only by denying the relational character of subjectivity and by relegating other viewpoints – different subjectivities – to invisible, subordinate, or competing positions'. [20] Elizabeth Bohls demonstrates that the discourse of disinterested disembodiment that anchored mainstream aesthetic theory was one of the 'universalizing vocabularies' that mediated the relations between imperial expansion, the birth of a modern British nation and the making of its ruling class. In particular, travellers took the vocabulary of the picturesque with them to England's colonial frontiers. The aesthetic discourses that structured descriptions of space and place found their 'figures of abjection in 'the laboring classes, in non-Europeans ... and ... in the feminine' – these are the 'others', the margins, against which was defined the property-owning 'man of taste' at the centre of the British Empire. [21] These hegemonic discourses, however, were unable to contain all elements of subversion and were disrupted in various ways. For example, the East sometimes emerges as resistant to its construction and consumption by the West: the empire writes back quite spectacularly in the case of the subversive subaltern discussed by Nigel Leask in his essay in this volume. Women writers challenged the assumptions of aesthetic discourse, especially in their valorisation of the detail, [22] and they critiqued and revised Burke's model of the sublime (as well as the categories of the picturesque and the beautiful). Thus Anne K. Mellor argues, for example, that women Romantic writers domesticated the sublime, and invested their landscape descriptions with 'an ethic of care'. [23]

If women revised asesthetic discourse, they did not, however, have the same latitude to wander as men: 'In many societies being feminine has been defined as sticking close to home. Masculinity, by contrast, has been the passport for travel.' [24] While men have textualised the experiences of mobility, women have stayed at home and articulated the discourse of absence. Although women certainly travelled in increasing numbers and produced some of the most significant travel texts of the period, they had to negotiate with the normative assumption that the travel writer was male and with the symbolic association of woman and home, an association that was increasingly valorised at this particular historical juncture and which engendered particularly 'feminine' ways of seeing. The influential conservative writer Hannah More thought that woman was best suited to seeing the world 'from a little elevation in her own garden, whence she makes an exact survey of home scenes'. [25] An important consideration for many women was how they could operate in the public sphere of travel and writing and yet still preserve their association with the private sphere. They might strategically exile masculine interests and authorities to the footnotes, as Lady Morgan does in her travel book *France* (1817), or authorise their political commentary in terms of acceptable feminine sensibility, so that politics becomes, as Helen Maria Williams puts it, 'an affair of the heart'. Gender, of course, is always imbricated in other discourses of difference: as Jeanne Moskal points out, one of the challenges for present-day critics is to confront the nationalistic or racial content of women's writing, as well as to examine, as Sara Mills has done in relation to the Victorian period, [26] the complex connections between discourses of femininity and imperialism in Romantic women's travel writing.

The insight that travel functions as one of the 'technologies of gender', a crucial discourse in the social construction of masculinities as well as femininities, informs many of the chapters in this volume, and is the central concern of Parts I and III (see also Jones and Chard in Part II). The chapters in Part I explore the socio-political implications of particular ways of looking at landscape. In the first chapter, Sara Mills takes up the question of a woman writer's revision of the prospect view, focusing specifically on gendered relations to the site of the sublime. Mills usefully surveys various theories of the sublime, and argues that a more negotiated model of the sublime than that traditionally acknowledged offers possibilities for female subject positions; following Gillian Rose's work on geography and gender, she theorises that women see landscape in more relational ways than men. Avoiding the essentialism that has marked psychoanalytic readings of the sublime, Mills's case-study of Wollstonecraft is a materialist feminist analysis which recognises 'the spatial [as] social relations "stretched out"' (Massey quoted by Mills). According to Mills, Wollstonecraft's landscape descriptions sometimes position her as a transcendent subject, while at other points her emotions seem to be written on to the landscape or her subjectivity dispersed and fragmented into the landscape, so that the landscape emerges as 'a relational zone'. Jacqueline Labbe complements Mills's concern with Romantic aesthetics: she demonstrates that Priscilla Wakefield's *A Family Tour Through the British Empire* traverses the textual terrain between 'feminine detail and masculine generality'. Labbe argues that in her 'Preface'

Wakefield presents herself as a rhetorically reluctant tourist: she authorises her (female) voice by invoking a juvenile audience, by asserting her dependence on previous texts and purporting to be merely an armchair traveller, thus strategically bypassing the cultural constraints on female travel. The result is an apparently conservative text: the 'family tour' undertaken by Mrs. Middleton, her daughters, sons, and their tutor, divides along traditional gender lines: the girls wait while the boys are on the move. However, Labbe observes the 'shadows' of an alternative, subversive discourse in the text; notably, the female eye is trained to distrust the open, prospect view and thus 'a new way of looking [that is, detailed inspection] can be insinuated into the landscape'. Dorothy McMillan further explores female dissatisfaction with orthodox modes of picturing; she argues that Ann Radcliffe's 'homely travel diaries', unpublished until after her death, displace the value accorded to the composed view of landscape in Radcliffe's romances and contributed perhaps to a loss of confidence in this fictive mode. Even Radcliffe's early account of her tour of the Lake District in 1794 displays uneasiness with 'the inexpressibility of the sublime [a common topos] and the difficulties attendant on the composition of prospects'. As McMillan points out, there is a difference between figuring the experience of the sublime as beyond language and experiencing the refusal of language to convey one's perceptions. In Radcliffe's travel writing, we find increasing attention to 'the particularities of actual place', which include the discontinuous details of landscape and the commonplace features of domestic interiors. The generic crossings between travel writing and novels help to map out a possible trajectory for Radcliffe's writing from 'the imaginary landscapes of Gothic romance ... [to] the busy real places of the nineteenth-century novel'.

While Labbe and McMillan challenge the putative exoticism of travel writing in their focus on domestic tourism, Part II turns to the itinerary of the European Grand Tour, particularly to various sites of enthralment in France and Italy which force the traveller to confront the boundaries between effeminacy and femininity, reason and passion, revolution and patriotism, pleasure and guilt, and in so doing, (re)construct British national identity in revolutionary Europe. Keith Hanley's chapter 'Wordsworth's Grand Tour' demonstrates that '*all* Wordsworth's journeyings are excursions or tours which loop back to "home at Grasmere"'.[27] Using a Freudian/Lacanian critical framework, Hanley argues that '"Grasmere" ... came to stand for an unbroken Imaginary relation with nature that provided him [Wordsworth] with a privately overdetermined version of full speech'; thus, the journeys of the *The Prelude* and *The Excursion*, and the accounts of tours of Scotland and the Continent, all enact Wordsworth's desire for a self-fulfilling language. Geographical sites are variously saturated with the self-empowering discourses of republicanism, nature, and nationalism, but the climax of Wordsworth's grand tour was the paradigmatic route of 'British reactionary politics – the path to "Rome"'. Ultimately, Wordsworth's 1837 tour made Rome the symbolic site for reconstituting 'the imaginary discourse of Anglican nationalism that was under stress at home'.

For Helen Maria Williams, the spectacle of liberated France was more inspiring than Rome (or England); her female republican heroines and the women who stormed the Bastille inherited the role of 'Roman matrons'. Williams's *Letters From France* (1790–96) provided for English readers a portrait of a society tearing down political and gender barriers; they demonstrate something of the geographic and disciplinary distances over which the familiar letter travelled in the eighteenth century (the letters contain mini-romances, accounts of military matters and constitutional arrangements). Chris Jones analyses Williams's canny exploitation of the feminine discourse of sensibility, arguing that her 'alternations between the internal and the external, domestic and collective, feeling and rationalism, are part of a strategy that imitates traditional feminine discourse in order to extend its bounds'. However, contemporary anti-Jacobin critics saw in her work the dangers of radical sensibility: in romancing the revolution she subverted 'British national values' and debased her sex. The spectactrice of the French Revolution became a demonic figure, the 'willing tool ... of French subversion' in contemporary satiric writings. In the chapter that follows, Chloe Chard discusses the boundary between spectacle and spectator in writings about southern Europe, noting the fascination with travellers, usually women, who transmute into tourist attractions. Chard concentrates on occasions when antiquity and femininity merge to produce especially intriguing sites of enthralment, as in Emma Hamilton's 'attitudes', which reproduce some of the poses of classical sculpture, thus confusing the boundary between the animate and the inanimate. While figures like Emma Hamilton and Paolina Borghese, in their self-presentation as near-naked spectacles, make possible the vicarious exploration of the pleasures and dangers of becoming an object of vision, Chard shows how most travellers, including Mary Wortley Montagu, Mary Wollstonecraft, Mungo Park, and Mrs Belzoni, disavow the 'allurement of excess' for 'the authority of restraint', and reclaim their role as subject of vision.

The chapters in Part III demonstrate, in Clare Brant's words, that 'Uneasy and incomplete distinctions between health and pleasure were tangled up in gender and class considerations', not to mention national ones. Brant focuses on Sir Nathaniel Wraxall's encounters with women of the north in his travels in Scandinavia and Russia in the mid-1770s.

Analysing a range of late eighteenth-century texts (including accounts by William Thomson, James Boswell, Eyles Irwin, Jemima Kindersley, and Edward Topham), Brant maps the cultural terrain through which Wraxall travels, in which 'femininity is used as a sign of national continence or moral hygiene'. On the other hand, women themselves are represented as impervious to cultural difference, and they thus hold out the possibility of a 'universal language', either one beyond the specificities of a particular tongue or one which privileges song and dance, whose expressivity transcends national boundaries. Such is the language of Safie, the foreign musical woman in Shelley's *Frankenstein*; this semiotic skill, however, does not empower the woman, rather the text demonstrates that cultural mastery is contingent on sexual, and racial, difference. The most eloquent and affecting women encountered by the travel writer are symbolically wordless: they are musical, or imprisoned, or, in the case of Wraxall's visit to a crypt in Bremen, dead. In this last, most extreme instance, Wraxall's subjectivity is forged over the embalmed body of an English countess and symbolically prefigures the gender ideologies of Romanticism. As Brant observes, travel writers thus played a key role in the process of the silencing of women that made 'femininity an object or sign expressive of a poetic masculine subject'.

The contributions by Jeanne Moskal and Beth Dolan Kautz take up different aspects of the relation between health and gender, and both take us back to more familiar European sites. Offering a wealth of historical detail about the gendered contours of travel and travel writing in the turbulent politics of the 1790s, Moskal argues that the 'pressures exerted by conservative reaction impacted particularly on women travel writers because the genre had been associated with French sympathisers Williams and Wollstonecraft ... and also because travel books conventionally took up the topic of "national manners", meditations often political in nature'. In Mariana Starke's *Letters From Italy* (1800), the domestic propriety of her occupation as nurse to an invalid relative guarantees her commitment to conservative ideology while it strategically 'blunt[s] the transgressive potential' of her political commentary. Her political (conservative) and religious (Anglican) concerns are steeped in the language of public health: commenting on what is clean and dirty, healthy and sick, Starke emerges as 'a nurse of national morals ... as well as the nurse of a consumptive relative'. Starke's concluding letters from Rome represent the city as dangerously unhealthy, for ultimately she considered Italian Catholicism a greater threat to British national health than French republican politics. While Moskal shows the intimate connections between discourses of health, religion, and nationality, Beth Dolan Kautz examines institutionalised, and masculinised, medical practice (strict regimen and authoritarian surveillance as purveyed by Dr Granville at Kissingen) in relation to alternative, aesthetic, healing strategies. She describes the two types of treatment Shelley explores on her travels, that is, the prescriptive regimens of Germany's spas and the balm derived from viewing picturesque landscape. Disempowered as a patient, we find Shelley empowered by her active relation with the landscape. The aesthetic healing that Shelley discovers depends on her version of Gilpin's 'picturesque eye', though she disrupts the picturesque frame in favour of a complex interaction with the scenery through which she travels. Like Mills, Kautz posits a gendered difference in looking at landscape, locating in Shelley's work the same relational impulse that Mills finds in Wollstonecraft's account of Scandinavia. Attempting to devise her own 'theory of self-healing', Shelley's geography of health traverses and challenges nineteenth-century discourses of medicine and aesthetics.

The final Part, 'Colonial and imperial cartographies', moves us both West and East to the geographical peripheries that were none the less central to British Romanticism's self-definitions. Wil Verhoeven analyses some of the transatlantic crossings that are so often marginalised in accounts of British history after the loss of the American colonies. He reads the 'hybrid' texts of Gilbert Imlay and Thomas Cooper – a mixture of epistolary travelogue, radical pamphlet, and emigration tract – in terms of their utopian 'construction' – and commodification – of America for a British audience. Their idealist post-American and post-French-Revolution vision was viable only in the brief period in which Britain remained potentially pre-revolutionary: in the counter-revolutionary backlash that ensued in the latter part of the 1790s 'emigrants' and 'refugees' were no longer defined as 'persecuted patriots', and the particular type of travelogue Verhoeven analyses perished with the radical spirit of which it was both document and agent.

The remaining three chapters explore versions of Romantic orientalism, including critiques of British national and imperial ideology.[28] Nigel Leask examines Francis Wilford's sensational articles on Hindu geography, which appeared in the journal *Asiatic Researches*, beginning in 1799, and thus 'in the midst of a "war of ideas" between Britain and revolutionary France'. Wilford extracted his geographical materials from literary sources collected for him by his pundit, and deployed a method of conjectural etymology in order to demonstrate that the 'Sacred Isles in the West', that is, the British Isles, were the origin of Indian religion and culture (indeed, Krishna, like Noah and Dionysus, turns out to be originally a British national!). As Leask points out, 'In the annals of British colonial discourse, it would be hard to find a more transparent care of cultural narcissism' than 'Wilford's mimetic "recognition" of Christian and British nationalist traditions in the (putative) texts of Sanskrit antiquity'. But Wilford's essays turned out to be based on forged sources provided by his unnamed pundit, and in order to explain this deception Wilford has to make visible the figure of the native informant who is normally occluded from authoritative ethnography. Leask argues that a postcolonial reading of the pundit's fabrication of evidence exposes the ambivalent power relations of colonial discourse.

Several chapters demonstrate how fluid were the boundaries between travel writing and other discursive modes – Brant invokes Shelley's *Frankenstein*, McMillan discusses the landscape aesthetics of Radcliffe's novels as well as her travel journals, and Priscilla Wakefield's text, discussed by Labbe, has 'the air of a real tour'. For Jane Stabler, the question of genre that haunts travel writing in view of the fluid boundaries between travel and fiction, philosophy, ethnography, medicine, etc., moves from the margins to the centre of the argument, if such terms can be appropriate for a chapter which deals with the ideological implications of digression. Stabler notes that contemporary reviewers were perplexed by the generic hybridity of *Childe Harold's Pilgrimage*: Byron's digressives asides, especially, the prose notes, destabilised two genres, the romance and the travelogue, 'which had both been associated with the consolidation of British nationalism'. Stabler takes us on a tour through some other contemporary travel writing (including Annesley, Gell, Irwin and Sir John Carr) which was 'structured around reference points in the wars against Napoleon or with a view to extending lucrative trade routes', and in which reflective asides validated British institutions. Stabler demonstrates that Byron's satiric digressions interrogate the early nineteenth-century rhetoric of British imperialism (or 'plunder' as Byron calls it), and that the form of Byron's poem offers a radical critique of contemporary travel literature.

If Wilford's Hindu geography is a colonial 'construction', *Alastor's* 'map of the East' similarly 'has no real referent'. Saree Makdisi argues that Shelley's poem, which takes the form of a travel narrative, invents the terrain it 'represents'. The poem narrates a journey beyond the limits of space and time, but it is also a journey informed by the anxious encounters on the imperial frontiers of its particular historical moment. As Makdisi points out, the complex spatio-temporal trajectory of Shelley's 'philosophical traveller' creates a map of the East in which the living cities of the Orient are rendered as preserved ruins which exist as signs to be read by the European explorer. The symbolic depopulation of the East grounds 'its reclamation as part of some suddenly invented "Western" heritage'. An essentialist notion of Time and History means that the colonised space of the East may be understood in terms of its cultural continuity with modern

Europe. Shelley's newly invented Orient is continuous with other European revisions of the East, an East detached from undesirable cultural and political associations either 'through the fires of revolution (as in Greece) or through the discipline of archaeological or philological research (as in India)'. But it differs from the Orient of Byron's *Childe Harold,* wherein the 'otherness' of other cultures is preserved and the East functions as a space from which to critique imperialist ideology. However, as in Wilford's texts, traces of otherness remain in *Alastor,* for example in the form of the Arab maiden whose haunting presence disrupts the smooth surface of orientalist discourse. Ultimately, Makdisi asks us to turn our gaze away from the nature of the quest itself, which has preoccupied critics of Shelley's poem, and focus instead on the terrain on which the narrative takes place, that is, an Orient emptied for European colonisation and inscription.

I have organised this book around a number of geographical and disciplinary sites, but obviously there are many other possible itineraries, which might focus on Rome, or the sublime, or northern Europe, or individual writers like Mary Wollstonecraft. Readers might pursue the unfamiliar terrains opened up by brief references to a little-known work or place or field of study, while exploration of areas under-represented here (the South Seas and Africa, amongst others) will supplement – and potentially challenge – the map of Romanticism outlined in this book.[29] The increasingly popular field of Romantic travel writing is likely to be considerably expanded when scholars have had time to explore the (soon to be digitalised) rare material available in the Corvey archive.[30] In their traversal of methodological, national, and disciplinary boundaries, the contributions that follow offer paradigms for reading this new material, as well as signposts to what may be the modern avatar of Romantic geographies – the multidisciplinary sites and simulated geographies of the World Wide Web.

Notes

1 Jane West, *A Tale of the Times* (1799), 3 vols, intro. Gina Luria (New York, 1974), 2: 24.

2 Andrew [Anders] Sparrman, *A Voyage to the Cape of Good Hope, towards the Antarctic Polar Circle, and Round the World: but chiefly into that country of the Hottentots and Caffres, from the year 1772, to 1776* (London, 1785), 1: iii–iv.

3 Mary Louise Pratt, *Imperial Eyes: Travel Writing and Transculturation* (New York, 1992), 138.

4 Though not concerned with our period, these issues of cultural geography are usefully explored in George Robertson, Melinda Mash, Lisa Tickner, Jon Bird, Barry Curtis and Tim Putnam, eds, *Travellers' Tales: Narratives of Home and*

Displacement (London and New York, 1994). Mary Louise Pratt observes that 'travel writing is one of the most polyphonous of genres' and as such is resistant to the 'disciplined' mediation of cultural differences ('Scratches on the Face of the Country; or, What Mr. Barrow Saw in the Land of the Bushmen', *Critical Inquiry* 12: 1 (1985), 141).

5 The rather arbitrary period demarcation depends on the earliest and latest texts discussed in detail in this book, that is, Wraxell's Scandinavian/Russian travel book, published in 1775 (see Brant's chapter), and Mary Shelley's European *Rambles* of 1844 (see Kautz).

6 Dennis Porter, *Haunted Journeys: Desire and Transgression in European Travel Writing* (Princeton, 1991), 19. Useful accounts of the Grand Tour are to be found in Jeremy Black, *The British and the Grand Tour* (London and Sydney, 1985), and Christopher Hibbert, *The Grand Tour* (London, 1987).

7 Elizabeth A. Bohls, *Women Travel Writers and the Language of Aesthetics, 1716–1818* (Cambridge, 1995), 265, n. 58, cites John A. Dussinger, 'Hester Piozzi, Italy, and the Johnsonian Aether', *South Central Review* 9 (1992), 49.

8 *Women Travel Writers*, 90. On Scottish tourism, see John Glendening, *The High Road: Romantic Tourism, Scotland, and literature, 1720–1820* (London, 1997).

9 On the politics of walking in the work of William Wordsworth and John Clare, see Anne D. Wallace, *Walking, Literature, and English Culture: The Origins and Uses of the Peripatetic in the Nineteenth Century* (Oxford, 1993).

10 *Wordsworth's Guide to the Lakes*, 5th edn (1835), quoted in Heather Frey, 'Defining the Self, Defiling the Countryside: Travel Writing and Romantic Ecology', *The Wordsworth Circle* 28: 3 (1997), 163. Frey usefully discusses the ecological aesthetics of Wordsworth and Radcliffe, and notes 'the *Guide's* powerful influence on environmental policy' as the origin of the Lake District National Park (*ibid.*). On Romantic ecology and the National Trust, see Jonathan Bate, *Romantic Ecology: Wordsworth and the Environmental Tradition* (London, 1991).

11 Harriet Guest, 'The Great Distinction: Figures of the Exotic in the Work of William Hodges', in Isobel Armstrong, ed., *New Feminist Discourses: Critical Essays on Theories and Texts* (London and New York, 1992), 296–341.

12 *Women Travel Writers*, 195.

13 See Homi K. Bhabha, *The Location of Culture* (London and New York, 1994), and Mary Louise Pratt, *Imperial Eyes.*

14 The titles, respectively, of the British Association for Romantic Studies conference held in Bangor, UK, in July 1996, and the North American Society for the Study of Romanticism conference held in Boston, USA, in November 1997: at both conferences, only a small number of papers dealt with travel writing *per se*; Mary A. Favret and Nicola J. Watson, eds, *At the Limits of Romanticism: Essays in Cultural, Feminist, and Materialist Criticism* (Bloomington and Indianapolis, 1994); Stephen Copley and John Whale, eds, *Beyond Romanticism: New Approaches to Texts and Contexts 1780–1832* (London, 1992).

15 *Limits of Romanticism*, 1.

16 Chandra Talpade Mohanty, 'Introduction: Cartographies of Struggle: Third

World Women and the Politics of Feminism', in Chandra Talpade Mohanty, Ann Russo and Lourdes Torres, eds, *Third World Women and the Politics of Feminism* (Bloomington, 1991), 34.

17 Frances Burney, *The Wanderer; or, Female Difficulties*, eds Margaret Anne Doody, Robert L. Mack and Peter Sabor (Oxford, 1991), 700. The novel was published in 1814 but is set in England during the period of the French Revolution.

18 *Ibid.*, 701.

19 John Barrell, 'Visualising the Division of Labour: William Pyne's *Microcosm*', in *The Birth of Pandora and the Division of Knowledge* (Basingstoke, 1992), 97, 98. Excellent discussions of the picturesque are to be found in Stephen Copley and Peter Garside, eds, *The Politics of the Picturesque: Literature, Landscape and Aesthetics since 1770* (Cambridge, 1994) and Malcolm Andrews, *The Search for the Picturesque* (Stanford, 1990).

20 R. Deutsche, 'Boys Town', *Environment and Planning D: Society and Space* 9 (1991), 7, quoted in Alison Blunt and Gillian Rose, eds, 'Introduction', *Writing Women and Space: Colonial and Postcolonial Geographies* (London and New York, 1994), 5.

21 *Women Travel Writers*, 82.

22 On the feminisation of the detail, see Naomi Schor, *Reading in Detail: Aesthetics and the Feminine* (London and New York, 1987). Schor discusses how the detail has been associated with the ornamental and the everyday, both domains traditionally marked as feminine; Reynolds's theories are discussed in chapter 1.

23 Anne K. Mellor, *Romanticism and Gender* (London and New York, 1993), 105. Mary Wollstonecraft's Scandinavian travelogue has emerged as a key text in recent feminist readings of the sublime; see, amongst others, Jeanne Moskal, 'The Picturesque and the Affectionate in Wollstonecraft's *Letters From Norway*', *Modern Language Quarterly* 52: 3 (1991), 263–94; Meena Alexander, *Women in Romanticism* (Basingstoke, 1989), 169–74; Bohls, *Women Travel Writers*, 140–69; Karen R. Lawrence, *Penelope Voyages: Women and Travel in the British Literary Tradition* (London and Ithaca, 1994), ch. 2. See also John Whale, 'Death in the Face of Nature: Self, Society and Body in Wollstonecraft's *Letters Written in Sweden, Norway, and Denmark*', *Romanticism* 1: 2 (1995), 177–92.

24 Cynthia Enlow, *Bananas, Beaches and Bases: Making Feminist Sense of International Politics* (Berkeley, 1989), 21.

25 Hannah More, *Strictures on the Modern System of Female Education* (1799), in *The Works of Hannah More*, 5 vols (London, 1834), 3: 202.

26 Sara Mills, *Discourses of Difference: An Analysis of Women's Travel Writing and Colonialism* (London and New York, 1991).

27 Dorothy Wordsworth's alternative perceptions of 'home at Grasmere' have been the subject of much critical attention in recent years; see, especially, Susan M. Levin, *Dorothy Wordsworth and Romanticism* (New Brunswick, 1987); Kurt Heinzelman, 'The Cult of Domesticity: Dorothy and William

Wordsworth at Grasmere' and Susan J. Wolfson, 'Individual in Community: Dorothy Wordsworth in Conversation with William', in Anne K. Mellor, ed., *Romanticism and Feminism* (Bloomington, 1988), 52–78 and 139–66.

28 Examination of the complex relations between British Romanticism and British imperialism is a rapidly developing area in Romantic studies. See especially two notable collections: Alan Richardson and Sonia Hofkosh, eds, *Romanticism, Race, and Imperial Culture, 1780–1834* (Bloomington and Indianapolis, 1996); and Timothy Fulford and Peter J. Kitson, eds, *Romanticism and Colonialism: Writing and Empire, 1780–1830* (Cambridge, 1998).

29 Two recent essays explore areas of the African continent. See Ashton Nichols, 'Mumbo Jumbo: Mungo Park and the Rhetoric of Romantic Africa' and Moira Ferguson, 'Hannah Kilham: Gender, the Gambia, and the Politics of Language', in *Romanticism, Race*, eds Richardson and Hofkosh, 93–113, 114–48.

30 A copy of the holdings of the Travel Writing Archive is available at the Corvey Web site: http://www.shu.ac.uk/corvey

Part I

Partial perspectives: landscape, aesthetics, and the politics of gender

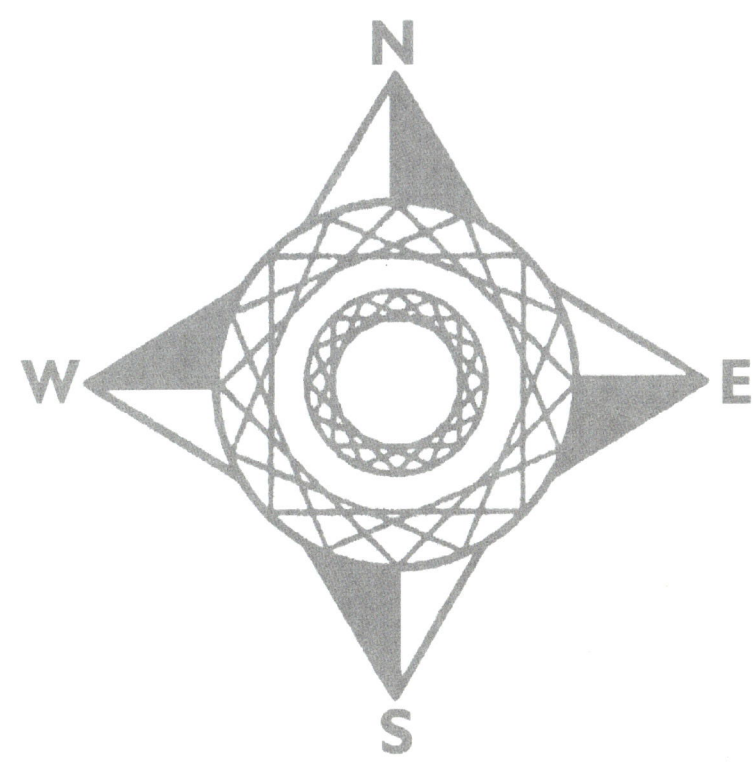

Written on the landscape: Mary Wollstonecraft's *Letters Written During a Short Residence in Sweden, Norway and Denmark*

Sara Mills

In this chapter I consider the interrelation between gender, aesthetics, and spatial relations.[1] In particular, by analysing Mary Wollstonecraft's travel letters, published in 1796 as *Letters Written During a Short Residence in Sweden, Norway and Denmark*, I will try to develop a materialist–feminist model for describing the representation of the sublime by considering the gendered nature of spatial relations.[2] By rooting my analysis in spatial relations which I argue are social relations, it is possible to move away from the tradition of analysing the sublime within psychoanalytical frameworks, which implicitly polarise and essentialise gender positions. I will be drawing on theoretical work on gender and space which has been developed by feminist geographers to examine the possibilities of developing a materialist feminist analysis of representational space which will be aware of the way that women and men negotiate their positions in space through their respective social positions. Much of the critical writing on representation of landscape and other countries has been undertaken in the area of colonial and postcolonial discourse studies, and another of my aims in this chapter is to investigate whether the vocabulary developed within that field has any implications for discussion of representational practices in the Romantic period, particularly in relation to the sublime.[3] Thus, I will be trying to fuse together models of analysis drawn from a variety of fields in order to analyse the spatial determinants of the sublime and the role that gender plays in constituting those spatial relations. I will be arguing that gender should be viewed not in essentialist terms, but rather, as Mary Crawford argues, as an activity or process which we perform.[4] Thus, I will not be arguing that all women writers draw on the language of aesthetics in the same way, but that for female and male

19

writers there is a process of negotiation and performativity in textual production.

Critics have asserted that Romantic women writers tended to write about subjects which were quite different from their male counterparts; rather than considering the limitations of language and the construction of a unified autonomous subject, 'women Romantic writers tended to celebrate not the achievements of the imagination nor the overflow of powerful feelings, but rather the working of the rational mind, a mind relocated – in a gesture of revolutionary gender implications – in the female as well as the male body'.[5] I will be arguing that there is not such a clear-cut division between male and female writers, but that socially-determined spatial relations are negotiated with differently because of class, race, and gender and one's access to certain discursive structures.[6]

Women and the sublime

The representation of experience of the sublime is crucial to discussion of women's relation to space, since the sublime subject is one who locates himself or herself in a particular spatial and power framework. Elizabeth Bohls comments on aesthetics as a whole: 'Aesthetics argues without arguing. Its vocabulary of visible surfaces represents power relations as natural and unchallengeable precisely by casting them as irrelevant to the compelling business of the quest for beauty through the senses and imagination.'[7] I would like to argue that psychoanalytic models of the sublime have tended to be seduced by this logic of the individual subject confronting the landscape and have therefore been unable to analyse the more general and socially-constituted power relations which the sublime entails. I will consider some of this psychoanalytical work briefly before proposing a different model of the sublime.

Moore argues that the sublime is 'probably Romanticism's most important and simultaneously least attainable ideal. It is unattainable because the sublime ego seeks ultimately to collapse the difference between subject and object, self and other.'[8] Moore argues that the sublime ego is never achieved, simply because this fusion is impossible except at an imagined level. Generally, critics have argued that the sublime is a moment of confrontation between a solitary individual ego and a landscape where these problems of conflict and otherness are resolved; it is a question of the subject controlling the landscape through controlling their visual sensations, thus consolidating their position as a unified seeing subject. Yaeger terms this encounter 'self-centred imperialism' and she states that the sublime is concerned with the attempt 'in words and feelings – [to] transcend the normative, the human'.[9] In this process of transcendence, the sublime subject is aggrandised and is ratified in its position of power.

There are particular types of sublime experience which Yaeger suggests are prototypically masculinist:

> Typically the male writing in the sublime mode will stage a moment of blockage which is followed by a moment of imagistic brilliance. That is, the mind fights back against the blocking source by representing its own inability to grasp the sublime object. This representation of inability becomes scriptive proof of the mind's percipience and stability – of the mind's willed relation to a transcendental order, and thus of the mind's powerful univocity – its potential for mental domination of the other.[10]

Thus, the landscape is represented as Other and merely as a device whereby control and transcendence of the individual ego may be foregrounded.

This psychoanalytic work leads to a certain essentialising move in descriptions of gender difference and the sublime. For example, Mellor states that the sublime is about the anxiety caused by the Oedipal recognition of the overwhelming power of the father, or about the annihilation of Otherness. For women writers 'the contemplation of sublime nature first produces the recognition that the self is separated from the Other. If the other is an oppressor the sublime arouses a sense of personal exaltation … If the other is beloved, then the experience of the sublime mediates a renewed connection with the lover.'[11] This type of theorising seems to categorise women as in essence different from men, rather than difference arising from processes of socialisation which attempt to restrict the movements of women.

Yaeger states that the sublime is in essence a masculine form of representation: 'the sublime constitutes a tradition that has not only been forbidden to women, but is inimical to their needs'; she suggests that in order to describe the sublime as expressed by a female writer we need to examine 'not … the old-fashioned sublime of domination, the vertical sublime which insists on aggrandising the masculine self over others, but instead … a horizontal sublime that moves towards sovereignty or expenditure, that refuses an oedipal, phallic fight to the death with the father, but expands towards others, spreads itself out into multiplicity'.[12] In her analysis of a poem by Marianne Moore, Yaeger considers the way that a new type of sublime may be constructed by female writers; she states that

> [Marianne Moore] signals her ability to stage a scene of empowerment in which the other is not obliterated or repressed. In place of this incorporation, she begins to invent a new kind of self – other dialectic

21

that allows the object ... to remain something other than the perceiving subject's conception of it, and allows that perceiving subject,
in turn, to become something other than a unified ego.[13]

Yaeger develops the term 'pre-oedipal sublime' to refer to this sublime of
nearness, which 'permits both a saving maintenance of ego-boundaries and
an exploration of the pleasures of intersubjectivity'.[14] This more negotiated
model of the sublime seems to offer interesting possibilities for describing
some of the subject positions taken up in women's writing, but it is necessary
for that difference of view to be located in women's experience of spatial
relations which are determined by the social structures within which we
live, rather than being located at the level of psychic relations.

Whilst recognising certain elements of this type of feminised sublime in
reading the sublime landscape in Wollstonecraft and other women writers
of the period, it strikes me that the situation is far more complex than
these psychoanalytical analyses can describe. Whilst it is clear that at many
points in their writings women do present a sublime landscape in this
feminised sense, there are other elements in their texts which mediate against
such a unified view.

The sublime moment is represented within psychoanalytic frameworks
as an ego experiencing a landscape in isolation from other humans; it is
seemingly a confrontation of the viewer and the landscape. However, a
more materialist analysis would be less concerned with the individual
subject, since it is clear that this is a discursive position;[15] instead, it would
be interested in the general discursive structures which empty that landscape
and distance the viewing subject from it. Bohls argues that 'Aesthetic
discourse disclosed a heightened potential for contributing to the colonial
project ... as travellers began to inscribe the concept of disinterested
contemplation on the landscape through scenic tourism. The effect was to
distance spectators from their surroundings and obscure the connection
between topography and people's material needs.'[16] This is very much Raoul
Granqvist's argument in his paper on Wollstonecraft's imperialism where
he suggests that she represents peasants either as 'moss-life, cave-life, fish-life'
in need of improvement by the West,[17] or she clears them from the
landscape in order to make way for the representation of her ego, a classically
imperialist move. This spectatorial position in relation to an empty landscape recalls Mary Louise Pratt's work on colonial landscape, where the
colonial male subject surveys the terrain often from a position of panorama.
Pratt states that the land in colonial writing presents itself to the viewer,
it shows itself or unfolds beneath his gaze; the landscape is not seen to be
one of human habitation or work, rather it is 'emptied' by the colonising
'improving' eye and 'made meaningful only in terms of a capitalist future

and of [its] potential for producing a marketable surplus'.[18] This analysis of colonial space is obviously not strictly appropriate for an investigation of the space of the sublime in Western countries; however, there are interesting parallels which perhaps foreground the importance of the land-scape of the sublime being emptied of other humans and the power relations that that emptying process entails.

Let us consider this discursive history briefly, since it is clear that the sublime consists of the collision of a number of different discursive frame-works. For Western travellers, there is a tradition of considering the relation between oneself and the landscape in particular ways, particularly in relation to walking.[19] In other cultures, where the landscape is considered in terms of its productive potential, walking across land does not have the same philosophical and self-reflective history.[20] This discursive tradition makes the right to wander and the relation between self-reflection and walking appear to be self-evident rather than culture- and class-specific practices. This supremely Romantic notion of situating oneself within, and traversing, a landscape developed at a particular moment of capitalist development, when intellectuals were attempting to carve out a space for themselves which was not as seemingly anti-individualistic and contaminating as the city.

Furthermore, the tradition of emotional reaction to landscape has con-notations of feminisation, and swooning and contemplation of mortality developed in relation to particularly awe-inspiring sights as McGreevy has shown in his analysis of Niagara Falls.[21] This almost spiritual, feminised aspect to Western apprehension of landscape is notably absent in many other cultures' views of landscape, and may stem from an already gendered discursive tradition of female mysticism and 'oceanic' feelings in relation to seemingly boundless space.

The position of imperialist mastery by the sublime subject is obviously one which is more familiar to those viewers already in positions of power, and particularly for those who have positions mapped out for them within the public sphere. Within Western culture, white middle-class gendered subjectivity is constituted on the terrain of the public–private sphere divide. The public sphere within Western cultures has been characterised as a sphere for men, where women on their own fear sexual attack, fear precisely not being alone. The private sphere is characterised as women's sphere, and this colours women's experience of being in a natural environment in a way in which men's experience is not. As Hamner and Saunders state: 'women's sense of security is profoundly shaped by our inability to secure an undisputed right to occupy that [public] space'.[22] However, it must be noted that this is true only for Western middle-class women; in other cultures, particularly where women are the farmers, the public sphere is viewed as women's terrain.[23]

The difference in the way that Western middle-class women and men see their position in relation to the site of the sublime is bound to have effects on the way that the sublime landscape is represented.

Women and space

The relationship between gender and space is becoming the subject of rigorous enquiry especially by feminist theorists.[24] Early feminist work on women and space tended to focus on women's confinement and restriction in movement; for example Iris Marion Young's article 'Throwing Like a Girl' stressed the way that women learn to situate themselves and move in space in a way which is significantly more restricted than men – even simple actions like sitting or walking are ones where the female subject is self-consciously not allowing herself to transcend the limits of the body as an object.[25] Similarly Marianne Wex has noted in a photographic essay on women in the public sphere that women attempt to take up as little space as possible by positioning their bodies in a restricted and confining fashion.[26] For Young, 'if there are particular modalities of feminine bodily comportment and motility, then it must follow that there are also particular modalities of feminine spatiality'.[27] She goes on to argue that because of this sense of restrictedness on motility, women as a whole experience their position in space as enclosed and confining and they see themselves as precisely positioned in space, that is 'in its immanence and inhibition, feminine spatial existence is *positioned* by a system of co-ordinates which does not have its origin in her own intentional capacities'.[28]

In contrast to this sense of the restrictedness of female space, Gillian Rose's work focuses on the interrelatedness of the spatial and power/knowledge and examines the possibilities that exist within this model of spatiality which women have exploited.[29] For her, whilst bodies are 'maps of the relation between power and identity', those maps do not simply trace subjection.[30]

Rose describes the work of many feminist theorists who have charted the ways in which women's sense of place within the public sphere is bounded by a fear of physical attack. But she adds to this an account of the work feminist theorists have done to try to explode the notion of a clear-cut division between the private and the public. Furthermore, in this context, women travellers by their very presence alone in the public sphere profoundly destabilise notions of a clear female/private – male/public sphere divide.[31] Space is encoded and policed/regulated in different ways for women and men and stereotypes of appropriate behaviour enforce these gendered divisions; however, it should be added that different groups of women have had different relations to space. Middle-class British women at various times in history were supposed to be chaperoned when in the public sphere, have seen the public sphere as a place of potential sexual attack, and have been taught to consider the domestic as primarily a female space. But working-class and upper-class British women in the same periods have not had the same type of restrictions. Furthermore, in contrast to these ideologies of the domestic sphere, even middle-class women have tested out, challenged, and transgressed the limits of these constraints. After all, the vast majority of women travellers were from the middle classes.

Rose also notes that women have tended to be represented as the space of the bodily, while male observation of nature takes place not from a bodily space but from a seeing space. This, as Rose goes on to show, is a space of power/knowledge, and this seeing position is more important in terms of the type of subject position that it maps out than for what is described.

Doreen Massey's work demonstrates the necessity of discussing women and men in space in materialist terms, for she states that 'what is at issue is not social phenomena in space but both social phenomena and space as constituted out of social relations'; we therefore need to think of 'the spatial [as] social relations "stretched out"'.[32] This notion of space being imbricated with social relations is important in considering women in space, because it moves discussion away from simple notions of women as a group having a consistent unchanging relation to spatial frameworks, and also thus to aesthetic judgements and the sublime.

Women and landscape

Rose's work on the landscape has been very important in understanding women's different access to that position of intelligibility which is the viewer of landscape. When describing fieldworkers and the landscape, Rose stresses that cultural geographers have begun to 'problematize the term "landscape" as a reference to relations between society and environment ... and they have argued that it refers not only to the relationships between different objects caught in the fieldworker's gaze, but that it also implies a specific way of looking'.[33] This focus on a specific way of looking and a specific form of subjectivity is especially important in considering the notion of the sublime, which is a peculiarly Western form of viewing. Many other cultures do not have a term for 'landscape' – that sense of a delimited terrain captured by a frame – and do not feel that this sense of distance involved in the viewing position pertains to them.[34] Even though, as Haraway has argued, the particularities of our visual capabilities are presented as universal, necessitating certain ways of processing and inter- preting visual stimuli, there are still marked cultural differences in relation to viewing landscapes.[35]

Rose argues that the 'domineering view of the single point of the omniscient observer of landscape' is one which is conventionally taken up by males and that women tend to see landscape in more relational ways; rather than seeking to subdue the landscape in their writings, they tend to see landscapes in relation to their domestic spaces and their networks of interaction.[36] She describes the work of Pollock on women artists who abandon the conventional wide landscapes of male painters for more confined spatial representations; she states that they rearticulate 'traditional space so that it ceases to function primarily as the space of sight for a mastering gaze, but becomes the locus of relationships'.[37] However, I would contest this view of women writers and artists representing landscape in a consistently different way to men. Sometimes, as Bergvall *et al.* have argued, when we focus on difference we may tend to polarise positions where there is in fact common ground or similar strategies, and exclude consideration of other elements which do not fit within this scheme.[38] They state: 'the problem with gender polarization is not that there are differences, but that these differences define mutually exclusive scripts for being female and male'.[39] What may be at issue here are other differences, for example, access to discourses of aesthetics, rather than the difference in description being due to gender. Although there may be a correlation between this access to discourse and gender, there will not be a complete fit.

Thus, through an analysis of the socially-constructed differences in middle-class women and men's access to the public and private sphere, it is possible to map out the parameters for the negotiations in which writers engage when they produce a textual space for the representation of the sublime landscape.

Mary Wollstonecraft's *A Short Residence in Sweden*

Mary Wollstonecraft's account of her travels in Sweden, Denmark, and Norway is a complex text defying easy categorisation. The text is composed of personal letters (revised for publication) to her lover Gilbert Imlay, the father of her child Fanny, who accompanies her on part of the visit. As Richard Holmes has convincingly shown, Wollstonecraft was undoubtedly in Sweden on a business mission for Imlay, which she successfully com- pleted.[40] The letters were sent to Imlay at a time when Wollstonecraft felt that their relationship was about to end and after she had attempted suicide; the subject matter of the letters wavers between concern about their relationship, concern about having left her child with her maid while she was travelling, concern about business matters in general, and more conventional manners and customs portraits of the countries through which she travelled. The concern about the business affair on which she was engaged is important, as Holmes states:

> Although never once referred to explicitly in the text, it exerts its unseen pressure on the text ... It gives Wollstonecraft's travels their secret urgency, their sense of a mysterious, almost nightmare pursuit. It adds immeasurably to the feeling of inexplicable anxiety, of gloomy foreboding which so marks Wollstonecraft's reflections on men and affairs and drives her continually to seek Romantic solace in the wilderness of the Scandinavian landscape, hoping to escape into a sublime vision of grand, impartial Nature: its magnificent forests, waterfalls and seashores, so remote from the petty concerns of man.[41]

Thus, from the very outset, Wollstonecraft's relation to landscape is marked as different to the position of the conventional sublime ego; she is not seeking a simple mastery over Nature, but rather she has been portrayed as trying to escape from worldly difficulties. And critics, following William Godwin's lead, have tended not to analyse Wollstonecraft's work in the way they would other Romantic writers; thus Godwin states, 'If ever there was a book calculated to make a man in love with its author, this appears to me to be the book.'[42]

The travels themselves are exceptional since they represent a woman travelling with her maid and young child and later completely alone, in a country which was considered a wilderness at the time. Wollstonecraft's text is a curious mixture of conventional sublime interludes with other types of more relational representational practices. However, it is important to stress that a great number of the descriptions which are represented in this text are of a conventional nature, where a stable ego gives an account of awe-inspiring vistas from a stable subject position; for example, in Letter Five she writes:

> It is not the queen of the night alone who reigns here in all her splendour, though the sun, loitering just below the horizon, decks her with a golden tinge from his car, illuminating the cliffs that hide him; the heavens also, of a clear softened blue, throw her forward, and the evening star appears a lesser moon to the naked eye. The huge shadows of the rocks, fringed with firs, concentrating the views,

without darkening them, excited that tender melancholy which, sublimating the imagination, exalts, rather than depresses the mind.[43]

Here the narrator describes natural phenomena which excite awe, and she positions herself in a straightforward position of knowledge/vision, in that it is the 'naked eye' which is located as the source of these phenomena. She locates herself within the discourse of aesthetics through the use of poetic language, and she describes the complex mixture of emotions that these phenomena excite within her, oscillating between melancholy and exaltation.

In her analysis of Letter Fifteen, Moore has shown that alongside these sublime passages there are other passages where the female subject is shown experiencing grief and sorrow rather than an uplift of spirits. She states: 'Letter 15 ... is remarkable for the overwhelming sense of lack and loss that contemplation of nature by a woman produces.'[44] However, I would argue that the position of Wollstonecraft and women writers in general in relation to the sublime is even more complex, since she is not simply expressing loss, in opposition to a supposed norm of a male exaltation when faced with nature, she is also challenging the very basis on which this experience of the sublime is based. Moore observes that 'The problem is how to categorise a sublime experience where the female subject is not empowered by her experience and is left utterly bereft.'[45] However, it is possible to see that in certain passages where Wollstonecraft expresses loss and mourning when faced with sublime landscapes, she is still exercising control of the landscapes; the reader is still confronted by an ego who describes the landscapes in terms of the emotions which the landscape evokes and which the narrator then describes in unitary terms, thus containing the landscape within his/her own limits of sensation. Thus, despite the fact that the sublime ego does not express exaltation, these passages seem to conform to a conventional unified subject position.

Alongside these conventional sublime passages there are also passages which seem to be challenging this unified subject who exercises scopic control over the landscape that he or she surveys, and seems to be challenging the simple ecstasy of the sublime viewer of landscape. Instead, emotional responses begin to be written on to the landscape so that the landscape becomes less a sounding board or means of asserting a controlling and unified subject, but rather becomes a way of negotiating and coming to terms with feelings of loss, and representing a gendered identity which does not conform to stereotype. For example, after a passage where Wollstonecraft has described aspens and junipers in a forest, she goes on to muse about the emotions which these landscapes evoke:

When a warm heart has received strong impressions, they are not to be effaced. Emotions become sentiments and the imagination renders even transient sensations permanent, by fondly retracing them. I cannot without a thrill of delight, recollect views I have seen, which are not to be forgotten – nor looks I have felt in every nerve which I shall never more meet. The grave has closed over a dear friend, a friend of my youth; still she is present with me, and I hear her soft voice warbling as I stray over the heath. Fate has separated me from another, the fire of whose eyes, tempered by infantine tenderness, still warms my breast; even when gazing on these tremendous cliffs, sublime emotions absorb my soul. And smile not, if I add, that the rosy tint of morning reminds me of a suffusion, which will never more charm my senses, unless it reappears on the cheeks of my child. Her sweet blushes I may yet hide in my bosom, and she is still too young to ask why starts the tear, so near akin to pleasure and pain? [46]

Thus, rather than the self here being presented as controlling and encompassing a landscape, there is more a sense of negotiation. The agency here is located in nature rather than the subject herself acting. The emotions themselves and the landscape begin to infiltrate each other, so that the colours of the morning sky and the blushes of her daughter are seen to be as one.[47] The landscape is made into a relational zone where, rather than human relations being excluded as in the masculinist phallocentric sublime ego, relations to other humans are seen to be an integral part of apprehension of the landscape.[48] In a further passage, it is the landscape itself which is given a sense of agency in terms of the production of emotion; whilst in conventional sublime passages, the landscape evokes certain emotions which are then mastered in order to contain the landscape, Wollstonecraft's descriptions seem more concerned with negotiating with the visual stimulations and her emotions than controlling them. She poses herself as an experiencing subject, but not one who is intent on focusing, controlling, and limiting her emotions:

Reaching the cascade, or rather cataract, the roaring of which had a long time announced its vicinity, my soul was hurried by the falls into a new train of reflections. The impetuous dashing of the rebounding torrent from the dark cavities which mocked the exploring eye, produced an equal activity in my mind: my thoughts darted from earth to heaven, and I asked myself why I was chained to life and its misery? Still the tumultuous emotions this sublime object excited, were pleasurable; and viewing it, my soul rose, with renewed dignity, above its cares – grasping at immortality – it seemed as

> impossible to stop the current of my thoughts, as of the always varying, still the same, torrent before me – I stretched out my hand to eternity, bounding over the dark speck of life to come.[49]

She suggests that her mournful thoughts are determined by the activity of the waterfall, and seems to fuse the unending nature of her thoughts with that of the water flowing. She also represents the moment of resolution when she mastered these thoughts using a peculiarly agentless phrase, 'my soul rose'.

Furthermore, Wollstonecraft is unusual in that, at times in her text, she positions herself as part of the landscape, as an element within the spatial dynamics, rather than as a controlling element set apart from and making sense of the observed landscape. Although Granqvist has asserted that this still locates her at the absolute centre of the landscape, I would argue that there is a more complex moving between this centring and dispersal at work here. For example, in the following passage she describes herself as situated within the landscape and then goes on to describe the way that she herself becomes diffused throughout the landscape:

> Here I have frequently strayed, sovereign of the waste, I seldom met any human creature; and sometimes, reclining on the mossy down, under the shelter of a rock, the prattling of the sea amongst the pebbles has lulled me to sleep – no fear of any rude satyr's approaching to interrupt my repose. Balmy were the slumbers, and soft the gales, that refreshed me, when I awoke to follow, with an eye vaguely curious, the white sails as they turned the cliffs, or seemed to take shelter under the pines which covered the little islands that so gracefully rose to render the terrific ocean beautiful ... Everything seemed to harmonise into tranquillity ... With what ineffable pleasure have I not gazed – and gazed again, losing my breath through my eyes, my very soul diffused itself in the scene – and seeming to become all senses, glided in the scarcely agitated waves, melted in the freshening breeze, or taking its flight with fairy wing, to the misty mountains which bounded the prospect, fancy tript over new lawns, more beautiful even than the lovely slopes on the winding shore before me – I pause again breathlessly to trace with renewed delight, sentiments which entranced me, when turning my humid eyes from the expanse below to the vault above, my sight pierced the fleecy clouds that softened the azure brightness; and imperceptibly recalling the reveries of childhood, I bowed before the awful throne of my Creator, whilst I rested on its footstool.[50]

Here Wollstonecraft locates herself at the centre of a vista, and she is unusual in this setting of herself within the landscape that she is to describe. As many feminist film theorists have shown, women tend to be the objects 'to-be-looked-at', and thus, she herself is positioned within the landscape, rather than being defined by her position of exteriority to the landscape. We may see this as reminiscent of Young's view that women are positioned in space rather than moving in a landscape; but here Wollstonecraft explicitly positions herself within a landscape rather than being positioned. She does locate herself as dominated by the power relations between herself and her 'Creator'; she positions herself on a lowly footstool in relation to a powerful throne. Furthermore, because Wollstonecraft chooses to describe her position of viewing, rather than the spatial relations presenting themselves as transparent, we are forced to be aware of the way that Wollstonecraft is seeing the landscape from a particular perspective. She sets herself low down on the approaches to a beach nestling into the hollow of a rock. From this position, which she is careful to describe as one of safety, since it is safe from the 'rude satyr', she describes the sea, the mountains, and the sky towering over her. So safe is this position that she represents herself as falling asleep. Rather than this position being one from which she describes the exalted emotions she experiences, she oscillates between describing the pleasure of a unified subject, the fragmentation of her self, the disappearance of the notion of difference between herself and the landscape which she observes and describing her lowly position in relation to the awe-inspiring throne of a superior power. In this sense, the subject here presented is at one and the same time subjected and dispersed. Rose details the way in which women have conventionally been seen as closer to Nature than men, and this may be one of the possibilities which Wollstonecraft makes use of in attempting to map out a textual space for herself.[51] By drawing on this association of the feminine with the natural, she is able, rather than taking a simple position of Culture/viewer to Nature/viewed, to take up a position which straddles this divide, seeing herself as viewer and viewed at the same time.

Thus, this analysis of Wollstonecraft's strategies has shown that there is no simple divide between male and female subjects when they are describing the sublime. Wollstonecraft frequently uses conventional sublime descriptions which position her as a controlling transcendent subject; at the same time, however, her text contains descriptions which negotiate far more with the subject positions available for the sublime subject; as I have shown, her emotions become far more a part of the landscape and the agency during these interludes is taken over by the landscape. She herself as a subject is at times dispersed into the landscape rather than maintaining a transcendent exteriority. In this sense, because of her marginalised position as a woman writer, Wollstonecraft is perhaps more able than male Romantic writers to foreground the variety of subject positions available to writers when describing the landscape. This variety of positions may help readers to re-analyse the male sublime ego in order to find greater variety within representational practices. As Rose states: 'A critical account of phallocentrism must argue that the phallocentric space of self/knowledge is not as stable or stabilising as the phallocentric subject desires.'[52] Thus, rather than simply accepting the monolithic and unified accounts of the masculinist sublime ego, it is important to re-analyse the male representation of the sublime to see whether in fact this impossible vision is challenged by other more negotiated forms of representation and subject positions.

Notes

1 I have given versions of this chapter as papers at the University of the West of England conference on Travel Writing, April 1998; The All Turkey university lecturers' conference on Travel Writing, May 1998. I benefited greatly from discussions at these two conferences. I would like to thank Tony Brown, Philip Cox, and Robert Miles for commenting on draft versions of this chapter.

2 By materialist–feminist I mean to refer to a type of criticism which is concerned not with the individual psyche as such, but rather with the socio-economic/historical/cultural context within which groups of women negotiate the parameters of subjectivity. Valentin Volosinov's work on the social construction of the individual psyche is of interest in this context. See *Freudianism: A Marxist Critique* (New York, 1976).

3 See Mary Louise Pratt, *Imperial Eyes: Travel Writing and Transculturation* (London, 1992), and Raoul Granqvist, 'Her Imperial Eyes: A Reading of Mary Wollstonecraft's *Letters Written During a Short Residence in Sweden, Norway and Denmark*', *Moderna Sprak* 91 (1997), 16–24.

4 Mary Crawford, *Talking Difference: On Gender and Language* (London, 1995).

5 Anne K. Mellor, *Romanticism and Gender* (London and New York, 1993), 2.

6 Perhaps one of the elements which I do not stress enough in this chapter is the sense of Wollstonecraft having to assert her ability to perform the language of aesthetics, which is a rational distanced form of controlled emotional response, rather than simply an emotional response to landscape. Thus, for women striving to position themselves as rational subjects, as Wollstonecraft so clearly is in her more political works, the emphasis on displaying ease within the language of aesthetics may have force which is lacking for males of a similar social status.

7 Elizabeth Bohls, *Women Travel Writers and the Language of Aesthetics, 1716–1818* (Cambridge, 1995), 65.

8 Jane Moore, 'Plagiarism with a Difference: Subjectivity in "Kubla Khan" and *Letters Written During a Short Residence in Sweden*', in Stephen Copley and

John Whale, eds, *Beyond Romanticism: New Approaches to Texts and Contexts 1780–1832* (London, 1992), 148.

9 Patricia Yaeger, 'Toward a Female Sublime', in Linda Kauffman, ed., *Gender and Theory: Dialogues on Feminist Criticism* (Oxford, 1989), 192.

10 *Ibid.*, 202.

11 *Romanticism and Gender*, 96.

12 'Female Sublime', 198, 191.

13 *Ibid.*, 196.

14 *Ibid.*, 205.

15 Many Western travel narratives are constructed as if the writer were alone, even when that patently is not the case. This discursive imperative to describe landscape as if alone is related to notions of ownership and also due to the Western obsession with individualism. In other cultures with more interrelational views of the self, this discursive exclusion of companions is not deemed to be necessary.

16 *Women Travel Writers*, 48.

17 'Her Imperial Eyes', 19.

18 *Imperial Eyes*, 61.

19 Robin Jarvis, 'Wordsworth and the Aesthetics of the Walk', *News From Nowhere* 1 (1995), 135–56.

20 Rick Rylance, 'Five go to the Wall: Auden and Walking' (paper delivered at Sheffield Hallam University, May 1998).

21 Patrick V. McGreevy, 'Reading the Texts of Niagara Falls: The Metaphor of Death', in Trevor J. Barnes and James S. Duncan, eds, *Writing Worlds: Discourse, Texts and Metaphors in the Representation of Landscape* (London, 1992), 50–72.

22 Cited in Gillian Rose, *Feminism and Geography: The Limits of Geographical Knowledge* (London and Minneapolis, 1993), 34.

23 See Daphne Spain, *Gendered Spaces* (Chapel Hill, NC, 1992).

24 See Allison Blunt and Gillian Rose, eds, *Writing Women and Space: Colonial and Postcolonial Geographies* (London and New York, 1994).

25 See Iris Marion Young, 'Throwing Like a Girl: A Phenomenology of Feminine Bodily Comportment, Motility and Spatiality', in Jeffner Allen and Iris Marion Young, eds, *The Thinking Muse: Feminism and Modern French Philosophy* (Bloomington, 1989), 51–70.

26 Marianne Wex, *Let's Take Back Our Space: Female and Male Body Language as a Result of Patriarchal Structures* (Berlin, 1979).

27 'Throwing Like a Girl', 62.

28 *Ibid.*, 64.

29 See *Feminism and Geography*, and 'Distance, Surface, Elsewhere: A Feminist Critique of the Space of Phallocentric Self/Knowledge' (paper delivered at Loughborough University, February 1995).

30 *Feminism and Geography*, 32.

31 See Sara Mills, *Discourses of Difference: Women's Travel Writing and Colonialism* (London and New York, 1991).

32 Doreen Massey, *Space, Place and Gender* (Cambridge, 1994), 2.

33 *Feminism and Geography*, 87.

34 See *Gendered Spaces*.

35 Donna Haraway, 'Situated Knowledges: The Science Question in Feminism and the Privilege of Partial Perspective', in Linda McDowell and Joanne P. Sharp, eds, *Space, Gender, Knowledge: Feminist Readings* (1988; London, 1997), 53–73.

36 *Feminism and Geography*, 112.

37 Griselda Pollock, cited in Rose, *Feminism and Geography*, 112.

38 See Victoria L. Bergvall, Janet M. Bing and Alice F. Freed, eds, *Rethinking Language and Gender Research: Theory and Practice* (London 1996).

39 *Ibid.*, 16.

40 Wollstonecraft was attempting to recover a stolen treasure ship which belonged to Imlay, which had been stolen by the Norwegian captain. There was a great deal of silver on board totalling a possible £3,500, equivalent to half a million pounds at current prices. See Richard Holmes, introduction, *A Short Residence in Sweden, Norway and Denmark*, by Mary Wollstonecraft (1796; Harmondsworth, 1987), 21–6.

41 *Ibid.*, 35.

42 William Godwin, *Memoirs of the Author of 'The Rights of Woman'*, with *A Short Residence in Sweden*, ed. Richard Holmes (Harmondsworth, 1987), 249.

43 *A Short Residence*, 94.

44 'Plagiarism', 149.

45 *Ibid.*, 152.

46 *A Short Residence*, 100.

47 However, it should be noted that, for some readers of this passage, the relationship between Wollstonecraft and her daughter becomes more distanced, precisely because it is dispersed through the landscape. It becomes almost an impersonal relationship because it acts as the vehicle for this aesthetic response.

48 It should be noted, however, that the landscape is imbued only with emotions towards other humans within Wollstonecraft's circle of friends and family rather than with emotions towards the inhabitants of the country.

49 *A Short Residence*, 152–3.

50 *Ibid.*, 110–11.

51 See *Feminism and Geography*.

52 'Distance, Surface, Elsewhere'.

'A species of knowledge both useful and ornamental': Priscilla Wakefield's *Family Tour Through the British Empire*

Jacqueline M. Labbe

In the 'Preface' to her *Family Tour Through the British Empire* (1804), Priscilla Wakefield outlines what she hopes to accomplish with her compendious volume: she wishes to give an impression and

> general idea of the variety of surface, produce, manufactures, and principle [*sic*] places of the British Empire; connected with its geography, and the addition of historical and biographical anecdotes: a species of knowledge both useful and ornamental, but so diffused in numerous publications, that a sketch, having the air of a real tour, and containing the prominent features of the subject, was thought likely to prove a valuable addition to the juvenile library.[1]

This prefatory remark is important not only for the straightforward and detailed way in which it lays out its objectives but also for the evasions and tensions it contains. As she does throughout her narrative, Wakefield both embraces and skirts her position as tourist; most significantly, she avoids appearing to be an actual tourist at all. Her 'sketch' has the 'air of a real tour', but is not real, just as its self-proclaimed position as a 'sketch' does not seriously challenge the 'numerous publications' whose 'diffuseness' she seeks to counter. Further, however, the epithet 'sketch' does not quite correspond to her opening pledge to provide her readers with details like 'produce, manufactures ... principle places ... geography ... [and] historical and biographical anecdotes', an avowal that itself would seem to go beyond 'general ideas' and impressions. In fact, this 'Preface' hovers between two extremes of behaviour, feminine detail and masculine generality;[2] it promises both 'prominent features' and 'general ideas', seeking to achieve the 'air' of a real tour, with its openness and expansiveness but

35

without sacrificing proper domestic retirement, and above all displaying a vast and intimate knowledge of the British Isles while presenting all details for the advantage of a juvenile readership. Even those rather uselessly 'diffused' prior travelogues become, in the next paragraph of the 'Preface', the 'great number of amusing and elegant tours that have formed a favourite department of British literature', and to which 'the author is indebted for her materials'.[3] Janus-like, Wakefield presents her readers with the paradox of generalisation and detail, mobility and stillness, knowledge and ignorance. Her *Family Tour* thus presents, albeit covertly, the tensions that often accompanied a female traveller as well as the frustrations attendant on reading her compartmentalised textual sisters.

Almost an embodied contradiction, the female traveller yet made up a small but significantly vocal part of the 'department of British literature' called travel literature. As Marie McAllister notes, travel books were read voraciously by women and even recommended as appropriate reading by sages of feminine behaviour;[4] Charles Batten, too, remarks that travel accounts were good for the 'youthful or inexperienced or female reader' because they stimulated otherwise ignorant minds.[5] Perhaps, also, encouraging the reading of travels involved discouraging actual travel: knowledge thus domestically gained could satisfy intellectual curiosity, function as lessons in geography, history, or the like (as Wakefield's text specifically purports to do), or simply provide 'innocent' entertainment, all in the privacy of one's closet. Intellectual roaming was thus both encouraged and corralled by the travel writer, who selected the views presented to the reader. Indeed, since the traveller or tourist 'was defined above all as a creature on the move', says Carole Fabricant,[6] and one womanly virtue was stillness, one recognises that perhaps to *read* of travels constituted the most valid method of travelling for the woman; one is reminded of the contradictions inherent in Wakefield's knowing enough detail of the facts *and* sights of the 'British Empire' to educate her readers about them while also, apparently, never stirring from her home.

The female reader of travel literature, moreover, often found herself presented with what might be called a foreign style of writing. Batten's account highlights certain narrative conventions to which travel accounts were expected to conform: travel literature sought homogeneity in its presentation of new or unusual facts, what one could call general(ised) knowledge. Such a style sought to avoid individual scenes in its quest for the whole story; the particular was dismissed in favour of the (imagined) universal. Batten's is essentially a masculinist model; the experienced-writer/ inexperienced-reader relationship fostered by travel accounts written out of the classical rhetorical tradition he describes forced female travel readers into a position of being virtually unable to identify with the writer: the reader's ignorance could overwhelm her. However, McAllister's characterisation of the style of women's travel writing provides an alternative. Almost as if deliberately, meaningfully, speaking the language of their (recommended) readers, women's travel writing during the Romantic period refused to focus around a central topic; it substituted a more receptive, less analytical approach, 'giving priority to the quotidien [*sic*] and ... relationships with fellow travellers and the people [the women writers] meet'.[7] Aware, perhaps, of the incompatibility between a masculine way of writing and their way of reading, women travel writers institute a design that more closely projects their own learned methods of viewing the world around them.

What Batten's fact-based, analytical, observant, centrally focused narrative pattern brings to mind is the general, disinterested prospect view.[8] McAllister's female travel writers also echo their own socialised viewpoint: their reliance on details, on the relation between their travelling selves and those with whom they travel, their very noticing of the people around them, are significantly aligned with expectations of feminine behaviour and ways of looking.[9] The privilege handed to the prospect viewer, however, assures 'him' of his power and superiority: even as Batten can write an entire analysis of eighteenth-century travel writing with only the barest glance at Lady Mary Wortley Montague and Ann Radcliffe, so too literary history elevates Batten's selection of travel style into the canon. The challenge to the masculine tradition implied by a female-authored travel narrative must be enacted over and over again, individual forays acting not cumulatively but, perhaps, distributively. Thus Wakefield in one breath criticises the 'diffuseness' of prior texts – the inaccuracies, the generalities, the forged connections? – and with her next acknowledges her 'indebtedness' to them. The irony of her debt is that she never mentions a debtor by name; the import of her debt is how extensive it implicitly is, since we are asked to believe, however tacitly, that Wakefield herself has not made the tour.

Thus the authority that she wields in *Family Tour* dislocates itself from Wakefield's position as a woman writing. McAllister notes that women writing about their own travel had to 'authenticate their voices', 'intermingling apology and assertion ... explaining their reasons for travelling and for writing, and the significance of their contribution to a crowded field'.[10] At risk, one might say, because of their autonomous movement both through the landscape and into print, female travel writers like Radcliffe, Helen Maria Williams, Sarah Murray and others, even as they include assertive strategies, yet 'affect' an amateurism that, one suspects, made it easier for their strategies to go undetected. Wakefield's own stratagem, however, is so large as to threaten to defeat her mobility. She accounts for her entrance into the 'crowded field' of travel writing by explicitly directing her narrative at a juvenile audience; her book even includes a glossary defining such terms as 'quartz' and 'bustard'. Again, in her 'Preface' she hopes that her text will correct the 'diffuseness' of previous accounts, bring them into control, impose order, clamp down any wandering structure – both her intended audience and her structure serve to provide her text with a reason to be. Meaning to entertain but more surely to instruct, she sets out a geography lesson (among others) in 437 pages. Her prosaic aims camouflage the broadness of her view: she extends her didactic eye over the entire island for the benefit of her young readers. And yet she remains, as far as her readers can tell, firmly at home, reminding one of Jane Austen's notorious two inches of ivory upon which she scratched an *oeuvre*. Wakefield may cover the British Isles, but she does not *actually*; she may describe, but she has never seen; she may be an author, but not an authority. Thus the steps her fictional family takes in their tour remain thoroughly textual, their sights 'indebted' to other tourists' accounts. Wakefield, finally, has no need to 'authenticate' or excuse her writing, since she has never really set forth at all.

However, as Carole Fabricant notes, literary works 'can incorporate subversive viewpoints and insights into their generally conservative overall approach: the degree through which the [works] function through disjunctions and inconsistencies that lay bare, and challenge, the very ideologies they seem most obviously to affirm'.[11] Wakefield seems to place herself and her text, within a patriarchal structure that recommends outdoor movement for boys and indoor quiet for girls. Reliant on others' authority, embracing her role as teacher in *Family Tour*, she seems to exist within bounds, constricting her eye to previous texts, her pen to a juvenile library. Indeed, Wakefield seems ultra-feminine, ultra-conservative, unwilling even to appear to step outside the domestic circle. The almost glaring subversion of this stance, however, remains the incredible scope of *Family Tour*, which, if nothing else, attests to a vast amount of reading and learning about Britain. More than that, it infuses the text with the conviction that Wakefield has indeed done at least some of the travelling represented in the text. The reader, confronted with the minute particulars of England, Scotland, Ireland, and Wales, cannot be blamed for forgetting the, on second glance, somewhat cursory obligation Wakefield implies to predecessors. Simultaneously closeted and unbound, Wakefield anchors her text from the very beginning in paradox, in subverted subversion. A 'creature on the move',[12] she neither stirs nor stays, and even in the authorial presence revealed in the 'Preface' disallows her reader an un-obstructed view.

Things get no better once in the text. Although her protagonists, Mrs Middleton, her children Arthur, Edwin, Catharine, and Louisa, and the boys' tutor Mr Franklin, set out on their journey as tourists, their aim is not to 'travers[e] ... as much territory, and ... [collect] ... as many sights, as could be crammed into a limited span of time'.[13] Instead, Mrs Middleton declares that her party will 'take sufficient time to inspect everything *worth observation*',[14] not content to rely, as Fabricant says the tourist was 'encour-aged' to do, 'on appearances and fleeting surfaces, on sights that could be apprehended in a single glance rather than ones that required extensive scrutiny or reflection, thereby threatening to become tedious and burden-some, or to slow down the progress of one's crowded itinerary by engrossing the attention for too long'.[15] Mrs Middleton, however, stresses observation, and furthermore distinguishes between that worth observing and that not: giving the eye importance but the mind's eye more importance yet. Rejecting the scrabbling for *meaningless* detail that characterises Fabricant's tourist, she directs that her family take the time to *inspect*. One senses that Wakefield taps simultaneously into a certain scientific disinterest and the involved curiosity attendant on seeing *into* – *in*specting – phenomena. In other words, she wants both inspection and understanding, not Batten's general disinterest.

Because Mrs Middleton assumes the guiding authority at the outset, one might conclude that Wakefield is perhaps locating her own knowledgeable power in the person of her main female character. Mrs Middleton is a widow of, as her name implies, the prosperous upper middle class. She and her family have no financial limitations, staying at the best hotels, free with their money under the correct circumstances, as when Catharine wants more geological specimens or a particularly worthy, but poor, peasant or factory worker has been brought to their attention. It is Mrs Middleton who directs the correct disposal of her money, and she who decides on the scope and purpose of their trip: an educational tour of the British Isles 'for the sake of collecting useful knowledge'; 'I only require attention to those objects of curiosity, whether of nature or of art, that the different parts of the country may present: imprint it on your memories, that we do not travel for the amusement of the moment', she directs.[16] Almost as soon as she assumes this directive power, however, she relinquishes it: we and the children learn that her 'particular friend', a Mr Franklin, will join the tour as the boys' tutor. Moreover, this 'family tour' is not exactly that, as she and the girls will 'take some cottage' on the borders of one of the lakes in Cumberland while the boys and Mr Franklin travel on to the 'northern counties'. Even though the girls regret this decision, they respect their mother's 'reason' too much to doubt its rightness:

> Catharine and Louisa were very sorry that their mother would go no further, but as they knew that her determinations were always founded on reason, and that when once fixed they were unalterable, they submitted without a murmur; at parting with their brothers, they entreated to have a constant account of everything they should see in their journey that was curious or instructive, as the only means of partaking with them the pleasure and improvement of their future travels. Mrs. Middleton approved the request, and having put her sons under the protection of Mr. Franklin, hastened the girls into the carriage, and proceeded to her favourite retirement near Windermere.
>
> Mr Franklin and his companions mounted their horses.[17]

One could, if reading no further, be excused for regarding Mrs Middleton and her creator as almost stagnantly conventional: the boys go north by horseback, expanding their field of movement, while the girls are bundled into enclosure (the carriage) and retreat, the 'favourite retirement' suggesting both meanings of the word: withdrawal and regression. The girls' very position on the 'borders' of a lake, in a 'superior' rustic's cabin, attests to their marginal and confined field of mobility; it is simply not reasonable to expect to travel any further. Surrounded by the 'sublime' lakes and mountains, they stall, liminal to the purpose of the tour, conveniently placed so as to receive the letters of Arthur and Edwin. They are thus dependent on their brothers' eyes and powers of inspection, bearing out the thought that while Mrs Middleton will 'spare neither expense nor trouble in promoting the improvement and happiness of her children',[18] such generosity applies mainly to Arthur and Edwin.

Not only the girls but Mrs Middleton too depends on the boys' far-reaching vision. Although she exercises her authority in deciding on her holiday home, making sure it is the right sort of rustic she chooses, it is Arthur who actually finds the place. During a sudden storm in the mountains Arthur goes looking for shelter for his mother and sisters and finds a secluded cottage, the inhabitants of which offer their hospitality. '[P]erceiv[ing]' that the inhabitants were of a class far superior to the day labourer', Mrs Middleton decides to settle in the cottage;[19] the end result is intellectual and visual confinement for the female contingent compared to the freedom of field granted to the males. Indeed, in what is perhaps by now a familiar move, Wakefield undercuts even Mrs Middleton's powers of observation. Although she has perceived her hosts' superiority, this is enhanced by their 'appearance of decency and plenty ... the man held a small farm ... The furniture was plain, but neat and convenient; and the manners of the farmer and his wife were gentle, and their conversation intelligent'. Mrs Middleton has deduced personal superiority from, first, appearances: personal objects, the surrounding farm, furniture, and manners. It is only after distinguishing such outward attributes that she notes intelligent conversation, last in the above-quoted sequence. Resembling Wordsworth's Michael, in fact, this man is defined by his property, but for the benefit of eyes other than his own: his status as landowner thus gives him an unmistakable superiority, to the point that this superiority is evident even before one knows of the land owned. Mrs Middleton's powers of perception are made dependent on the appearances that provide clues to the reality, and, although she is vindicated by the manners and conversation of the rustics, one senses that her perception has been exposed as, perhaps, somewhat superficial. It was, after all, Mrs Middleton's specific injunction to her children that they take sufficient time to inspect everything worth observing; her actions when approving the rustics seem to belie this instruction. Perhaps this demystification of her perception allows us to question her reason as well: might not that superficiality extend to her decision that it is 'reasonable' to keep the girls at Windermere? By undercutting the female character invested not only with reason but with convention, Wakefield subverts the proprieties that cause Mrs Middleton to make the decision she does.

The question remains problematic, however; Wakefield also allows the tutor, Mr Franklin, to assume didactic authority, leaving Mrs Middleton room only to mention, here and there, the famous (and mostly male[20]) personages of the regions through which they pass. In addition, once Mr Franklin takes over Mrs Middleton's authority, Arthur and Edwin become more prominent in the narrative. The girls, Catharine and Louisa, are not eliminated, but they are often elided (and this is before the group splits up at the lakes), becoming anonymous parts of the group, sometimes silently erased from the group: when visiting the astronomer Herschel,[21] we are told that 'they' explore the observatory; the only specific mention is of Mr Franklin's pupils, however, who would be just the boys. It is not made clear who 'they' are, but the significance works both ways. While the girls are not specifically mentioned, neither are they specifically excluded. Once again, Wakefield eludes a definite statement.

Wakefield's strategy of elision and suggestion leads to some creative instances of narrative avoidance. For example, when Mrs Middleton finally leaves the lakes with her daughters to meet her sons, the female travellers make a detour through Wales, in the company of a Swiss émigré and his daughter. Not surprisingly, the émigré makes the physical explorations of the peaks and caverns they encounter, while Mrs Middleton and the girls sit in inns, but the trip to Wales is interesting for more than who it shows climbing mountains and descending into caverns; it is also remarkable for how it is presented in the text. The journey up until the separation at Windermere, and the boys' rambles in Scotland, have been narrated as they occurred, the narrator as it were accompanying the tourists and faithfully recording their adventures. The trip through Wales, however, is narrated via Catharine's journal, which she keeps only during the journey towards reunion with their brothers. It is, therefore, already limited to Catharine's rendering of what was seen in Wales, and while the omniscient narrator keeps guard over Arthur, Edwin, and Mr Franklin, the same is not done for Catharine, Louisa, and Mrs Middleton. Once Catharine's journal is produced, it is then selectively read by Mrs Middleton who 'omits' certain portions at her discretion when they merely recapitulate what the boys have already seen – on a larger scale – in Scotland. Furthermore, certain of the more manly sights seen solely by M. Rougemont, the émigré, are available only through his description, transcribed by Catharine into her journal, and then read aloud by Mrs Middleton; and, compared to the space devoted to what the boys see in Scotland, the descriptions are short and general. The girls' journey is truncated narratively, reliant on second-hand inform-ation and only read aloud piecemeal. Moreover, the journey is fragmented in time, triply removed from the present-time narration given to the boys' journeys: one must negotiate one's way through the time passed, the substitution of journal-narration, and the changed narrator-reader: Mrs Middleton for Catharine for the narrator. Effectively defusing – and collectivising – the experiences the girls have had in Wales, this strategy of narrative-stitching transforms into a story Catharine's records of, for example, passages over dangerous mountain roads: the experience is re-corded from memory in a journal, then read aloud long after the fact, given reality for the group as a whole only once it has passed into a kind of fiction. The girls' journey, in many ways approximating the boys', recedes into the past, becoming a literary exercise that in microcosm reminds the reader of *Family Tour* as a whole. Read this way, Wakefield's text remands any challenge it may be making to readers accustomed to gendered behav-iours; her own authorship again defuses itself, becomes as non-threatening (because unassertive), and as derivative as Catharine's journal.

It seems that Wakefield works so hard to protect herself from any charges of non-conformity that she reduces her text to stereotypes. As if to under-score this point, she carefully blocks the girls and their mother from enjoying uninhibited prospects in Wales as their brothers so often do in Scotland.

For the female travellers, prospects are meaningless: Wakefield enlarges on the theme only when she later permits Mrs Middleton and the girls to '[mount] a tedious ascent to the summit of a mountain … without observing any striking object'.[22] The various strategies by which the female eye is debarred from viewing the landscape underscore the ease with which Wakefield's male characters claim that privilege. Not only when with the women, but also on their single-sex trips through Scotland, Ireland and Cornwall, the men ascend every possible hill or mountain and enjoy the view thus spread out, most times 'boundless' or 'command[ing] a charming prospect'. The female contingent's privileged position as moneyed travellers opens up potential prospects, but their gender seems to render those prospects too difficult, tiring, or uninteresting to reach. Thus one is not surprised to find, at nearly the volume's end, the 'family' trip suddenly described as Mrs Middleton's '*son's* tour of Great Britain', cancelling Catharine, Louisa, and even Edwin as viable members of the tour.[23] Arthur becomes the beneficiary of a journey, the original purpose of which was to 'collect knowledge' on all their parts. The battle Wakefield has waged with herself over the question of female participation and authority would seem decided.

But because Wakefield herself has called this struggle, the outcome cannot be so easily determined. Donna Landry points out when writing about Mary Collier that 'if a woman addresses the public by writing rationally and eloquently, she *may* be read, and her audience's consciousness altered accordingly'.[24] Likewise, if a woman addresses the problem of female travel protocol by writing conventionally and eloquently, she may be able to register her dissatisfaction with that protocol even as she seems to observe it. In an approximation of *l'écriture féminine*, she writes almost invisibly, using the spaces occupied by the dominant, expected discourse to shadow in an alternative discourse. Yet, if she wants to be read, the shadows must remain fleeting; 'incorporat[ing] subversive viewpoints and insights into [a] generally conservative overall perspective' still requires the dominance of conservatism.[25] Strangely enough, the female reader of a narrative like *Family Tour*, because she can only catch glimpses of shadows sabotaging the convention, becomes a kind of tourist herself, dependent here on 'fleeting surfaces, on sights that [can] be apprehended in a single glance'.[26] Tying in with the limited power of the eye normally granted women and revealed so thoroughly in *Family Tour*, the quick glances encouraged by the subtext of *Tour* ensure that reading it will not overtly interfere with the business of being a woman reading travel narratives in lieu of travelling. One suspects, however, that the information thus conveyed enlarges the understanding more flexibly than the seeing of actual sights. What is being worked on is the response of the viewer to custom, to convention. Even as Fabricant's potentially destructive tourist is allowed glimpses of what he can never reasonably attain – property – in the hopes of defusing his desire simply to take that property, so travel narratives function on one level as palliatives for the woman constrained from actual travel. Narratives such as Wakefield's, however, and others that challenge the accepted parameters of eighteenth-century travel writing, can achieve the opposite: by subtly training the female eye to distrust the open view, the dominance of the prospect, by encoding the textual landscape with a discourse that dismisses the importance of the prospect, a new way of looking can be insinuated into the landscape. Revolutionary in its import, such a practice yet depends on the willingness of the eye to be diverted from the prospect, from the dominant way of seeing. It depends on the capacity of the eye to recognise the existence of the shadow behind the shapes written.

Wakefield participates in this unspoken, nearly invisible practice characteristically. As much as she limits her female travellers' points of view and physical mobility, confining them to stereotyped exclamations of delight over flower gardens and 'covered walk[s] ... lined with shops, where the richest and most elegant toys ... [are] displayed with the greatest taste and variety';[27] as much as she pushes her male characters up hills, into caverns, and over the sea, she remains the final authority, the ultimate director – and describer – of the journey. Arthur writes how glad he is that his sisters were saved from the terror of underground shaking rocks, but Wakefield has both contrived the situation and put Arthur there to experience it. She not only accompanies her characters up eminences to prospects, she creates the mountain and the view. And while she employs strategies that sink the women's trip to Wales into a second-hand recital, she also portrays Mrs Middleton as a widow who takes – pays for – Mr Franklin on her tour, and who does nearly the same for M. Rougemont in Wales: it has been 'pity' that induced her first to become friendly with the émigrés, and pity implies condescension, implies that Mrs Middleton holds herself and her daughters in a class above the Rougemonts. The end result is a travelling group that looks correct – male chaperon/authority, mother, her children – but whose internal dynamics, at least financial, are reversed; subversion shadows the convention. Accompanying this is internal evidence that suggests Wakefield's desire to limit the mobility her male tourists would seem inherently to own. Each sea voyage the boys and Mr Franklin take, from Scotland to an outer island, from England to Dublin, from Ireland back to England, is disrupted by wild and dangerous storms that, perhaps fortuitously, land them on some part of the island they had not expected to explore, but also threaten to end their tour altogether. The unexpectedness of each storm and the life-threatening danger each poses indicates that Wakefield may be criticising the mobility she allows her male travellers; that they barely live to see the Outer Hebrides, the Isle of Man, or Cornwall suggests not only the folly of sea voyages but an implicit punishment for those who take that voyage – her male characters invested with male authority and the privilege to travel where and when they will.

In fact, Wakefield never allows her reader to decide one way or the other. Her paramount strategy is to evade definition: to present men and women as they are expected to travel and to act, and to undermine that presentation, and to subvert that undermining – a double evasion that preserves her independence from orthodoxy *and* protest. The popularity of the book – the British Library lists at least fifteen editions up to 1840 – probably indicates that more readers were comforted by the stereotypes and informed by the lessons than were startled by the subversions of each; the under-writing[28] remains unobtrusive, though present. What persists is an interpretatively elusive travel author, demure in her 'indebtedness' to previous authors,[29] simultaneously incredible in her knowledge of the British Isles and her presentation of that knowledge. Although we are told from the outset that her narrative is a fictional sketch, the completeness of the text and its familiarity with everything it presents to our view encourages us to forget this.

Wakefield's text, published in 1804, closes a decade that saw the publication of four other important travelogues by women. Ann Radcliffe's *A Journey Made in the Summer of 1794* came out in 1795, Mary Wollstone-craft's *Letters Written During a Short Residence in Sweden, Norway and Denmark* in 1796, Helen Maria Williams's *A Tour in Switzerland* in 1798, and Sarah Scott Murray's *A Companion and Useful Guide to the Beauties of Scotland* in 1799. How well do Mrs Middleton, Catharine, and Louisa mirror Radcliffe, Wollstonecraft, Williams, and Murray in their actions; does their restricted movement represent a more conservative reaction against the very freedom that takes the earlier women to the Continent, Scotland, and Scandinavia? Clearly, the four texts present their authors as intrepid travellers, but then so, in many ways, is Mrs Middleton, despite her voluntary marginalisation; and as if to prove McAllister's point that very few female travellers really travelled *alone*, only Wollstonecraft, whose life has already involved the rejection of so many conventions, breaks this one as well: Williams travels with male guides and companions, Radcliffe 'in the company of her nearest relative and friend',[30] and Murray, whose text does contain some radical departures from the feminine norm, 'with [her] maid by her side, and [her] man on the seat behind' her carriage.[31] Aligned with Mrs Middleton in their retention of male companionship, only Murray, it would seem, competes with her in economic mastery, her reference to 'her man' plainly identifying him as her servant, in her employ. By contrast, Radcliffe's self-conscious self-presentation as a wife in most ways dependent on her husband is heightened by her prefatory statement that 'where the oeconomical and political conditions of countries are touched upon in the following work, the remarks are less her own than elsewhere'; Radcliffe establishes the presence of a co-writer as well as co-traveller at the outset of her narrative, subsuming her authority in the plural 'we' here and throughout the text, and telling us she omits her husband's name only at his request and to forestall any accusations of 'design[ing] to attract attention by extraordinary novelty'.[32] While not husbands, Williams's male companions prove invaluable to her as well; she even credits one, M. Ramond, with the 'philosophical discussion' she feels incapable of after a particularly gruelling mountain ascent to view a glacier.[33] Left behind while her male companions explore the glacier, Williams is further disempowered when they descend another part of the glacier and leave her stranded until after dark, her mule slips his bridle and escapes, and she must be, once retrieved from her borderline position, carried down the mountain by the guides, since 'to walk down the valley was for [her] impossible'. In the end, the men fashion a litter of shrubs 'in leathern girdles fastened' to walking sticks (a fine metaphor for the usefulness of walking sticks to female travellers) and 'not without some apprehension' she is carried safely down.[34]

The similarity between Williams's sojourn on the edge of the glacier and Mrs Middleton's on the edge of a lake (a kind of thawed glacier?), while the menfolk explore the sublime heights of glaciers and Scotland, reinforce the properly feminine position of marginal stasis. As the female Middletons learn of Scotland through the boys' letters, so Williams learns of the glacier through the 'charming writing' of M. Ramond, who overcomes the feminising epithet through his masculine freedom of mobility. Radcliffe, too, finds ascension difficult and overstraining, for although in the decorous company of her husband she reaches several summits, her prose dwells on the terror and danger involved in scaling the heights. '[T]remendous chasms' beckon them with mesmerizing sound; 'the length and precipitance of their course ... hurr[ies] the sight with them into the abyss' and, through nervous sympathy, encourages the body to follow until 'we recoil from the views with involuntary horror'.[35] Although the Burkean sublime requires a certain amount of terror to be genuine, it also allows for the viewer's certainty of personal safety; Radcliffe's experience does not, which disables the sublime and leaves only risk. Wollstonecraft's thoroughly anomalous position, however, opens the prospect to her without hazard on several occasions, while Murray is perhaps the most unusual in that she insists on the availability of prospects, not just for herself but for any female traveller *properly prepared* with such accoutrements as sticks, 'a little attention', and, one suspects, a will equal to that of Murray herself. Yet even Murray encodes some discomfort with the prospect view in her travel book: Chapter Two purports, in both the contents page and chapter heading, to conclude with 'The Views from Calton Hill, and Arthur's Seat', yet neglects to do so, while another viewpoint seems to open to the sight of no one at all. 'After climbing the hill of Moncrief, and two miles north of the Brig of Earn, then comes the charming prospect ... and which, on taking a short turn round a hill, at once opens to the sight', says Murray, and the reader is left to wonder – who, exactly, climbs? [36]

Indeed, Wakefield not so much revises a tradition but exposes it, articulating and emphasising the slippages, elisions, and outright – and self-imposed – restrictions of her predecessors. Williams and the others, while assuming greater freedom and autonomy than Wakefield allows to Mrs Middleton and her daughters, remain to greater or lesser degrees hampered, whether by skirts, the lack of crampons, deficient knowledge of 'oeconomical and philosophical conditions', even fear of heights. Again, the exception is Wollstonecraft, who experiences only two similar episodes: once she admits the possibility of rape (something her contemporaries, with their male companions, seem protected from), and once she records with evident delight her host's comment that she converses like a man. Wakefield in her turn highlights the very unmanly behaviours sketched, hinted at, or suppressed in the earlier books, fulfilling in Mrs Middleton, at least part of the time, a stereotype of the proper lady traveller. The difficulties and restrictions implied in the earlier texts become literally textual in Wakefield's *Family Tour*, integral to the plot, to the structure of her little family, to the lessons she teaches her juvenile readership. Yet always complicating such a project in a way not possible to the 'real' travels narrated by the 1790s travellers is Wakefield's authorial status, her presence as creator not just of Mrs Middleton and her daughters but of Mr Franklin and his charges; her position as author means that even as she restricts the movement of her female characters she rather widely extends her own, encompassing the journeys of all her characters easily and without dissembling. Not even Wollstonecraft accomplishes this.

At one point the readers of *Family Tour* learn that education provides the mind with a 'vast compass of knowledge',[37] a mental prospect view that opens the world up for inspection. With the emphasis on critical inspection, not general knowledge, of that vastness, Wakefield's opening injunction via Mrs Middleton that her children/readers 'take sufficient time to inspect everything worth observation' translates into a challenge to her readers to decipher the language she uses to illuminate *and* cover her project; as she says of Erse reapers, 'one song constantly used ... corresponds to the action'.[38] Understanding the song can help to understand the action, and vice versa. It is up to the reader to take sufficient time to inspect Wakefield's text, to learn the song, and thereby uncover the meaning of the action. The best way to learn is to experiment for oneself; the best way to learn about the British Isles is to travel them. Wakefield refuses to make it easy for us – we must decide if her work reinforces or exposes the strictures on male and female travel and, one suspects, education. Only our close inspection, she implies, will make the result, whatever we decide it to be, worth looking at.

Notes

This essay appears in expanded form in my book, *Romantic Visualities: Landscape, Gender and Romanticism* (Basingstoke, 1998).

1 Priscilla Wakefield, *A Family Tour Through the British Empire; Containing some Account of its Manufactures, Natural and Artificial Curiosities, History and Antiquities; interspersed with Biographical Anecdotes. Particularly adapted to the Amusement and Instruction of Youth* (London, 1804), unpaginated 'Preface'.

2 For an enlightening discussion of the gendering of the detail as feminine, see Naomi Schor, *Reading in Detail: Aesthetics and the Feminine* (London and New York, 1987). John Barrell characterises the prospect view and the general or abstract as a function of masculinity in several works; see especially *An Equal, Wide Survey* (London, 1983); *Poetry, Language and Politics* (Manchester, 1988); and 'The Public Prospect and the Private View: The Politics of Taste in Eighteenth-century Britain', in Simon Pugh, ed., *Reading Landscape: Country – City – Capital* (Manchester, 1990), 19–40. See also Peter de Bolla, 'The Visibility of Visuality: Vauxhall Gardens and the Siting of the Viewer' (paper delivered at the University of Pennsylvania, September 1991).

3 *Family Tour*, unpaginated 'Preface'.

4 Marie McAllister, 'Woman on the Journey: Eighteenth-century British Women's Travel in Fact and Fiction' (diss., Princeton University, 1988), 1.

5 Charles L. Batten, Jr, *Pleasurable Instruction: Form and Convention in Eighteenth-century Travel Literature* (Berkeley, 1978), 28.

6 Carole Fabricant, 'The Literature of Domestic Tourism and the Public Consumption of Private Property', in Felicity Nussbaum and Laura Brown, eds, *The New Eighteenth Century: Theory, Politics, English Literature* (New York, 1987), 259.

7 'Woman on the Journey', 100.

8 For a full discussion of the cultural and literary politics of the gendered viewpoint, see my book *Romantic Visualities*.

9 For a number of essays that investigate the feminisation of these and other important social constructs, see Michelle Zimbalist Rosaldo and Louise Lamphere, eds, *Woman, Culture, and Society* (Stanford, 1974).

10 'Woman on the Journey', 9.

11 'Literature of Domestic Tourism', 274.

12 *Ibid.*, 259.

13 *Ibid.*

14 *Family Tour*, 2 (emphasis added).

15 'Literature of Domestic Tourism', 259–60.

16 *Family Tour*, 2.

17 *Ibid.*, 65.

18 *Ibid.*, 117.

19 *Ibid.*, 65 (emphasis added).

20 It is worth noting that when a female luminary is described, Mrs Middleton is the speaker: she takes note of women such as Hannah More, Aphra Behn, various countesses and noblewomen, and Susanna Centlivre, among others.

21 Wakefield is careful to include notice of Herschel's sister Caroline, who lives with him and assists him in his work.

22 *Family Tour*, 337.

23 *Ibid.*, 348 (emphasis added).

24 Donna Landry, 'The Resignation of Mary Collier: Some Problems in Feminist Literary History', in Nussbaum and Brown, eds, *The New Eighteenth Century*, 112.

25 Fabricant, 'Literature of Domestic Tourism', 274.

26 *Ibid.*, 259.

27 *Family Tour*, 393.

28 I use the hyphen in 'under-writing' to recall the shadow writing I observe to be Wakefield's version of *l'ecriture feminine*. However, the additional meaning of 'endorse' also pertains, and acts as a furtherance of Wakefield's slippery ideology.

29 Internal evidence of other debts, for instance a faithful-dog story Wakefield credits to the *Monthly Magazine* for April 1802, makes one wonder if the entire book may not be a pastiche, an instance of literary japanning suitable for a lady's afternoon occupation. One also wonders if that is exactly the impression Wakefield wants to convey.

30 Ann Radcliffe, *A Journey Made in the Summer of 1794, Through Holland and the Western Frontier of Germany, with a return Down the Rhine: to which are added Observations During a Tour to the Lakes of Lancashire, Westmoreland, and Cumberland* (London, 1795), unpaginated 'Preface'.

31 The Honourable Mrs Murray of Kensington, *A Companion and Useful Guide to the Beauties of Scotland, to the Lakes of Westmorland, Cumberland, and Lancashire; and to the Curiosities in the District of Craven, in the West Riding*

of Yorkshire. To which is Added, a More Particular Description of Scotland, Especially that Part of it, called the Highlands* (London, 1799), 42.

32 Radcliffe, *Journey,* unpaginated 'Preface'.
33 Helen Maria Williams, *A Tour in Switzerland; or, A View of the Present State of the Government & Manners of those Cantons: with Comparative Sketches of the Present State of Paris* (London, 1798), 2: 15.
34 *Ibid.,* 13, 14.
35 Radcliffe, *Journey,* 455–6.
36 *Companion and Useful Guide,* 178.
37 *Family Tour,* 218.
38 *Ibid.,* 180.

The secrets of Ann Radcliffe's English travels

Dorothy McMillan

Christina Rossetti, who admired Mrs Radcliffe, was asked by the publisher Macmillan to write her biography. She began enthusiastically 'Radcliffing' in the British Museum.[1] After a summer of this activity, she gave up for want of material: Mrs Radcliffe did not apparently have enough life to write about. This want of material was also felt while she was alive, by those who had been seduced by her romances and who, throughout the silence between the publication of *The Italian* in 1797 and her death in 1823, awaited more with decreasing hope. The silence was tantalisingly peculiar, given the success of *The Mysteries of Udolpho* and *The Italian*. Yet that very silence gave a continued lease of life to the terrors and sublimities that she had authorised – what was not known about Mrs Radcliffe was freely invented. She suffered the 'honours of posthumous fame' while she still lived: 'Her unbroken retirement suggested to those, who learned that she still lived, a fancy that something unhappy was connected with her story, and gave occasion to the most absurd and groundless rumours, respecting her condition ... some spoke of her as dead, and others repre-sented her as afflicted with mental alienation.'[2] In a way Radcliffe had only herself to blame, for her novels had sanctioned a way of reading which encouraged the desire to uncover guilty secrets in half-known lives, and this offered a model for reading her own life. Unsurprisingly, one guilty secret was felt to be that her fictional encounters with terror had driven her mad. Even after her death, some were unwilling to relinquish this notion of the revenge of the unconscious upon 'the Great Enchantress'.[3]

But Mrs Radcliffe's secret is perhaps not to have had one or, to put it in another way, to have lived in a manner that called in question the potential subversiveness of her fictions. For she was certainly not doing nothing for twenty-six years: to live a life of retirement is not to do nothing. She was with her husband, William, a lawyer turned owner and editor of *The English Chronicle*, 'thankfully enjoying the choicest blessings of life – with a cheerfulness as equable as if she had never touched the secret springs of horror, and with a humility as genuine as though she had not extended the domain of romance, for the delight and benefit of her species'.[4] Specifically, she was between 1797 and 1822 making twice-yearly carriage and walking excursions with her husband chiefly in the south of England, extending the travels that she had begun in Holland, Germany, and the English Lakes in 1794. She published an account of the early travels in 1795: this is fairly early for published travels in the English lakes – William Gilpin's account of his travels in the Lake District had appeared in 1786 but Wordsworth did not publish his *A Description of the Scenery of the Lakes* until 1822, although his introduction to Joseph Wilkinson's collection of scenes drawn in the Lake District was privately published, without Wordsworth's name, in twelve monthly instalments in 1810. Radcliffe's more homely travel diaries remained unpublished until after her death, when selections from them were included in the 1826 volume along with the romance *Gaston de Blondville*, the metrical romance *St Alban's Abbey*, and some poems. These travels, both published and private, are, I want to suggest, not merely what filled in the time of public silence but also what in part explain it; for there is some evidence that the processes of travel, the observation of actual landscape and the effort to render it and its effects, worked towards a loss of conviction in the landscape strategies of the novels. Radcliffe's secret then may be to have presaged in her silence, in her privacy, the death of her own mode.

Certainly it was her own mode. Radcliffe's construction of nature in her romances, particularly in *The Romance of the Forest* (1791), *The Mysteries of Udolpho* (1794), and *The Italian* (1797), is dependent on existing literary and visual models but there is no gainsaying the originality of her deployment of them. Her originality is signalled by Scott, who hailed Radcliffe as 'the first to introduce into her fictions a beautiful and fanciful tone of natural description and impressive narrative which had hitherto been exclusively applied to poetry'; Radcliffe had a title 'to be considered the first poetess of romantic fiction'.[5] The poetry derived from the use of scenery to provide atmosphere, and to convey thought and feeling, and this in prose fiction as opposed to verse is new. Later Ruskin, despite his dislike of an aesthetic of the visual based on modes of feeling rather than moral responses, recognises the novelty of Radcliffe's procedures. Ruskin speaks of Radcliffe's 'love of natural scenery, which although mingled with what was merely dramatic … was still itself genuine and intense, differing altogether in character from any sentiments previously traceable in literature'.[6] The natural scenery in the novels is, however, in another sense, unnatural, wholly a cultural construct. There is a certain irony in the insistence in the novels on the superiority of nature to art since Radcliffe's nature is wholly an effect of art. Radcliffe's scenery in France and in Italy, as is commonly known, is derived from the travel writings of others, the paintings of Claude, Gaspard and Nicolas Poussin (for harmonious and beautiful effects) and Salvator Rosa (for the evocation of the sublime), the whole validated by Burke's aesthetic of the beautiful and the sublime. So well did Mrs Radcliffe render these landscapes that her contemporaries were persuaded into taking as actual scenes what were imitations of previously pictured ones. *The Critical Review*, for example, praises the verisimilitude of the descriptions in *The Romance of the Forest* of a country which Mrs Radcliffe had never seen, 'the accounts of Savoy in this novel are often beautiful, and seem to be drawn from personal experience';[7] as late as 1823 in *The Edinburgh Review* there is a footnote to the effect that Radcliffe's husband had been attached to one of the British embassies and that she had accompanied him to Italy where she 'imbibed the taste for picturesque scenery, and the obscure and wild superstitions of mouldering castles, of which she has made so beautiful a use in her romances'.[8]

The willingness of her readership to be fooled by second-hand pictorialism is an indication of how powerful this pictorialism had become as a way of seeing and reacting to the external world. Certainly, Radcliffe in her novels does nothing to unsettle the orthodoxies of the late eighteenth-century pictorial modes or the pressure they exerted on ways of seeing nature. In her characterisation of landscapes Radcliffe is always writing out of an unquestioned orthodoxy; she never imagines in her fiction, or indeed in her travel writing, that her readers will not understand what she intends by characterising scenery as sublime or picturesque or beautiful (and this despite the shifts in meaning that the picturesque in particular underwent in the course of the eighteenth century).[9] She never writes as one arguing her readers into a position but always as one who knows that she can command assent to her propositions about landscapes. In *The Romance of the Forest* the heroine, Adeline, who has spent much of her early life immured in a monastery, deprived of the consolations of nature, may be taken as a paradigm of Mrs Radcliffe's expectations of her readership:

> The fresh breeze of the morning animated the spirits of Adeline, whose mind was delicately sensible to the beauties of nature. As she viewed the flowery luxuriance of the turf, and the tender green of the trees, or caught, between the opening banks, a glimpse of the varied landscape, rich with wood, and fading into blue and distant mountains, her heart expanded in momentary joy. With Adeline the charms of external nature were heightened by those of novelty: she had seldom seen the grandeur of an extensive prospect, or the magnificence of a wide horizon – and not often the picturesque beauties of more confined scenery.[10]

Adeline instinctively responds to what the reader is expected to recognise as worthy of a response. What she looks at is pictorially conceived with a varied foreground partially opening on to the obscure splendour of the heights behind; the eye of the reader is led into the picture by Adeline, the figure in the landscape. The reader is expected to comprehend both the potentially sublime in 'the magnificence of a wide horizon' and the more limited, yet delightful possibilities of 'more confined scenery'. The gaze of Adeline is, despite being untutored by actual experience, wholly confident – it knows what it sees. The reader then may assent to Radcliffe's pictures not because they confirm the results of their own experiences of external nature but because they coherently exploit a convention.

Against the confidence of Adeline's assimilation of the landscape and its significances here might be argued the uncertainties that attend Emily's encounters with the sublime landscapes of Udolpho. Emily's approach to Udolpho is attended by fears that make the Apennines a less secure source of the sublime for her than were the Alps. Yet I would contend that Emily, like Adeline, assimilates the landscape with the kind of confidence that derives from an encounter with comprehended picture rather than from the processes of engaging with the fearful unknown. Montoni announces his castle with the gesture of a connoisseur pointing out the best piece in his salon: '"There", said Montoni, speaking for the first time in several hours, "is Udolpho".' We might think of Ferrara and the portrait of his last Duchess. Here is how Emily sees:

> Emily gazed with melancholy awe upon the castle, which she under-stood to be Montoni's; for, though it was now lighted up by the setting sun, the gothic greatness of its features, and its mouldering walls of dark grey stone, rendered it a gloomy and sublime object. As she gazed, the light died away on its walls, leaving a melancholy purple tint, which spread deeper and deeper, as the thin vapour crept up the mountain, while the battlements above were still tipped with splendour. From these too, the rays soon faded, and the whole edifice was invested with the solemn duskiness of evening. Silent, lonely and sublime, it seemed to stand the sovereign of the scene, and to frown defiance on all, who dared to invade its solitary reign. As the twilight deepened, its features became more awful in the obscurity, and Emily continued to gaze, till its clustering towers were alone seen, rising over the tops of the woods, beneath whose thick shade the carriages soon after began to ascend.[11]

Emily's gaze assimilates the castle in the landscape, effectively neutralising its threat. Radcliffe's suggestiveness in the use of half-heard sounds may create a sense of danger, but the framed pictorialism of her landscape mode contains and orders, never allowing for what may be seen out of the corner of the eye.

The uses to which Radcliffe puts her pictures are, of course, less derivative than the aesthetic that sanctions them and in some ways prefigure the concerns of the male Romantic poets. She is certainly in the older sentimental tradition when she associates landscape and feeling and when feeling is itself close to a synonym for moral response. Nor do the villains, male or female, ever have a feeling response to the beauties or the sublimities of nature. The Marquis of Montalt, in many ways the most vile of the Gothic oppressors of young, innocent women, places the abducted Adeline in a chamber fitted out with exotic artificiality: 'The hangings were of straw-coloured silk, adorned with a variety of landscapes and historical paintings, the subjects of which partook of the voluptuous character of the owner.'[12] Since Radcliffe is offering as natural landscapes pictures of a more decorous nature, we are unfortunately reminded of the limitations of her pictorialism.

Montoni is unaffected by the sublime surroundings of Udolpho: the characteristics of Udolpho which fit the Burkean criteria for the sublime are for him merely utilitarian, since from his mountain fastness he can pursue his career in banditry and terrorise his wife and her niece. In *The Italian* neither Schedoni nor his evil accomplice, the Marchesa di Vivaldi, is susceptible to the powers of landscape to evoke feeling: 'The Marchesa reclined on a sofa before an open lattice; her eyes were fixed upon the prospect without, but her attention was wholly occupied by the visions that evil passions painted to her imagination.'[13] Response to natural beauty then acts as a moral indicator in a manner consonant with the conventions of the sentimental but neither beauty nor sublimity has the property of modifying the sensibility of those not already predisposed to respond.

But Mrs Radcliffe pushes somewhat beyond this by locating this predisposition within childhood experience. Clara, in *The Romance of the Forest*, is born 'amid scenes of grandeur and sublimity' in the Alps and has 'quickly imbibed a taste for their charms, which taste was heightened by the influence of a warm imagination'.[14] Emily's attachment to nature is formed in the bosom of the family among scenes of domesticated loveliness which lead naturally on to an appreciation of the sublime and the divine:

> It was one of Emily's earliest pleasures to ramble among the scenes of nature; nor was it in the soft and glowing landscape that she most delighted; she loved the wild wood-walks, that skirted the mountain; and still more the mountain's stupendous recesses, where the silence

and grandeur of solitude impressed a sacred awe upon her heart, and lifted her thoughts to the GOD OF HEAVEN AND EARTH.[15]

Emily's walks are solitary but they come out of communal familial experience. Her father has himself derived his love of nature from boyish attachments: 'such was his attachment to objects he remembered from his boyish days, that he had in some instances sacrificed taste to sentiment'.[16] He is horrified when his brother-in-law, the worldly M. Quesnel, proposes to cut down a chestnut tree that 'encumbers his chateau'. ' "Good God!" exclaimed St Aubert, "you surely will not destroy that noble chestnut, which has flourished for centuries, the glory of the estate! ... How often, in my youth, have I climbed among its leaves, while the heavy shower has pattered above, and not a rain drop reached me!" ' [17] The history of the self is thus located in the history of known and loved places; Emily inherits this sensibility from her father, and her travels from her home, La Vallée, are always accompanied by her memories of her happiness there. Since the love of nature then derives from the sociability of the family it promotes further sociability, and Emily and Valancourt are initially bonded, as are Ellena and Vivaldi in *The Italian*, through their mutual love of landscape.

Anne Mellor in *Romanticism and Gender* identifies what she calls 'the positive Radcliffean sublime'; 'For Radcliffe the experience of the sublime in nature is one that is finally *beyond* language, one that impresses the finite self with the presence of an inexpressible other.' [18] The confrontation with the divine that is the invariable accompaniment of sublime feelings in Radcliffe 'elevates the perceiving self to a sense of her or his own integrity and worth as a unique product of divine creation'. Since it is then grounded in self-esteem, 'the Radcliffean experience of the positive sublime can produce a sympathy or love that connects the self with other people'.[19]

But the topos of inexpressibility which Mellor here invokes as Radcliffe's method of validating the uniqueness of the individual self, may from another position be seen as blurring the distinctions upon which uniqueness might seem to depend. And Radcliffe's other resource, the composed picture, is also limited in the very repetitiveness of its conventional variety. These limitations become particularly worrying if Radcliffe's use of landscape is felt to provide a model for subjectivity. David Punter suggests that such a use is made in the view from the turret-room in the convent of San Stefano, to which 'Ellena retreats during her imprisonment, and in which she derives comfort from the scenes of sublime grandeur with which the convent is fortunately surrounded. Radcliffe cannot and does not seriously try to explain how it is that Ellena is allowed this retreat; and this is surely because the turret-room is largely an image for the interior of Ellena's own mind.' [20] Elsewhere too Radcliffe places imprisoned characters at windows from which they can view the world outside and it does seem plausible to suggest that Radcliffe is offering to the character a window out, and to the reader a window in. But the window is also a framing device and what Ellena sees from her window is characteristic of the composed landscape and entirely characteristic of what is seen by others from other windows:

> These precipices were broken into cliffs, which, in some places, impended far above their base, and, in others, rose in nearly perpendicular lines, to the walls of the monastery, which they supported. Ellena, with a delightful pleasure looked down them ... till her eye rested on the thick chestnut woods that extended over their winding base, and which, softening to the plains, seemed to form a gradation between the variegated cultivation there, and the awful wildness of the rocks above.[21]

It becomes problematic then if unique female subjectivities are conveyed either by asserting the impossibility of conveying them or by acts of repetition of an orthodox method of picturing.

When Radcliffe came to make her actual journeys, she was, of course, unsurprisingly still powerfully influenced by the culturally constructed way of seeing and of describing that inform her fiction. The real landscapes of England are pronounced sublime or beautiful or picturesque with usually the same confidence that the reader will share comprehension and approval of these characteristics. But some uneasiness begins to show, and her account of her tour of the Lake District shows her increasingly aware of problems in the inexpressibility of the sublime and of the difficulties attendant on the composition of prospects. The countryside will not always yield itself to the habit of composition, the eye cannot retain that grip of the prospect that picturing demands:

> Ullswater in all its windings, which give it the form of the letter S, is nearly nine miles long; the width is various, sometimes nearly two miles and seldom less than one; but Skelling-nab, a vast rock in the second reach, projects so as to reduce it to less than a quarter of a mile. These are chiefly the reputed measurements, but the eye loses its power of judging even of the breadth, confounded by the boldness of the shores and the grandeur of the fells, that rise beyond.[22]

Even when prospects do offer themselves, they sometimes do so with a profligacy that defeats description: On Skiddaw she finds that 'the prospects that burst upon us from every part of the vast horizon, when we had gained the summit, were such as we had scarcely dared to hope for, and must now rather venture to enumerate, than to describe'.[23] Enumeration is here a courageous, even assertive way of refusing the potentially fallacious descriptive mode:

> We stood on a pinnacle, commanding the whole dome of the sky. The prospects below, each of which had been before considered separately as a great scene, were now miniature parts of the immense landscape. To the north, lay, like a map, the vast tract of low country, which extends between Bassenthwaite and the Irish Channel, marked with the silver circles of the river Derwent, in its progress from the lake. Whitehaven and its white coast were distinctly seen, and Cockermouth seemed almost under the eye. A long blackish line, more to the west, resembling a faintly formed cloud, was said by the guide to be the Isle of Man, who, however, had the honesty to confess, that the mountains of Down in Ireland, which have been sometimes thought visible, had never been seen by him in the clearest weather.[24]

The care with which what may be seen is thus enumerated is a protection from the merely conventional; similarly the guide refuses to see merely because others have conventionally claimed to be able to do so.

Nor does Radcliffe fudge her difficulties with the potentially repetitive element of description. Near the head of Ullswater she finds that 'It is difficult to spread varied pictures of such scenes before the imagination. A repetition of the same images of rock, wood and water, and the same epithets of grand, vast and sublime, which necessarily occur, must appear tautologous, on paper.'[25] It is one thing in the absence of actual landscape, to figure the sublime as inexpressible and another to be repeatedly confronted, within real landscapes, by one's inability to express it, the refusal of language to accommodate one's perceptions; the helpless consciousness of repetition begins to call in question the validity of the figuring procedure.

Radcliffe also has to face up to the uneasy recognition that the perception of the sublime and hence the sublime feelings that are supposed to attend that perception are not available in real physical danger – 'attention is sometimes unpleasantly engaged by a precipice, from which the road is not sufficiently secured'.[26] Of Skiddaw, too, she ruefully admits: 'our situation was too critical, or too unusual, to permit the just impressions of such sublimity. The hill rose so closely above the precipice as scarcely to allow a ledge wide enough for a single horse. We followed the guide in silence, and, till we regained the more open wild, had no leisure for exclamation.'[27] There is some self irony here – in actual scenery we can only be awed, as it were, from a position of comparative security and comfort.

It is true that *The Italian* was written after Radcliffe had made and published her tour of the Lake District, and that in it she still does not

choose to deviate from her customary mode of pictured imaginary landscape. But her accounts of the problems involved in rendering her
perception of actual scenery begin, I think, to explain the feeling of
exhaustion, even boredom with her own earlier methods, that betrays itself
in *The Italian*. *The Italian*, because of its treatment of the villain, Schedoni,
is usually characterised as the last and best of Mrs Radcliffe's published
romances. In truth, I think, the praise lavished on this novel at the expense
of the subtler *Udolpho*, reflects a rather superficial response to grand villainy;
but even if the success of Schedoni be granted, then it must be allowed
that it is achieved by sucking the life blood out of everything else. Ellena
is merely a more perfunctory version of Emily, and the disquisitions of
Ellena and Vivaldi on nature scarcely even pretend to take place in the
open air:

> 'See,' said Vivaldi, 'where Monte-Corno stands like a ruffian, huge,
> scared, threatening, and horrid!' ...
> 'Mark too,' said Ellena, 'how sweetly the banks and undulating
> plains repose at the feet of the mountains; what an image of beauty
> and elegance they oppose to the awful grandeur that overlooks and
> guards them!'[28]

No clearer indication of the near absurdities of pictorialism need be sought:
the manner is that of the art critic in a gallery, except that Vivaldi has
become fixated on Rosa and Ellena on Claude. The reader has overwhelmingly the sense of being presented with a wholly assimilated aesthetic object
rather than the results of the exploration of unique differentiation.

It seems to me then no wonder that Mrs Radcliffe should have withdrawn
from further acts of pictorial repetition, should have lost confidence in her
own mode, should have found herself 'without sufficient excitement to
begin on an extended romance'.[29] Yet elsewhere in these Lake tours, in her
persistent, private travel writing, and in the posthumously published
romance, *Gaston de Blondeville*, she may be found, perhaps unwittingly,
foreshadowing a solution to the impasse into which her earlier treatments
of landscape had led her. For increasingly we find her meticulously, if
tentatively, attentive to the particularities of actual place, striving to transfigure the commonplace, romancing place by lovingly attending to the real,
rather than finding romance in the flight to the imaginary. This goes along
with an increasing awareness of the pressures of place on people and a
sense of the paradoxical significance of the prosaic, fleeting, contingent
detail.

Her tentativeness is suggested by the frequency in the Lake tours with
which the confident gaze is replaced by the gentler 'peep'. Of course, some

of this is still conventional as mountains peep over the landscape or cottages peep through it but the humans within the scenes also hazard 'peeps'. The tentative approach, however, insists on carefulness about detail and Radcliffe is always precise about the naming of places and persistently aware of that local naming which allows those who live within the landscape to possess it in ways not available to the mere tourist: 'Not only every fell of this wild region has a name, but almost every crag of every fell, so that shepherds sitting at the fire-side can direct each other to the exact spot among the mountains, where a stray sheep has been seen.' [30]

The local people, indeed, come alive in ways which will surprise those familiar only with the operatic peasants of her novels. Some of her remarks are in a conventional eighteenth-century moralising strain about the virtues of simplicity and independence (although they still strike with thoughtful veracity and often would not embarrass Wordsworth), but she is also sensible of the difficulties that impressive landscapes put in the way of 'the intercourse and business of ordinary life'.[31] More tellingly she is moved by the genuine good will and friendliness of the local people; records the voices of singing children; the farmer working side by side with his hands; the old farmer on Skiddaw sheltering in the lee 'of an heaped up pile of slates, formed by the customary contribution of one from every visitor', who, although he lived in a neighbouring vale, had made the climb for the first time; and for the guide who took them up Skiddaw she offers this moving advertisement: 'Why should we think it trivial to attempt some service towards this poor man? We have reason to think, that whoever employs, at Keswick, a guide of the name of Doncaster, will assist him in supporting an aged parent.' [32]

Again in contrast to the generalised sublime, these travels give evidence of the careful struggle for precision. This often occurs where the detail of colour is at issue: 'The grey stones, that grew along the heath, were spotted with mosses of so fine a texture, that it was difficult to ascertain whether they were vegetable; their tints were a delicate pea-green and primrose, with a variety of colours, which it was not necessary to be a botanist to admire.' [33] Or: 'the gleamings of the water, close on the left, between the foliage ... was ever changing its hue, sometimes assuming the soft purple of a pigeon's neck, at others the silvery tint of sunshine'.[34] The attention to colour here includes a new sense of the relativity of perception in actual landscape which undermines the fixities of the pictorial mode:

> In the descent, it was interesting to observe each mountain below gradually re-assuming its dignity, the two little lakes expanding into spacious surfaces, the many little vallies [*sic*], that sloped upwards from their margins, recovering their variegated tints of cultivation,

the cattle again appearing in the meadows, and the woody promontories changing from smooth patches of shade in to richly tufted summits.[35]

Even Radcliffe's adverse comments are attentive and may bring the scene vividly before us: 'its [Derwentwater's] mild bosom is spotted by four small islands, of which those called Lords' and St Herbert's are well wooded, and adorn the scene, but another is deformed by buildings, stuck over it, like figures upon a twelfth-cake'.[36] Radcliffe concedes that not all human intervention in the landscape is regulated by aesthetic principles but the humble analogy forgivingly pulls the landscape into a relationship with domestic life.

As I leave Radcliffe in the Lake District and turn to her private travels, I like to think of her not in contemplation of the inexpressible sublime but sitting rather in an inn in Thelkeld before a blazing hearth in a clean sanded parlour, eating preserved fruit with cream, 'an innocent luxury, for which no animal has died'.[37]

The reviewer of Radcliffe's posthumous volume in *The Monthly Review* is rather intemperately disappointed by her defection from the landscape modes of her fiction. The volume's editor comments on the relaxed, informal style of these journal extracts that they 'exhibit her mind in its undress – show her feelings as they were undisguised':[38] the *Monthly* reviewer has no time for Radcliffe without her enchantress's disguise. He concedes that she probably enjoyed herself on these homely excursions in the south of England but is sure that

> The beauties of Gravesend, Rochester, and Chatham, the undulations and richness of landscape which characterise the road to Sittingbourn [*sic*], the attractions of Barham Downs, and the antiquities of Dover, can hardly be objects of curious inquiry at this time to any person, except those very industrious and praiseworthy gentlemen who are engaged in compiling the county histories, or books of the road.[39]

But this is, of course, the very point, for these gentlemen are not the old men, as it were, but the new.

The *Literary Chronicle*, more aware perhaps of current trends, merely prints Radcliffe's description of Blenheim as a taster for the volume. It is the transfigured familiarity of the mode of these journals that is particularly remarkable. And familiarity may be understood in various senses. Radcliffe has not wholly deserted the inexpressible sublime but the references to it except in one important case become increasingly mechanical: the special case subdues the sublime into the personal and familiar. When Mrs Radcliffe is led by the melancholy grandeur of the sun setting behind the vast hills at Seaford to contemplate the unknowable promise of the great God of order, her disquisition quickly slips into her personal grief: 'In this month, on the 24th of July, my dear father died two years since; on the 14th of last march, my poor mother followed: I am the last leaf on the tree!' [40]

However, generally the familiarity of the journals is more cheerfully sociable; the reader is constantly reminded of the presence of her husband and of her dog. Radcliffe, tired at Beachy Head, rests while her husband pushes on:

> the white precipices beautifully varied with plants, green blue, yellow and poppy. Wheatears flew up often from the beach: Chance [the dog] pursued them. At length William returned, having been nearly, but not quite in front of the great promontory. Slowly and laboriously we made our way back along the beach, greatly fatigued, the day exceedingly hot, the horizon sulphurous, with lowering clouds; thunder rolled faintly at a distance.[41]

There is a delicious appropriateness in the dog's name given the haphazard nature of his pursuit: the unshaped, the discomposed is displacing the value normally accorded in the fiction to composition.

Moreover, the private journals continue the attention that I have re-marked in the Lake Journals, to lovely, shifting colour: 'the vast sea-view – the long shades on its surface of soft green, deepening exquisitely into purple; but above all that downy tint of light blue, that sometimes prevailed over the whole scene, and even faintly tinged the French coast, at a distance. Sometimes, too, a white sail passed in a distant gloom, while all between was softly shadowed.' [42] Throughout there is an increasingly intense sense of the physicality of being in places: on the Needle Point, or Alum rock, Radcliffe writes, 'You have a wonderful and rather a painful sensation of the narrowness of the earth that bears you, though it may be half a mile or more in width'. Or delightfully on Dover cliff: 'Proceeding to the point of the cliff, had no longer the protection of a railing; the bushes of hawthorn, mossed with yellow, alone fence the precipice. Putting our hands on the ground, we peeped over, ledge below ledge, abrupt down.' Everywhere, too, Radcliffe attends to those contingent discontinuities that arrestingly transfigure the commonplace: the sails in the Channel 'tacking in all directions'; the 'he-hoes of the sailors, afar in the channel and the boatswain's shrill whistle'; the lights from ships 'like glow-worms'; the implements of the Woodman and his thatched hovel; the waggons and cheese piled up in the dusk for 'the morrow's fair'; and 'a hasty dish of very good tea'.[43]

Here, finally, is Radcliffe with her husband in Portsmouth in a situation which comes wholly out of the special characteristics of the particularity of place:

> Went to the George Inn, a very handsome house, with many galleries and staircases. Handsome furniture and excellent accommodation, except you could get nothing when you wanted it. We had fish brought without plates, and then plates without bread. All this owing to a vast throng of company, two hundred vessels or more being detained by winds, besides many ships of war. Nothing but ringing of bells and running about of waiters. If you ask a waiter a question, he begins a civil answer, but shuts the door before you have heard it all. It was very diverting to hear the different tones and measure of the ringings, particularly about supper time, and the next day about five, when everybody happened to be dining at one and the same time, to hear them all ringing together, or in quick succession, in different keys and measure, according to the worn out, or better, patience of the ringer. These different keys enabled me to distinguish how often each bell was rung before it was answered; also the increasing impatience of the ringer, till, at the third or fourth summons, the bell was in a downright passion.[44]

Leaving Radcliffe here, we leave her, I think, not in the imaginary landscapes of Gothic romance but in the busy real places of the nineteenth-century novel.

While, then, Radcliffe's contemporaries anxiously wanted to believe that the special characteristics of her novels were born out of her experience of real places, what I am suggesting is that her experience of real places is what may well have put an end to her fiction. Obviously this is speculative but what we do securely have are these travel diaries and the half-articulated stories they tell. We have also the awkwardness of the only fiction Radcliffe located in a place that she had visited – the posthumously published *Gaston de Blondeville*.

The romance was begun in 1802 after a visit to Kenilworth: it comes out of the imagination working on actual place. Two friends, Willoughton and Simpson, are walking in the forest of Arden. Willoughton is a Romantic antiquary and laments the failure of the real forest to come up to Shakespeare's imagined world; Simpson is more down to earth, thinks of his dinner, and sometimes drifts into waking slumber during his friend's reflections. Near the ruins of Kenilworth, where the real becomes more Romantic, they meet an old, garrulous villager who tells them about the sexton's having found a buried chest containing a curious old book. The book proves to be an illuminated manuscript of the thirteenth century containing the 'Trew Chronique of Gaston de Blondeville', which story of the reign of Henry III then follows. The story takes place in a romanticised version of the forest in which the travellers discover the manuscript and it is thus situated, as it were, between Willoughton's desire to be claimed by the romance of the forest and Simpson's sceptical detachment and desire for 'a little Warwickshire ale'.

Gaston de Blondeville is not the first of Radcliffe's novels to be framed by the story of the story: *The Italian* opens with a group of English travellers in Naples who are given, by an Italian gentleman, the volume which contains the story which forms the principal narrative. But in *Gaston de Blondeville* the temporal distance between the frame and the tale is much greater, centuries rather than decades, and the narrative manner of each is quite different. Contemporary reviewers of the romance were generally so concerned to point out the relative feebleness of the romance, notwith-standing its introduction of a 'real' ghost, that they failed to notice the displacement of the centre by the frame: they may have felt let down by the romance partly because the framing introduction is uncharacteristically lively and up-to-date. Willoughton's tendency to wish away recalcitrant fact in the pursuit of romance is consistently exposed and gently mocked:

> 'I am doomed to disappointment in Arden. For many miles, I could not discover any thing like a forest-shade, that might have sheltered a banished court, or favourite ... I cannot even catch a gleam of the torches, which, on such an occasion, might have thrown their light on the woods and towers of the castle, and have quivered on the waters over which they passed.'
>
> 'No, Sir,' said the old man, 'it would be a hard matter to find any thing of all that now. Cromwell's people would have knocked all that o' the head, when they drained off the water, if such things had been there then.' [45]

The creation of pleasing pictures in and of the past is shown sometimes to depend on excluding truths about human nature from the frame:

> 'What a noble sheet of water,' exclaimed Willoughton, 'with lawns and woods sloping to its margin and reflected on its surface!'
>
> 'Yes, Sir, all that on the opposite side was a deer-park then, as I've heard from the account of some book, except that low ground further on, and that was pasture for cattle.'
>
> 'For cattle!' exclaimed Mr Simpson, – 'how they would poach such ground as that!'
>
> 'But what a beautiful picture they helped to make from the castle windows here,' said Willoughton; 'when, on a summer's noon, they

lay under those shades, or stood in the cool waters of the lake.'
'Ay,' said Mr Simpson, 'to such as did not value the land.'[46]

On the other hand, the natural world presented in this introductory chapter is derived directly from Radcliffe's private travels. Here the aged stranger draws the travellers' attention to an ancient ivy: '"Why, there is an ivy tree now against that old wall there, partly as old as the wall itself. Look, Sir, it is as grey, and almost as sapless as the stone it crawls upon, though the trunk is such a size, and hardly shows a green leaf, spring or summer."'[47] Here Radcliffe gives the version of the ivy that she saw herself in 1802: 'The trunk of some of this ivy is of great thickness, and it is so old, that in some places, the branches are sapless and leafless, and the grey stalks seemed to crawl about the ruin in sympathy.'[48] This kind of seeing is a feature of the frame but not of the romance which follows; there the natural world tends to be reduced to scenes from, as it were, peculiarly cloying tapestries:

> The rustic seats of the king and queen were raised on turf, not carpeted with tapestry, but strewed with flowers, and, for their canopies of estate, they had arching branches of chesnut, wreathed with sweet woodbine. The wine was brought in beechen cups, carved from that noble tree, that stretched forth its mighty branches over the king's tent, and then sent out its spray, so lightly and so proudly above the flag of England waving there.[49]

This is a debased pictorialism measured by the standards of the earlier fiction and seems to confirm my contention that real travel undermined the Radcliffean formula, made for an increasing loss of conviction on Radcliffe's part in what had previously been felt to be her strengths. The pity of it is, first, that she should not have taken further the talent for witty exploration of the contemporary scene that seems to be peeping out of her travel writing and out of the frame of *Gaston de Blondeville* and second, that we should not have been permitted more of the personal travel writing. It is with enormous regret that we read that the journal of a tour in the autumn of 1798 to Portsmouth, the Isle of Wight and Winchester which she seems to have particularly enjoyed 'is too minute to give entire'.[50] The decision to refuse the minute detail has resulted in apparently irrecoverable loss and may have made the secrets of Ann Radcliffe's travels more obscure than perhaps they might have been.

Notes

1 Mackenzie Bell, *Christina Rossetti: A Biographical and Critical Study* (London, 1898), 92.

2 Ann Radcliffe, *Gaston de Blondeville; or, The Court of Henry III Keeping Festival in Ardenne: A Romance. St Alban's Abbey: A Metrical Tale, with some Poetical Pieces*. 'To which is prefixed a Memoir of the Author, with extracts from her Journals' (London, 1826), 4. References to the memoir and journals are given as *Memoir* in subsequent notes. References to the tale are given as *Gaston*.

3 The *Memoir* points out an erroneous rumour credited by *The Monthly Review* that Mrs Radcliffe had 'died in a state of mental alienation not to be described'. *The Monthly Review* reviewer of *Gaston de Blondeville* defensively claims that the medical evidence adduced in the memoir to prove that Mrs Radcliffe was in full possession of her faculties until just before her death at least shows that she was not fully in possession of them at her death. See *The Monthly Review*, n.s. 2 (1826), 282–3.

4 *Memoir*, 4.

5 Sir Walter Scott, *The Prose Works*, 3 vols (Edinburgh, 1834), 3: 341–2.

6 John Ruskin, *The Complete Works*, 12 vols (London, 1904), 12: 120.

7 *The Critical Review* 4 (1792), 459.

8 *The Edinburgh Review* 38 (May 1823), 360.

9 See Malcolm Andrews, *The Search for the Picturesque: Landscape, Aesthetics and Tourism in Britain, 1760–1800* (Aldershot, 1987).

10 Ann Radcliffe, *The Romance of the Forest*, ed. Chloe Chard (Oxford, 1986), 9.

11 Ann Radcliffe, *The Mysteries of Udolpho*, ed. Bonamy Dobrée, notes by Frederick Garber (Oxford, 1980), 227–8.

12 *Romance*, 163–4.

13 Ann Radcliffe, *The Italian*, ed. Frederick Garber (Oxford, 1968), 292.

14 *Romance*, 248.

15 *Udolpho*, 6.

16 *Ibid.*, 4.

17 *Ibid.*, 13.

18 Anne K. Mellor, *Romanticism and Gender* (London and New York, 1993), 95.

19 *Ibid.*

20 David Punter, *The Literature of Terror: A History of Gothic Fictions from 1765 to the Present Day* (London, 1980), 78.

21 *Italian*, 70.

22 Ann Radcliffe, *A Journey Made in the Summer of 1794, Through Holland and the Western Frontier of Germany, with a return Down the Rhine: to which are added Observations During a Tour to the Lakes of Lancashire, Westmoreland, and Cumberland* (London, 1795), 410.

23 *Ibid.*, 457.

24 *Ibid.*, 457–8.

25 *Ibid.*, 419.

26   *Ibid.*, 463.
27   *Ibid.*, 457.
28   *Italian*, 158.
29   *Memoir*, 89.
30   *Journey*, 422.
31   *Ibid.*, 396.
32   *Ibid.*, 460, 461.
33   *Ibid.*, 403. Cf. Keats's impressions of the Ambleside waterfall: 'What astonishes me more than any thing is the tone, the coloring, the slate, the stone, the moss, the rock-weed; or, if I may so say, the intellect, the countenance of such places', in Maurice Buxton Forman, ed., *The Letters of John Keats*, 4th edn (London, 1952), 156.
34   *Ibid.*, 413.
35   *Ibid.*, 460–1.
36   *Ibid.*, 450.
37   *Ibid.*, 423.
38   *Memoir*, 16.
39   *The Monthly Review*, n.s. 2 (1826), 283.
40   *Memoir*, 39.
41   *Ibid.*, 42.
42   *Ibid.*, 19.
43   *Memoir*, 21, 16, 27, 31, 44, 47, 30. Interestingly Keats follows an assertion that he is getting 'a great dislike of the picturesque' with a passage about the beautiful movement of boats: 'The Regent in his Yatch ... was anchored opposite – a beautiful vessell – and all the Yatchs and boats on the coast, were passing and repassing it; and curcuiting and tacking about it in every direction – I never beheld any thing so, silent, light, and graceful' (*Letters*, 371).
44   *Ibid.*, 75.
45   *Gaston*, 27.
46   *Ibid.*, 26–7.
47   *Ibid.*, 18.
48   *Memoir*, 58.
49   *Gaston*, 129.
50   *Memoir*, 23.

Part II

The Grand Tour: sites of enthralment

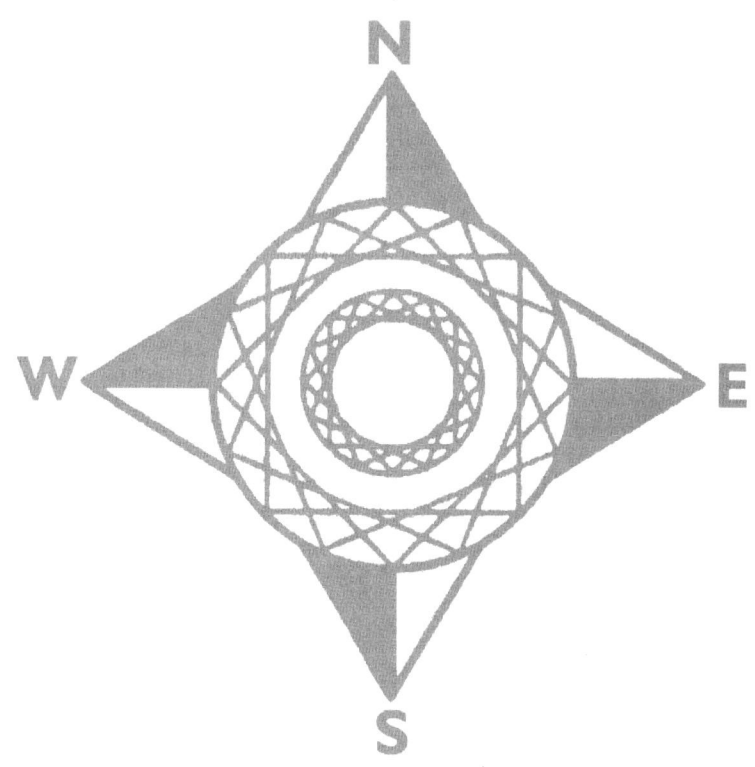

Wordsworth's Grand Tour

Keith Hanley

In a previous essay I argued that Freud's open letter entitled 'A Disturbance of Memory on the Acropolis' describes an Oedipal structure in the 'after-effect' of arrival at destinations of climactic cultural prestige that helps characterise the similar Wordsworthian experience of 'derealisation':

> those obstinate questionings
> Of sense and outward things,
> Fallings from us, vanishings;
> Blank misgivings of a Creature
> Moving about in worlds not realised.[1]

For Freud, one's reading of such culminating symbols of incredulous fulfilment ('What I see here is not real'[2] – which he calls *Entfremdungs-gefühl*) is undercut by guilt at 'having gone such a long way': 'there was something about it that was wrong, that from earliest times had been forbidden. It was something to do with a child's criticism of his father. It seems as though the essence of success was to have got further than one's father, and as though to excel one's father was still something forbidden.'[3] He summarises that 'what interfered with [his and his brother's] enjoyment of the journey to Athens was a feeling of *filial piety*'.[4]

Following the Lacanian revision of Freud, I suggest that a retelling of Freud's Acropolis experience might see it as a replay of the original entry into the Symbolic order, when language itself was the object of aspiration. The word 'Acropolis' (*akron*, top + *polis*, city) would itself stand for the domain of cultural power that language constructs and that has to be negotiated with the father: a symbol, that is, for the whole empowering system of signification. The effect of derealisation might, I suggest, result from a disorientating reversion to the first rudimentary stage of subjectivity, the Imaginary, and as a result, place-names that are impregnated with cultural prestige might particularly commemorate the subject's successful (but vestigially remorseful) inscription in the Symbolic order.

Yet while such eloquent travels as Freud describes would predictably be accompanied by traces of primal alienation and restless splitting, what remains extraordinary about Wordsworth's equivalent accounts is that they

71

usually end by reaffirming the triumphant adequacy of the language so symbolised. The meandering journey of *The Prelude*, the provisional instalment of the *chef d'oeuvre*, *The Excursion*, and the memorials of his various tours in Scotland and on the Continent can all be followed as varying replays of a shared history of language acquisition that he is seeking to acknowledge *on peculiar terms*: of self-fulfilment. Whatever 'Blank misgivings' Wordsworth entertains, his hanging back from external reality shows a will to detain the evolution of the castrative fear and guilt of Oedipal conflict and victory thereby attained. Instead, the symbols of wholly acceptable self-expression that he does acclaim come after all to convey an originating 'visionary gleam', 'That dream-like vividness and splendour which invest objects of sight in childhood',[5] and to reflect what in the 1802 Preface to *Lyrical Ballads* he refers to as 'the structure of [the poet's] own mind', from which they 'arise in him without immediate external excitement',[6] creating an internal power-base from which to govern external reality. What stands revealed in such moments of self-affirmation is a language of impunity, so gloriously oblivious of any sense of transgression that it appears almost wholly unalienated and inherent in objects themselves: things become symbols.

Uneasiness is attached rather to the degrading claims of 'reality', which turns out to be what proceeds from the disjuncture between word and thing, when the imaginary structure is disrupted into a premonition of otherness. In what is commonly taken to be the epigraphic lyric for 'Ode: Intimations of Immortality', 'My heart leaps up', Wordsworth explicitly narrates the self-originating myth of his own particular progression to subjectivity that underwrites all his poetry of the imagination, when he expresses his wish for this pre-Oedipal formation to inform a continuingly uncontested relation with language and culture:

> The Child is father of the Man;
> And I could wish my days to be
> Bound each to each by natural piety.[7]

Wordsworth's elision of a rivalrous undercurrent was so complete and had been effected so early that he had come to feel his piety was owed to that alternative formation rather than to any other presence that might disturb its ascendancy.

Seen in this way, *all* Wordsworth's journeyings are excursions or tours which loop back to 'home at Grasmere'. His Lakes childhood and youth had trained him for his more extensive undertakings, as Thomas West had suggested in his *Guide*: 'those who intend to make the continental tour should begin here; as it will give, in miniature, an idea of what they are to meet there, in traversing the Alps and the Appenines [*sic*]'.[8] The place-name, 'Grasmere', came to stand for an unbroken imaginary relation with nature that provided him with a privately overdetermined version of full speech – one not replete with semiotic significance (in Kristevan terms), but rather reflective of an extraordinarily powerful investment in a specific subject-formation that had preceded language-acquisition. I am arguing that all Wordsworth's travels were radically in search of such self-reflective imaginary discourses, and that they were repeatedly retraced over the years to revise earlier discursive misrecognitions and negotiate new inscriptions in different discourses so as to make them all end up at the same desired destination. In this way, Wordsworth's travels may be mapped as a series of place-names, of localities large and small, that at various times functioned as symbols of appropriate cultural empowerment.

His journey to 'France', for example, was originally towards the self-fulfilment of republican idealism, and, when it turned into the alienating sign of Revolution, substitute routes towards an alternatively self-expressive organic nationalism were pursued inland, back to 'the Lakes' and 'Scotland'. The redirection entailed a compositional return over the territory of his first Continental trip, which had then terminated in 'France', to enable the later 'discovery' that his true destination had all along been the natural sublime of 'the Swiss Alps'. At different or overlapping times, republicanism, nature, and nationalism had all reflected unbelievably satisfying self-empowerments, but encompassing all the itineraries in which they were inflected was a grand narrative to which all paths seeking an unproblematised and undisrupted European traditionalism ultimately led. At first rejected and deliberately replaced, and then finally subscribed to, was the paradigmatic tour of British reactionary politics – the path to 'Rome'.

If the trauma of the loss of Wordsworth's mother in his eighth year replayed the original self-division of symbolic castration, the result, as I have argued previously, was a denial of that primary rupture by an insistence of the rudimentary formation of the Imaginary which took the form of a lasting preoccupation with the experience of derealisation.[9] Richard Onorato has observed that 'The journey-metaphor' in Wordsworth's poetry 'begins with the death of the mother and her "disappearance" from the original vale',[10] but it is a journey Wordsworth did and did not wish to make. His arrest would, of course, tend to elide the subject's inscription in language – the Symbolic order – and the consequent sense of lack. Words for him would have to seem to subserve a stronger self-representation that preceded them, leading to the Wordsworthian re-invention of childhood as, in effect, the insulation and protraction of early infancy, before language had opened up the condition of self-division. For this ego, evidence of violence and destruction served only to call forth and inflate the enjoyment of an unusual impunity, oblivious of intimations of mortality.

In the summer of 1790, when Wordsworth broke free from the irksome restraints of his university studies, including a specialisation in Italian, to go in search of the Alpine sublime, he was enjoying a shoe-string equivalent of the historical practice that by the eighteenth century had come to represent the process of cultural maturation and the attainment of political authority in England: the Grand Tour. The pattern was that of fathers dispatching sons, either instead of or after the conclusion of their university studies, to attain the necessary grounding for positions of social influence. In its full-dress version of tutorial bear-leader, several years' sojourn, bought connoisseurship and Italian portrait, it fully dramatised the rites of social passage that are epitomised by Freud's experience on the Acropolis. Boswell, for example, records Johnson as summarising the assumptions that lay behind it: 'A man who has not been in Italy, is always conscious of an inferiority, from his not having seen what it is expected a man should see. The grand object of travelling is to see the shores of the Mediter-ranean.'[11] The symbol for completed self-inscription was the arrival at Rome (Figure 1).

Dennis Porter, in his study of travel writing since 1750, has pursued the complicating ideas of transgression and guilt that are attached to travellers' rejection of their inherited cultural discourses. Here I wish to develop an individual writer's relation to the presiding narrative of European travel in his time as one that characteristically evades such transgression. Porter himself writes that 'in the geopolitical imagining of Europeans down to relatively recent times at least, there is a hegemonic geometry of center and periphery that conditions all perceptions of self and Other. Thus the Grand Tour may stand as a paradigm of travel undertaken to the center of a self-confident cultural tradition for the purposes of self-cultivation and the reaffirmation of a common civilised heritage.'[12] Throughout the nineteenth century, the Grand Tour continued to operate automatically as a metaphorical substitution for Oedipal themes of self-empowerment, and key Wordsworthian narratives – of entitlement, restitution, and self-authorisation – are motivated in its terms. Overall, Wordsworth's own Oedipalisation slid from an assumption of entitlement during childhood and youth, to a relegitimising creativity of restitution following his trau-matic self-misrecognition in revolutionary discourse, to a proto-Tractarian affinity to the authority of Catholic traditionalism.

Wordsworth and his companion, Robert Jones, accomplished an extra-ordinary feat of energy on his first Continental trip of 1790, walking over

From an Original Drawing by Gr.....   Published as the Act directs

WELLADAY! is this my SON TOM!

1 'Welladay! Is this my son Tom!'. British Museum Caricature Archive.

fifteen hundred miles through France, Switzerland, and the north of Italy. He was, of course, familiar with the conventions of the gentleman's inland tour in Scotland and the Lakes, and at one time he contemplated a career as a travelling companion, even engaging in it by accompanying William Calvert round the West Country in 1794. But whereas art and music on the shores of the Mediterranean had been the original goal of this rite of passage into social and political status, by the later eighteenth century, as an awareness of the educational benefits of nature was coming to the fore, the route had been optionally revised in order to accommodate the new vogue for mountains and glaciers. Earlier, after Rome had become the centre of Western Christendom, the Alps had been simply a barrier on the way from northern Europe to Italy and were often avoided, as by Addison in 1699, by taking a sea-voyage from Marseilles to Genoa. Switzerland, for example, warranted only a few pages in Nugent's four-volume *The Grand Tour* (1756). By the mid eighteenth century, however, particularly after the upsurge in numbers of visitors there following the conclusion of the European war in 1763, the revulsion the Alps had inspired in the previous century was reversed, and they themselves became an established feature, even a climactic one, of an alternative European Tour that bore Protestant overtones.[13]

The new interest was enabled by improvements in accessibility, and it was pioneered by Enlightenment scientists and topographers, but it also came in answer to deep psychological and aesthetic transformations. The Alps were becoming an important symbol in the myth of 'nature' that a pre-Romantic reaction to Enlightenment intellectualism was beginning to construct: a domain seemingly immune to human design. Another cause and consequence of this diversion was that visitors were distracted from the inevitable destination of Rome, the traditional focus of humanist culture, to a more modern consideration of Swiss republicanism. It has been claimed that William Coxe's *Sketches of the Natural, Civil, and Political State of Switzerland: A Series of Letters to William Melmoth, Esq.* (1779), which Wordsworth knew in several versions, marked a new era of Swiss travel, catching a new tone of reverence to replace the excited *frissons* of horror that had previously been the commonest response. Coxe describes travelling through the Furca Pass in soulful terms: 'I frequently quit my party, and either go on before or loiter behind, that I may enjoy uninterrupted, and with a sort of melancholy pleasure, the sublime exhibitions of nature in her most awful and tremendous form.'[14] But Coxe also shows great interest in the social and political life of the Swiss that strongly invests Wordsworth's own first account of the tour in his *Descriptive Sketches* (1794) when the discourses of republicanism and nature had seemed one and the same.

When Wordsworth had left for the Alps without taking his degree in 1790, he was affirming his right to ascend an eminence of his own in the face of the other urgent interpretations of worldly self-definition sponsored by his family and the university authorities. The idea of 'Crossing the Alps' was emphatically transgressive for him, 'An open slight / Of college cares and study'.[15] The rivalrous superiority to which he was laying claim was inscribed in an itinerary culminating in the natural sublime that for him exceeded in its promise the realisation of 'Cambridge', whose signifieds had effectively turned out to bar imaginary self-representation. Yet the completion of his rite of passage in his own exceptional terms entailed precisely the culminating adequacy of 'the Alps' in sustaining the deflection of any sense of alienation and guilty struggle.

'The Alps' therefore was a site of plural meanings, which Wordsworth's own readings were obliged to distinguish between his first visit and his various descriptions, of 1794 and the *Prelude* accounts in Book 6 of 1804–05. What he came to encounter in the course of his later descriptions, however, was precisely his power (the Wordsworthian imagination) of insisting on a continually imaginary reflection in *different* discourses, so that, though 'the Alps' might cease satisfactorily to represent a particular discourse that he had formerly seen in them (revolutionary idealism), they would still support the self-representation that he most fundamentally needed in substitute discourses (crucially the literary sublime). The discourse that facilitated the translation was that of the natural sublime which was chiastically associated with both the earlier and later discourses involved.

In 1790 Wordsworth's initial response to the eagerly anticipated scenes had been one of recurrent disappointment. A letter to Dorothy relating the comparative failure of his visit to the Rhine Falls at Schaffhausen sets the tone: 'Magnificent as this fall certainly is I must confess I was disappointed in it. I had raised my ideas too high.'[16] The same letter contains a distinctly unimpressed reference to Lake Geneva, and the travellers' reaction to Mont Blanc, as he relates in *The Prelude*, was similarly deflating:

> That day we first
> Beheld the summit of Mont Blanc, and grieved
> To have a soulless image on the eye
> Which had usurped upon a living thought
> That never more could be.[17]

The eye/I mirrored in the act of perception was not the imaginary subject, with the result that 'Mont Blanc' ceased to be an imaginary signifier. Yet the disappointment was established as part of a pattern, according to which the Imaginary *was* more gradually reasserted, as in this instance, when an enormous field of fixated silence cancelled the threatened disjunction between thing and word, and

> The wondrous Vale
> Of Chamouny ...
> With its dumb cataracts and streams of ice –
> A motionless array of mighty waves,
> Five rivers broad and vast – made rich amends,
> And reconciled us to realities.[18]

In the succeeding passage on the Crossing of the Alps over the Simplon Pass this oscillation is repeated on a far larger scale, so that what 'never more could be' becomes the recreative potential of 'something evermore about to be'.[19]

What is at stake may be related to two opposed approaches to the sublime which Thomas Weiskel influentially defined as 'negative' and 'positive', and which may be different stages of a single complete response, as classically theorised by both Burke and Kant.[20] The *negative* impresssion is that which in Wordsworth's case produces an underlying realisation of his alienation within the Symbolic order, of his subjectivity in flux. For Wordsworth, however, the fuller experience rehearses the aftermath of the psychological trauma which in the full process of its unfolding can lead to an active rereading of the sublime as *positive* – as, after all, the self-fulfilling reflection of his particular subject-formation. This further perception came to depend on the understanding not only that significant place-names require creative discursification in order to contain traumatic alienation but also that such alienation is the necessary motor for re-establishing them as imaginary signifiers.

The Crossing of the Alps passage in Book 6 of *The Prelude* forms the pivot in Wordsworth's writing – the point at which he arrives at the axial insight that his own necessary version of the positive *literary* sublime relies on his recognition that the natural sublime is incident to historical and personal reading: that his original imaginary relation with natural objects must (and can be satisfactorily) transferred to one with language. The Alps, as the climax of *his* Grand (de)Tour, in actuality fall short of imaginary self-representation, and at first disappointingly draw excessive attention to their general symbolic status. The episode begins with the travellers' losing their way, followed by a disheartening interrogation of a peasant who explains that, without even registering it, they had already achieved the end of their youthful enterprise:

> Hard of belief, we questioned him again,
> And all the answers which the man returned
> To our inquiries, in their sense and substance
> Translated by the feelings which we had,
> Ended in this – that we had crossed the Alps.[21]

These travellers' difficulty with belief resulted from their experience being only too real. Wordsworth refers to the experience as one of 'dejection ... / A deep and genuine sadness', when 'something of stern mood, an under-thirst / Of vigour, never utterly asleep' had been frustratingly awakened.[22] The expected realisation of the fabulous potency of the Hannibalesque (and Napoleonic) phrase, 'Crossing the Alps', is suddenly anti-climaxed by a mundane actuality.

Alan Liu has written influentially on the subtextual presence of Napoleon's passage through the Alps during the Italian campaign of 1800, explaining that it represents a suppressed revolutionary discourse by 1804, when this account was written.[23] Wordsworth's contrary investment in Hannibal's earlier journey at this later date might be seen as deepened by a common opposition to the Republic. Certainly for J. M. W. Turner, the struggle between Rome and Carthage was explicitly to figure the rivalry between France and England. Freud noted that 'Napoleon lines up with Hannibal, owing to their both having crossed the Alps'.[24] For Freud, of course, the Oedipal theme is primary, and the association of the two generals helps explain the resolution of Napoleonic transgression by Hannibalesque restitution in his own case. As Porter points out, 'Freud on the Acropolis finds himself moved to echo a legendary remark Napoleon is supposed to have made ... to his brother: "What would *Monsieur notre Père* have said to this, if he could have been here today?"'[25] The Wordsworthian resolution is to discover that playing between discourses may alleviate the trespass so that the rebellious feat becomes overdriven by a piety too deep for guilt (or 'tears').

In the act of rewriting his Alpine experience in March 1804, it suddenly comes to Wordsworth that the imaginary signified may be re-articulated in an alternative discourse. The subject-formation had been confirmed within the Symbolic order, emerging without Oedipal struggle because always already there, and the mist that appeared to be witholding power simply dissipates itself as it becomes transformed into the figure of his own 'unfathered' endowments:

> Imagination! – lifting up itself
> Before the eye and progress of my song
> Like an unfathered vapour, here that power,

> In all the might of its endowments, came
> Athwart me. I was lost as in a cloud,
> Halted without a struggle to break through,
> And now, recovering, to my soul I say
> 'I recognize thy glory'.[26]

The passage on Wordsworth's entry into London ('that vast metropolis, / The fountain of my country's destiny / And of the destiny of earth itself'[27]) originally illustrated this resolution of Wordsworth's disappointment as part of the account retained in Book 6 before being shifted to Book 8. In his chapter on 'The Nation of London' in his *Autobiographical Sketches*, which is a tissue of Wordsworthian allusions, De Quincey indirectly offers an expanded commentary on how this imaginative control of metaphoricity can handle the threat of alienation. He describes his own first visit to London: 'It was a most heavenly day in May of this year (1800), when I first beheld and first entered this mighy wilderness, the city – no! not the city, but the nation – of London'; his account ghosts Wordsworth's apprehension of a huge sense of otherness that may or may not confirm one's expectation: 'Already at three stages' distance (say, 40 miles from London), upon some of the greatest roads, the dim presentiment of some vast capital reaches you obscurely, and like a misgiving. This blind sympathy with a mighty but unseen object, some vast magnetic range of Alps, in your neighbourhood, continues to increase, you know not how.'[28] For Wordsworth, too, London had emerged from his 'Blank misgivings' as the alternative destination of an Alpine journey. His 'blank sense of greatness passed away' had been ultimately met by 'weight and power, / Power growing with the weight'.[29] The potency of the effect of arrival on De Quincey, however, is fully admitted by him only when it is considered comparable to the greatest imaginable (Roman) experience, so that 'London' (which Wordsworth treated as a metaphor for the full unfolding of the Alpine achievement) has itself after all become a metaphor for 'Rome'. London represents 'a pomp to which there is nothing corresponding upon this planet, either among the things that have been, or things that are. Or, if any exception there is, it must be sought in ancient Rome.'[30] Through De Quincey's text, it may be seen that Wordsworth's crossing issued in a version of cultural magnitude that would most automatically be named as 'Rome'.

Wordsworth's diversion to 'London' as the textual terminus of his crossing the Alps represents the substitution of a nationalist discourse for an earlier revolutionary internationalism. By 1804–05, when it so emerges in the process of rewriting, it is the epic voice which controls the evocation of religious discourse. In Book 6, the succeeding description of the consummation of his overall Alpine experience (the walk through the Gondo Gorge) is the apocalypse of Wordsworthian subjectification, when Wordsworth finds an entirely fulfilling self-representation in the dyadic correspondence between the original natural and the subsequently recuperated literary sublime of Milton and the Bible. What is most significant about the equation is that it has been almost unnoticeably effected by a parallel discursive transition: Wordsworth has brought Milton's exemplary appropriation of the language of Revelation ('I am Alpha and Omega, the beginning and the end, the first and the last') in *Paradise Lost* ('On earth joyn all ye Creatures to extoll / Him first, him last, him midst, and without end' [31]) into relation with his own imaginary touchstone of the Alpine sublime:

> Characters of the great apocalypse,
> The types and symbols of eternity,
> Of first, and last, and midst, and without end.[32]

Wordsworth's prophecy had indeed come to pass. His original subject-formation had asserted its indomitable continuity in seeing itself reflected in a myth of self-creation that he had not needed to invent, but which was already there to speak for him, as for Milton, like nature itself.

Freud's identification with Hannibal, who, of course, never made it to Rome, was with a figure of both victory and defeat. When Hannibal crossed the Alps with 35,000 select troops and his famous elephant corps, the culminating triumph of Cannae lay ahead, but so also did his eventual suicide rather than enduring extradition to Rome. It is significant that on his approach to Rome in 1897 Freud felt he had done enough when he turned back at Lake Trasimeno, the scene of Hannibal's great victory. On the one hand, the Carthaginian leader offered a powerful identification, who promised a memorable assault on the seat of what was to become the empire, but on the other he failed to conquer it in the end. The subtextual presence of Hannibal's triumphant failure figures the compromise between originality and conformity in the act of revisionism that constitutes Wordsworth's 'Crossing the Alps'.

It is Turner, in the sudden explosion of his *Snow Storm: Hannibal and his Army Crossing the Alps* (1812), who has most memorably fixed the sublime treatment of Hannibal's crossing as the highpoint of the narrative of the second Punic Wars. The painting represents a vortex of man and elements which arrests Hannibal's progress in such a way as to incorporate the rest of the story – its mastery and defeat. (Turner's vignettes of this scene that illustrate Rogers's *Italy* (1830) similarly isolate a moment in which an extended history is frozen in epitome.) By the time of executing it, Turner believed that human greatness, including his own artistic mission, was necessarily bound up with *struggle*, represented by his particular interpretation of the sublime. His series of works on Carthaginian history are commonly viewed as examples of the negative sublime, in that they seem overwhelmingly to signify the inevitable unfolding of a violently originated history. Yet Turner read the hostility between Carthage and Rome through Virgil as the outcome of Pius Aeneas's dutiful desertion of his lover, Dido, in the fulfilment of his father's injunction to found a new nation. Accordingly, Turner's Hannibal is swept up in the complex legacy of violence initiated by an act of filial odedience, echoed in Hannibal's continuation of the grand design of his own father, Hamilcar Barca. Though the violence remains unexorcised, it nevertheless is partly legitimised for Hannibal's warring by a conscious counter-piety that is even free of the guilt of Aeneas's complicating act of betrayal. A widening mythological reading situates Hannibal's invasion as a credible narrative of restitution, and the triumphalist potential of crossing the Alps causes it to signify something in excess of the threat of destructiveness. Though doomed, Hannibal's attempt remains more than a sign of defeat: it succeeds in radically problematising the legitimacy of Roman dominion, while establishing an alternative claim to figure more than is apparently resolvable – to become, that is, a version of the positive sublime.

Hannibal's career offers a revision of the narrative of the Grand Tour, that should issue in the arrival at Rome, but that has become waylaid by an optional and equivocally achieved destiny of incompletion. Those who were to proceed to Rome had, with more or less difficulty, to put the identification aside. In disowning any Hannibalesque parallel in his approach to Rome, Gibbon, for example, was being slyly self-deprecatory about his own heroic pretensions: 'I climbed Mount Cenis, and descended into the plain of Piedmont, not on the back of an elephant, but on a light osier seat, in the hands of the dextrous and intrepid chairmen of the Alps.' [33] Ironically, however, by evoking but not shadowing the fate of Hannibal he was already opening up the possibility of becoming *more* successful than the great general in his own command of Roman civilisation, by turning himself into *the* authority on the whole area: 'Perhaps I might boast that few travellers more compleatly armed and instructed have ever followed the footsteps of Hannibal.' [34]

For Freud, the investment was deeper. In order to identify with the semitic Hannibal as an idealised father-figure, he could stress the victorious side without also in effect empowering an opponent (whom he would have to outdo if he were indeed to go to Rome). Freud was interested in usurping the seat of Roman authority that had castrated this father-figure, and thereby he carried out the figure's own frustrated ambition: he had to surpass Hannibal in order to realise the piety of restitution. When his psychoanalytical system was complete, he was prepared to overcome a crucial paternal presence who had always been contaminated by a lingering history of inferiority by taking the emasculating power of Christian humanism by storm. Freud's victorious entry into Rome, which entailed the resolution of his own Oedipal story as one of restitution, was his eventual execution of Hannibal's intent.

When Wordsworth crossed the Alps in 1790, as recorded in *The Prelude*, he was not to go on to Rome, nor was he in an important way to complete his passage at all. Rather, his Hannibalesque élan, at first frustrated and then redirected, was to be *its own reward*:

> Our destiny, our nature, and our home,
> Is with infinitude – and only there;
> With hope it is, hope that can never die,
> Effort, and expectation, and desire,
> And something evermore about to be.
> The mind beneath such banners militant
> Thinks not of spoils or trophies, nor of aught
> That may attest its prowess, blest in thoughts
> That are their own perfection and reward.[35]

He had advanced on the Alps in 'something of stern mood, and under-thirst / Of vigour' that seemed spoiling for contest, and his disappointment appeared to result from the lack of any sense of climactic triumph that the mountains had offered. He had, however, failed to perceive the character of the actual recalcitrance that was confronting him. The bar to his imaginary progression had in fact been the shock of symbolic alienation, when the hugely evocative phrase, 'Crossing the Alps', was reduced to a simple literalism, 'that we had crossed the Alps'.[36] And yet, his realisation of the power of the imagination is based on the memory of one guiding signified that proves capable of being revitalised within the same signifying phrase following a shift in discursive definitions. The passage into the Symbolic order Wordsworth describes continues to insist on the representation of a peculiar mental topology. Unlike Lacan's Borromean knots, for example, Wordsworth's great emblems of the mind, here and in 'The perfect image of a mighty mind' that he depicts in the Ascent of Snowdon in Book 13,[37] do not effectively construct a scientific model of total psychic reality so much as manifest the structure of an enormous private compulsion, in that they will only acknowledge a domain that reflects the idiosyncratic repetition of his founding imaginary overdetermination.

Wordsworth's identification with Hannibal consequently takes the form of a conquering recalcitrance of inscription in the Symbolic order taken forward into the Symbolic order, which it recognises only in its own revisionist terms. It works with and against the grain of the powerful languages into which it enters, both to enjoy and to bypass them. The upshot of his crossing is that there is no ultimate destination beyond the private recession of 'something for ever more about to be', as the imaginary subject inoffensively invades all further territory. Having re-established his subject-position, his crossing abuts on to a protracting pass, the Simplon Pass, with its

> immeasurable height
> Of woods decaying, never to be decayed,
> The stationary blasts of waterfalls ...
> ... all like workings of one mind.[38]

Wordsworth was aware that what I have defined as a pioneering assertion of the Imaginary was thereby proclaiming a new and surrogate legitimacy for his own imaginative system. When, in the *Essay, Supplementary to the Preface* (1815), he came to consider what made an author (like himself) great and original, he argued, after Coleridge, that he 'has had the task of *creating* the taste by which he is to be enjoyed', and continues: 'The predecessors of an original Genius of a high order will have smoothed the way for all that he has in common with them; – and much he will have in common; but, for what is peculiarly his own, he will be called upon to clear and often to shape his own road: – he will be in the condition of Hannibal among the Alps.'[39]

Rome did not lie within Wordsworth's prospect either actually in 1790 or imaginatively in the *Prelude* account of crossing the Alps as, having successfully confirmed the alternative satisfactions of a self-deflecting 'path / Which, in the main, was more circuitous', he returned home northwards along 'delightful pathways' past Locarno and Como without proceeding on the 'Giro d'Italia', the Italian part of the Grand Tour.[40] In 1820, when Wordsworth undertook another Continental tour in the company of Dorothy, Mary, and several of his wife's relatives which again took in the north of Italy, together with Belgium, Germany, Switzerland, and France, the same structure of self-limitation was corroborated, though by then it had come to inform later symbolic representations, particularly the discourse of British national traditions and institutions that had become increasingly confident between Trafalgar and Waterloo. The party crossed the Alps by the St Gotthard, visited Airolo, Maggiore and Como, Milan, and Domodossola, before leaving Italy through the Simplon Pass. Going over the same terrain in later years, in a poem from *Memorials of a Tour on the Continent, 1820*, 'Stanzas Composed in the Simplon Pass', he writes how he was prepared to proceed exultingly southwards through a landscape layered with literary and historical associations. Yet, he acknowledges, his 'sadness' in having to turn from Vallombrosa, Florence, and Rome was just, as he piously bends to a familiar discipline:

> Toward the mists that hang over the land of my Sires,
> From the climate of myrtles contented I go ...
> Each step hath its value while homeward we move: -
> O joy when the girdle of England appears! [41]

The practical opportunity of pursuing the full Italian tour had been available between the close of the Seven Years War in 1763 and the Napoleonic Wars, but was no longer feasible at the time of writing his account of the journey in the early 1800s. The French-occupied Continent had already been cut off when he and Coleridge had chosen instead to visit Germany in 1798–99. But by May of 1803, '[a] thousand Grand Tourists were caught in France, and a number of them were interned at Verdun until 1814'. [42] Coleridge, on his way back to England early in 1806, was one of the few Englishmen to pass through Rome during these years: hours after his departure all the other English visitors were arrested. The Treaty of Paris in 1814 was finally to mark the end of the Grand Tour on the old pattern, but in the early 1820s Wordsworth was willingly accepting the restricted horizon that by turning the former Continental travellers inwards, towards Scotland and the Northern Tour of England, was effectively empowering the images of his own past as the object of a larger contemporary quest for Britain as well as of his autobiography. In turning back, it is Milton again who emerges as the exemplary case-history of the British Grand Tourist, travelling for education and to equip himself for state service, who had been forced to abort his tour and return home by the threat of the Civil War. As with Milton, national – though by now not specifically republican – interest calls him home, and the more powerful bidding of the paternal order which emerges from the mists is now safely located in a specific nationalist discourse for which 'England' stands.

In his later sixties, however, Wordsworth did eventually travel to Rome, and in the Fenwick note he dictated for a sequence of commemorative poems, *Memorials of a Tour of the Continent, 1837*, he justifies his claim to the lifting of a long-imposed self-denial: 'During my whole life I had felt a strong desire to visit Rome and other celebrated cities and regions of

Italy, but did not think myself justified in incurring the necessary expense till I received from Mr Moxon, the publisher of a large edition of my poems, a sum sufficient to gratify my wish without encroaching upon what I considered due my family.'[43] In 1827, Sir George Beaumont had in fact left him an annual bequest for travelling, but an obscurer (and 'just') impediment to the realisation of this project was associated with the financial settlements that Wordsworth had had to make on his unofficial French family deriving from the transgressive travels of his youth. It was only in 1835 that Wordsworth was able to end the annuity he had paid for his illegitimate daughter since 1816 'with a capital settlement'.[44] And yet poignantly, when he did get off, he repeatedly confessed to Crabb Robinson, who accompanied him on the journey, that he *did*, after all, regret his feeling of inalterable unfulfilment: 'It is too late.'[45]

His securities had become so firmly circumscribed by the ties of family, local attachment, and national constructions that, as Crabb Robinson reports, 'It often happened that objects of universal attraction seemed chiefly to bring back to his mind absent objects dear to him'.[46] Nevertheless, while his responses to the immediate objects of admiration were still overdetermined by discursive pacts which carried his major self-investment, crises of imaginary indeterminacy re-admitted on other cultural ground did problematise those preformulations, threatening trauma, however diminished, and triggering the characteristic anxiety of his revisionary process. What is most interesting is that Wordsworth should *at that moment* feel impelled to try to extend himself in this way, though the tedium of this secondary discursive struggle evidently weighed on his powers of reaction, especially in relation to the Catholic overtones of Italian culture which his profound commitment to Anglicanism as the foremost embodiment of his imaginary nation had previously strongly deprecated.

In order to encounter 'Rome' as the sign of further imaginary self-fulfilment, Wordsworth needed to re-enact the paradigm of his imaginative re-creation as it had been established in completing *The Prelude* in 1805. Predictably, after he had finally reached his goal, the initial result was disappointment, as he recorded in 'At Rome'; like Hazlitt, he found that the everyday reality emptied the names of their spell: 'In Rome', Hazlitt had written in 1825, 'you are for the most part lost in a mass of tawdry, fulsome *common-places*'.[47] Yet, as usual, Wordsworth's expectation is 'mocked' by the actual experience, only to be subsequently reconfirmed by the insistence of the interrupted structure in the operation of imagination, so that those who transcend the 'depression' are 'not unrecompensed'. The return of imaginary fulfilment within the Symbolic order depends on the mind's power to restore what preceded fragmentation, and in Wordsworth's case his reconstruction of a generalising 'comprehension of the past' (as he puts it in a note attached to the poem) was his imaginative response to a new spirit of literalism that other poems in this commemorative sequence written in the early 1840s rise up against. 'At Rome. – Regrets. – In Allusion to Niebuhr, and Other Modern Historians', for example, insists on sustaining the fabulous content of 'Rome' (largely derived from Livy's *History*) in the face of Niebuhr's methods of historical source-criticism in his *History of Rome* (1811–32), thus replaying in terms of Roman historiography the structure of loss ('The glory of infant Rome must disappear, / Her morning splendours vanish') and recompense ('One solace yet remains') first fixed in 'Intimations of Immortality'.[48] Any republican affinities of Wordsworth's earlier classicism have gone, but the lingering regard for the virtues of Roman stoicism represent a newly embattled traditionalist mind-set.

More generally at this time, the Renaissance construction of Rome as the centre of humanism was becoming overdetermined by the nineteenth-century return to the idea of the medieval pilgrimage to Rome as the custodian of 'belief', while the interest in classical 'antiquities' was shifting to Greece. Wordsworth's disappointment with the contemporary reconstruction of Roman antiquity was becoming offset by the encounter with an originary site of the discourse of Christian assent and faith – more archaic than its assumption as a nationalist language – which, after Milton, he encountered particularly in Tuscany. What he now called for was rather the reinstatement of the Imaginary within the discourse of his national religion, appealing to the continuing tradition for which 'Rome' still stood in the England of the 1840s – an alternative discourse of 'belief' that turns out, after all, to be attached to the institution of Catholicism.

The 1830s were dogged by events, both personal and national, that badly tried Wordsworth's imaginary reclosures in the Symbolic order. The decade started with his gloominess over the French Revolution of 1830. While his literary reputation had become solidly established (sales and reprints were at their height, and academic honours were loaded on him), with the deaths and declines of family and friends he more than ever needed the support of the discourses he had painstakingly prepared to withstand such shocks; but the tide of political change, with a privately desperate irony, was at the same time threatening precisely those personal investments. Private needs and national trends were uncomfortably at odds, even in regard to the institution on which his sense of security most depended – the Established Church of England.

His Anglicanism was 'in the High Church tradition ... which in practice sometimes seemed to put more emphasis on the institution than on anything the institution might involve',[49] and he was open about his 'Misgivings' ('O dearer far than light and life are dear'), and about his 'fear / That friends, by death disjoined, may meet no more!').[50] Yet Wordsworth was deeply opposed to the current tradition of Erastianism, 'which made the Church a department of the state, an *imperium in imperio*'.[51] Rather for him the Church embodied the whole fabric of the British establishment – 'Britain' – most particularly as the representation of the Anglican nationalism that after completing the 1805 *Prelude* had become the chief discursive translation for his imaginary subject. During the Church reforms of the 1830s, however, it was in danger of failing to live up to its hegemony over alternative national institutions. The consequence of 'improvement' was the familiar check to expectation, with the corollary of symbolic alienation: England had become a state which was in urgent danger of no longer representing the Wordsworthian constitution.

Christopher Wordsworth's comments in the *Memoirs* that his uncle was 'predisposed to sympathize with a form of religion which appears to afford some exercise for the imaginative faculty' is suggestive of the contestation between what the poet conceived of as the primacy of 'the imaginative faculty' and the churchman's preferential investment in a specific discourse.[52] Wordsworth gave an interesting account to a young friend of why he cultivated an incompleteness of theological definition that was frequently regarded as indicating a discrepancy between his vehement avowals of orthodox attachment to Christianity and the doctrinal vagueness of his poetry:

> He ... explained it by stating that when in youth his imagination was shaping for itself the channel in which it was to flow, his religious convictions were less definite and less strong than they had become on more mature thought; and that, when his poetic mind and manner had once been formed, he feared lest he might, in attempting to modify them, become constrained. He added that on religious matters he ever wrote with great diffidence.[53]

Though these are presumably not Wordsworth's exact words, the ambiguity over the object of his attempted modification – his own 'poetic mind and manner', or his 'religious convictions', or both – suggests the nature of the problem that occasioned his sense of 'constraint'.

Radically, the institution of Anglicanism had over time come to represent a formation that was peculiar in the degree of its insistence; but that representation had been secured as the resolution of former passages through a series of other discourses – pantheism, republicanism, and nationalism among them. The journey between these discourses had had to be propelled by continual acts of imagination if their abandonment were not to expose them traumatically to an alienated literalism. A sustained process of translation was called for whereby each revision demanded the renegotiation of entry into the Symbolic order in such a way as to ensure the dominance of the imaginary subject-position. The position he ascribed to Southey was intimately known: 'Christian faith / Calmed in his soul the fear of change and death.'[54] In order to effect such seamlessness and establish 'a repose that ever is the same',[55] and following the same indeterminate gradualism that marked his journey to political reaction, Wordsworth intuitively avoided the precision of theological niceties that might reveal contradictory stances and so advertise a volte-face that he was deeply interested in eliding.

The crisis of depression that had occurred in 1835, when Mary Wordsworth begged Henry Crabb Robinson (immediately he had returned from a Continental trip) to come and help relieve her husband, had resulted in the plan to go to Rome. It was no mere distraction, but a journey that Wordsworth was being drawn to undertake in part to reconstitute the imaginary discourse of Anglican nationalism that was under stress at home. The Church of England was itself under reform during the brief Tory government of Sir Robert Peel in 1835 and subsequently under that of Lord Melbourne when an Ecclesiastical Commission, notably advocated by C. J. Blomfield, the Bishop of London, was set up to modernise the national Church. Wordsworth felt the Church was in danger of a provincialising Evangelical takeover, and was intuitively seeking out a new basis for its authority. In the words of one Church historian: 'in the 1830s the most serious question about the Church of England was: "Can these dry bones live?"'[56] From the process of improvement in the reorganisation of revenues, pluralism and non-residence, sinecures and nepotism, the 'Anglican revival' of spiritual values proceeded through the Oxford Movement.

Wordsworth was following a similar trajectory towards the rediscovery of a more universalist religious tradition within his Anglicanism. Like Hilaire Belloc, who seems to allude to Wordsworth's Wanderer ('But in the mountains did he *feel* his faith'), Wordsworth had crucially '[seen], as it were, [his] religion in the Alps',[57] but he also fully apprehended that much of its history lay in Italy beyond and was centrally institutionalised in Rome. The tour of 1837 enlarged Wordsworth's view of the Catholic tradition. If the success of his private mission involved the Romanisation of Anglicanism, it depended more fundamentally on his imaginative re-creation of Italy as the centre of an imaginary tradition that embraced his reading of Anglicanism, and so also on the Anglicanisation of 'Rome'.

He was in effect engaged in an act of cultural revisionism that reflected his desire to sustain the discursive continuity of his own construction of his nation by seeing it represented in a symbolic 'Rome' that would after all live up to the fulfilment anticipated by his imaginary subject. By the 1840s, Wordsworth had completed his revision of the Grand Tour, and he had eventually arrived at the charisma of 'Rome' on his own terms.

Notes

1 'Ode: Intimations of Immortality', *The Poetical Works of William Wordsworth*, eds Ernest de Selincourt and Helen Darbishire, 5 vols (Oxford, 1940–49), 4: 283, ll. 142–6. See my essay 'Describing the Revolution: Wordsworth, Freud and Lacan', in C. C. Barfoot and Theo D'haen, eds, *Tropes of Revolution: Writers' Reactions to Real and Imagined Revolutions 1789–1989* (Amsterdam, 1991), 90–113.
2 Sigmund Freud, 'A Disturbance of Memory on the Acropolis', in *Complete Psychological Works of Sigmund Freud*, trans. under the general editorship of James Strachey, 24 vols (London, 1953–74), 22: 244.
3 'Disturbance', 247.
4 *Ibid.*, 247–8.
5 *Poetical Works*, 4: 280, 463–4.
6 William Wordsworth, *Lyrical Ballads,* eds R. L. Brett and A. L. Jones (London, 1965), 256.
7 *Poetical Works*, 4: 279.
8 Thomas West, *A Guide to the Lakes in Cumberland, Westmorland, and Lancashire* (Kendal, 1821), 4.
9 See my essay, 'Crossings Out: The Problem of Textual Passage in *The Prelude*', in Robert Brinkley and Keith Hanley, eds, *Romantic Revisions* (Cambridge, 1992).
10 Richard Onorato, *The Character of the Poet: Wordsworth in 'The Prelude'* (Princeton, 1971), 72.
11 James Boswell, *Life of Johnson*, ed. R. W. Chapman, new edn, corrected by J. D. Fleeman (London, 1976), 742.
12 Dennis Porter, *Haunted Journeys: Desire and Transgression in European Travel Writing* (Princeton, 1991), 19.
13 See Paul P. Bernard, *Rush to the Alps: The Evolution of Vacationing in Switzerland* (New York, 1978), 16–17.
14 Quoted in W. E. Mead, *The Grand Tour in the Eighteenth Century* (Boston and New York, 1914), 239.
15 *The Prelude* (1805), eds Jonathan Wordsworth, M. H. Abrams, and Stephen Gill (New York, 1979), bk 6, ll. 342–3.
16 To Dorothy Wordsworth, 6 and 16 Sept. 1790, *The Letters of William and Dorothy Wordsworth*, ed. E. de Selincourt, 2nd edn, *The Early Years 1787–1805*, rev. Chester L. Shaver (Oxford, 1967), 35.

17 *The Prelude*, bk 6, ll. 452–6.
18 *Ibid.*, bk 6, ll. 456–61.
19 *Ibid.*, bk 6, l. 542.
20 Thomas Weiskel, *The Romantic Sublime: Studies in the Structure and Psychology of Transcendence* (Baltimore, 1976), 26–33, 48–62.
21 *The Prelude*, bk 6, ll. 520–42.
22 *Ibid.*, bk 6, ll. 491–2, 489–90.
23 Alan Liu, *Wordsworth: The Sense of History* (Stanford, 1989), 24–31.
24 *Psychological Works*, 4: 198.
25 *Haunted Journeys*, 197.
26 *The Prelude*, bk 6, ll. 525–32.
27 *Ibid.*, bk 8, ll. 746–8.
28 Thomas De Quincey, *Autobiographical Sketches*, in *Works of Thomas De Quincey*, 16 vols (Edinburgh, 1862–71), 14: 179.
29 *The Prelude*, bk 8, ll. 744, 705–6.
30 *Autobiographical Sketches*, 179–80.
31 *The Poems of John Milton*, ed. Helen Darbishire (London, 1961), bk 5, ll. 164–5.
32 *The Prelude*, bk 6, ll. 570–2.
33 Edward Gibbon, *Memoirs of My Life and Writings*, eds A. O. J. Cockshut and Stephen Constantine (Keele, 1994), 159.
34 This sentence from Draft C is printed in *Memoirs of My Life*, ed. Georges A. Bonnard (London, 1966), 132.
35 *The Prelude*, bk 6, ll. 538–46.
36 *Ibid.*, bk 6, ll. 489–90, 524.
37 *Ibid.*, bk 13, l. 69.
38 *Ibid.*, bk 6, ll. 556–8, 568.
39 *Poetical Works*, 2: 426.
40 *The Prelude*, bk 6, ll. 679–80, 617.
41 *Poetical Works*, 4: 190, ll. 19–20, 29–30.
42 Brian Barefoot, *The English Road to Rome* (Malvern, 1993), 136.
43 *Poetical Works*, 3: 489.
44 Stephen Gill, *William Wordsworth: A Life* (Oxford, 1989), 299.
45 Quoted in *Poetical Works*, 3: 490.
46 *Ibid.*
47 'Notes of a Journey Through France and Italy', in *Complete Works of William Hazlitt*, ed. P. P. Howe, 21 vols (London, 1930–4), 10: 232.
48 *Poetical Works*, 3: 213, ll. 11, 10; 3: 494; 3: 213, ll. 5–6, 10.
49 Katherine M. Peek, *Wordsworth in England* (Bryn Mawr, 1943), 102–3.
50 *Poetical Works*, 2: 37, ll. 5, 3–4.
51 *Wordsworth in England*, 103.
52 Christopher Wordsworth, *Memoirs of William Wordsworth*, 2 vols. (London, 1851), 2: 151.
53 *Wordsworth in England*, 124.

54 'Inscription for a Monument in Crosthwaite Church, in the Vale of Keswick', *Poetical Works*, 4: 278, ll. 17–18.
55 'Ode to Duty', *ibid.*, 4: 85, l. 40.
56 Alec R. Vidler, *The Church in an Age of Revolution: 1798 to the Present Day* (Harmondsworth, 1978), 48.
57 *Poetical Works*, 5: 15, l. 226; *The Path to Rome* (London, n.d.), 159.

Travelling hopefully: Helen Maria Williams and the feminine discourse of sensibility

Chris Jones

In late eighteenth-century Britain the future was another country. America and France had outstripped the tardy progress of England in forming a new political society. Travellers, always aware of displacement in time as well as place, took new bearings when judging their destinations by their progress in civilisation. Replying to a sceptical correspondent, Helen Maria Williams, in the first volume of her *Letters from France* (1790), asserts the political motivation of her pilgrimage to a site more inspiring than those of Rome or, by implication, England:

> If I were at Rome, you would not be surprised to hear that I had visited, with the warmest reverence, every spot where any relics of her ancient grandeur could be traced; that I had flown to the capitol; that I had kissed the earth on which the Roman senate sat in council: And can you then expect me to have seen the Federation at the Champ de Mars, and the National Assembly of France, with indifference? Before you insist that I ought to have done so, point out to me, in the page of Roman history, a spectacle more solemn, more affecting, than the Champ de Mars exhibited, or more magnanimous, more noble efforts in the cause of liberty than have been made by the National Assembly.[1]

Mary Wollstonecraft estimated the progress of Scandinavia by reference to France and made disparaging remarks about the regions of Britain. Wordsworth was drawn to the Continent by the sublimity of the Alps and the commensurate spectacle of liberated France. They shared a sense of the Revolutionary sublime, the evermore about to be, that characterised a radical sensibility. Burke's sublime stimulated fear and protective preservation of the masculine ego within established power relations which it further consolidated. The sublime of radical sensibility looked to an extension of human faculties, especially of the 'social passions' that would realise new forms of society. In tune with the moral and humanitarian movements of the time, it hoped to see oppressive distinctions of power and wealth diminish.[2] Burke's sexual distinctions, like all socially constructed divisions, were open to deconstruction in the prospects opened up by the French Revolution. Only when the defeat of France was foreseen could Scott send Waverley on his journeys in time and place within Britain, confident that England would dictate the future. By then France could be presented as an absolutist military state, fulfilling Burke's prophecies, and the traditional discourses of family, rank, and sex that Burke had consolidated returned with a vengeance. The principal female protagonists of Scott's novel, Flora MacIvor and Rose Bradwardine, embody the antithetical traits of Burke's sublime and beautiful, and the plot suitably punishes Flora's pretensions to the sublime, masculine prerogatives of political intervention and self-determination. Waverley's renunciation of the 'romance' of Flora, military glory, and political activism for the 'reality' of Rose and the domestic life of a man of taste and feeling demonstrates the importance of such gendered traits in a context that does not confine them to one sex. Scott's fiction, published at a time when the term 'romance' was giving way to 'novel', presents political action in the context of feminine transgression and indulgence in romance. He 'returns' Waverley to a domestic reality and a merely aesthetic representation of doomed revolution. Waverley is left with a painting to commemorate his masculine exploits in fancy dress and a set of arms to be used as an ornament. Scott may be 'masculinising' the novel but he is also colonising the feminine, contributing to what Gary Kelly sees as the feminised, middle-class cultural (anti-Revolutionary) revolution.[3]

Helen Maria Williams played a considerable role in establishing this Romantic formation, as much by her complicity with established conventions as by her flagrant breaches of their limitations. Her efforts to placate her British readership with a feminine discourse of pure sympathy belied her own more dissident, intellectually based political principles and she became a model of the dangers of errant female sensibility. Her insistence on her role as a *spectactrice* encouraged an aesthetic, voyeuristic interest in the lurid and sentimental tales in which she captured the violence and elation of the Revolutionary period. My purpose is not primarily to show how Williams subverted a supposedly uniform feminine discourse of sensibility, or how her work remained a prisoner of its conventions. I am more interested in her canny and sophisticated exploitation of the ambiguities of sensibility to grasp the progressive possibilities of the age. Though her work was re-assimilated to the dominant discourses of post-

Revolutionary Britain, her efforts were continued in the work of the Shelleys and Sydney Owenson, and she made a lasting impression on Wordsworth.

Williams well knew the common ploys of sentimental discourse and often employed them strategically to deflect criticism. She attempted to use, rather than be used by, the established 'feminine' discourses and extend them into new territory. The role of *salonnière* in the tradition of Georgiana, Duchess of Devonshire, or of Manon Roland develops into the enabling function Williams performs for others' writings, both in the hospitality of her *Letters* and as a channel to English publishers. Manon Roland's political partnership with her husband is similar to Williams's equal participation in John Hurford Stone's commercial ventures in an unlicensed but long and faithful union. In valuing French culture for its intellectual vitality and its sociability she seems to take little heed of criticisms of its moral corruption, attributed by many to 'courtly' habits of female sexual influence. The situation becomes more complicated by Williams's tendency, in her growing disillusionment with the French, to associate them with the negative characteristics of conventional feminine sensibility. This chimed in with the concerted Anti-Jacobin attack on sensibility in England, and reinforced the stigmatisation of revolutionary zeal as feminine: emotionally unstable, extreme, and violent. While Williams was in France during this development, Wollstonecraft reacted by retreating from her androgynous ideal into a defence of female virtue corrupted by man. Vivien Jones charts a similar trajectory for both writers, doing justice to their transgressive celebration of 'libidinised' fulfilment and their hopes that sympathy held the possibility of breaking the cycle of violence and retribution.[4] But she sees them as haunted by the dominant construction of the female, 'vulnerable to abduction and corruption',[5] and eventually reinscribing her within the respectable middle-class body politic.

Gary Kelly and Anne Mellor have attempted to assimilate Williams into a feminine discourse of the private virtues and domesticity, despite her notorious flouting of the marriage bond.[6] Here Williams seems to have succeeded in grafting a universal benevolence and sympathy on to the stock of a restricted sentimentalisation of the family. Jones's use of a sentimental novel scenario of transgression and repentance does acknowledge, with Nicola Watson, that the triumphant domestic tableaux that frame Williams's mini-romances are reclaimed from transgression or tragedy only by the Revolution.[7] This relieves the exiled Du Fossés from the threat of a *lettre de cachet* and allows Madelaine to escape taking the veil and to marry the man rejected by her family. The disagreements of critics reflect the ambiguity of the work as a subversion or extension. Mary Favret's response is similarly ambiguous. In a lengthy study she suggests that Williams is prisoner to the form of the sentimental letter, condemned by her self-representation through feeling to mirror the feelings of her readers. In 'domesticating' French events Williams must celebrate the British constitution as the model of their aspirations. When they exceed this, the sentimental letter form experiences a 'fall' into multivocal experience (novelistically epistolary) which leaves Williams a spectator on the sidelines of history.[8] Favret's earlier article, focusing on the use of interior/exterior space in the *Letters*, poses some interesting doubts about the limits of Williams's vision and aims. There is a translucence, an echoing, of the interior, domestic life in evocations of public festivals and a similar permeability in her domestic settings to the symbolic rites and situations of national life, be they festivals or prisons. This translation of French experience is made through feelings claimed to transcend nationality, and is based on the possibility of a state 'constituted in terms of affective relationship'.[9] This more utopian scenario seems in keeping with sentimental fictions designed not only to procure reader-identification but to extend the reader's sympathies by their capacity to entrance, challenge, and embarrass. Initially reluctant to take part in the Du Fossés' pageant (shades of *Mansfield Park*!), Williams modestly takes a non-speaking part, but that part is the figure of Liberty. The domestic situation of the performance is extended to the local fête of which it is a part, involving all ranks and sexes on the estate. It becomes one of those *fêtes bocagères* represented in the novels and poems of the eighteenth century celebrating spontaneous social harmony, which Roland Mortier has seen as preludes to the fêtes of the Revolution.[10]

Williams's alternations between the internal and the external, domestic and collective, feeling and rationalism, are part of a strategy that imitates traditional female discourse in order to extend its bounds. 'That form of politics must be best by which those I love are made happy', she asserts, but the apparent restriction is jeopardised when her affections are aligned with 'the common feelings of humanity' as a 'citizen of the world'.[11] As her contemporaries realised, such expanded sympathies were associated with the 'universal benevolence' of writers like Godwin and Wollstonecraft who attacked the form of the traditional family and state. Williams projects, and sometimes over-projects, the image of the sentimental, merely social woman, just as she cultivated a manner and appearance that struck observers as a parody of affected sensibility. Her head-dresses were legendary. Beneath her camp exaggeration and equivocation, however, she is seriously committed.

Williams's *Letters* are not informal, emotional responses any more than Burke's *Reflections* is a private letter. Availing herself of the form and feminine register of the letter, she goes beyond both. She considered herself not a passive observer of the Revolution but an active force within it, celebrating, criticising, and furthering it. Her literary acts drew her into peril under the Terror, antagonised Napoleon, and provoked political censorship. She championed Manon Roland, who campaigned for war and the dethronement of the king; she justified the king's trial (though not his execution), and she welcomed the disestablishment of religious institutions. The most conspicuous talents of the day were gathered into her salon as the ruling spirits of the age to be.

Her narratives challenge conventional frames as Revolutionary France becomes the swiftly changing setting for trials and resolutions impossible in traditional society. In one of her narratives a priest disappointed of office under the old regime becomes a military chaplain. After a defeat, wandering through the disputed borders of Germany and France, he becomes a pedlar, then successfully enters a competition for the role of schoolmaster, much to the astonishment of those who deride his ragged appearance. His feelings lead him to marry his female assistant, but in illness his conscience makes him contact his relatives, who reinstate him in his priestly role. Imprisoned under Robespierre, his life-giving solace is the meals brought to him by his cast-off 'wife' and Thermidor reunites them in a tranquil old age. Here the domestic affections transgress family and social regulation and the drama of inner change is echoed in the changing boundaries of the Revolution, disrupting traditional distinctions and enabling the triumph of true feeling. The learned pedlar of this tale, foreshadowing Wordsworth's philosopher-pedlar of the 'Ruined Cottage', provides a typical radical conflict of social decorum. Williams reverses conservative romance conventions. In her mini-romance the *nostos*, or return to home, original status, and identity, is an imprisonment within the forms of a creed outgrown. The family members who come to conduct the married schoolmaster back to his true place lock the door while they interrogate him, foreshadowing his later incarceration under the Terror. Both the institutions of the old regime and the rule of Robespierre block an emerging revolutionary society in which individuals learn to unite love and service to the community. After the demonic romance stories of the prisons, generically similar to the gothic romance stories of former oppression, Thermidor gives Williams another opportunity to celebrate the triumph of feeling and the poetic justice of romance. Yet these stories are true. In renouncing novel-writing for the *histoires* of history Williams finds herself writing romances. Posing as mere narrator she becomes the voice of Revolution, sweeping away social and generic distinctions. The *Gentleman's Magazine* was largely justified in maintaining that even in 'recording' the events of the Revolution, Williams was subverting British traditional values and the discourses associated with them, debasing 'her sex, her heart, her feelings, her talents'.[12]

One of the obvious ways in which the *Letters* incorporates wider responses than the feminine is in the inclusion of letters by male writers, Stone and Christie,[13] and of documentary appendices. This could be seen as feminine self-abrogation in the service of truth, which is better comprehended by a witness or male authority. But it is remarkable that in such a 'dialogic' presentation there is so little variation of view. It could be seen as a more masculine editorial job, selecting and commissioning evidence to support the dominant line. Even some of the disagreements contribute to eventual unity. She seems to alter her view of the 'traitor' Dumaurier in the light of his correspondence, becoming progressively more sympathetic to his alienation from Parisian demagogues as she herself appreciates the threat of Robespierre. Offences against masculine duty and honour are palliated by a feminine exercise of rational discrimination.

The male contribution that most differs from her own views is the lengthy political analysis of the stages of the Revolution by Christie. He insists that a constitutional monarchy after the English pattern was the goal of the first Revolutionary uprising and that, since then, events had been swayed by conflicts within French society. He praises the solid, English middle class as the essential bulwark of order. This was obviously designed to reply to Burke and placate English critics. It was not Williams's view. She tends to concentrate on the intelligentsia and the peasantry in her letters. Her tentative criticism of the English commercial middle class is expressed in the hope that England would follow the same path as France by reason, not violence, and that she may 'direct that full tide of wealth which rolls through the land, to visit it in more equal streams; and may there be "no leading into captivity, and no complaining in her streets"'.[14]

For Williams the Girondist republican programme was the inspiration of the Revolution and in several places she looks forward to a state that would demonstrate 'ideas even more enlarged, and philosophy more liberal' than America. But even in her first letters she is aware of the accusation hanging over her head in the shape of a reply from a correspondent: 'you accuse me of describing with too much enthusiasm the public rejoicings in France, and prophesy that I shall return to my own country a fierce republican'. In response to this she makes one of what Vivien Jones calls her 'ritual apologies' for a woman's inadequacy when faced by political arguments: 'my political creed is entirely an affair of the heart; for I have not been so absurd as to consult my head upon matters of which it is so incapable of judging'. Taking refuge in this 'feminine' response, she goes on to make some decidedly political observations about those who repeat 'the trite remark, that the French have gone too far, because they have gone farther than ourselves; as if it were not possible that that degree of influence which is perfectly safe in the hand of the executive part of our government, might be dangerous, at this crisis, to the liberty of France'.[15]

Constitutional arrangements were important to Williams as the form that might express and contain the feelings which were the motive power of the Revolution. She hoped that the French might

> form a system of politics, which like a modern ship of discovery, built upon principles that defy the opposition of the tempestuous elements ('and passions are the elements of life' –) instead of yielding to their fury makes them subservient to its purpose, and sailing sublimely over the untracked ocean, unites those together whom nature seemed for ever to have separated.[16]

She admits that the success of the venture is problematic and to many 'chimerical' since such a 'principle of perfection' has hitherto 'only served to adorn the page of the philosopher'. In the case of other countries she favoured the French standing aloof and allowing a constitution to be freely worked out which, she thought, would incorporate as much of the principles of liberty and equality as national traditions might tolerate. She reacted against the French imposing their own political ideas on occupied countries under the specious familial description of 'fraternization'. This she scanned as 'persecuting their new allies with theories of which they themselves do not know the result'. The French were progressing not too far but too fast, and she feared that 'the stubborn habits of this generation must pass away, which they scarcely will but with the generation itself, before these great principles of liberty and human happiness give all the benefits to be expected from them, on the soil even where they are sprung'.[17] This element of realism, admitting the limited truth of Burke's appeal to national tradition and prejudice, has been insufficiently appreciated by commentators who, like the anti-Jacobins, see her exclusively as an apologist for the French.

In the case of France, Williams looked forward to a speedy end to abuses that were obnoxious to the civilised world, such as the system of *lettres de cachet*, the achievement of measures which the progress of reason and humanity anticipated, such as the abolition of the slave trade and the introduction of universal education, and the evolution of an egalitarian society which would purge the French character of its national faults while leaving intact its reputation for sociability. It is in the last of her hopes that Williams demonstrates most that ambivalence that prejudices her characterisation of Revolutionary France as demonstrating an ideal balance of reason and feeling, masculine and feminine. The national character of the French had always been reproached for effeminacy by the British. In the vanguard of intellectual progress, France was even more renowned for the graces of life, the easy sociability that attracted writers of sensibility, the amorous intrigue and concern with surfaces that affronted moralists. Much as she wished to acclaim such a fusion, Williams could not resist ascribing the failures of the Revolution to French levity and passion, the dangerous excesses of a 'feminine' sensibility.

Generally Williams portrays a society that is throwing down political and gender barricades. She appreciates the carnivalesque variety of activities and classes tolerated in the main square of Orléans, without the restrictions that would be thought necessary by any English municipality. In Paris the coffee-houses, the Lycée, the Assembly, are open to women. French men and women have transcended their national and courtly habits of foppish display and sexual gallantry. 'Engrossed by political concerns which involve the fate of their country', men seem to prize a negligence in dress and exchange sexual compliments for politics as the staple of their dinner conversation. 'Not only the age of chivalry, but the age of petits maîtres is past', she comments with satisfaction.[18]

Stone, in his capacity of reporter on military affairs, repeats this account of the transformation of the French character: 'The gallants whom I have seen parading in the public walks with their mistresses, in all the style of foppery and dissipation, are now transformed into hardy soldiers.'[19] It is the same transformation that Wordsworth describes in Beaupuis, as narrow gendered and social values evolved into extended sympathies for 'man as man'. Beaupuis seemed to have transferred the passion and gallantry 'which he, a soldier, in his idler day / Had paid to woman' to the obscure and mean.[20] For Stone 'the effeminacy of the Sybarite' has been changed into 'Roman firmness'.[21] Williams uses the masculine discourse of the classics not only for a long appendix on Rome under the emperors but to characterise her female republican heroines. Manon Roland and Charlotte Corday were inspired by Roman examples, and the women at the taking of the Bastille behaved like 'Roman matrons'.

Perhaps the most audacious departure from conventional feminine discourse is Williams's account of military matters. As the daughter of a soldier and a Scottish mother whose line prided itself on fighting for the Covenant, she makes only the most perfunctory gesture of feminine reluctance to engage in descriptions of warfare. Despite her declared intention of relying on male authority, she discusses in some detail the campaigns of Dumourier and Miranda and gives a sublime description of the French army singing the Marseillaise before battle. She even justifies invasion of an enemy's territory as part of the 'defensive' war thrust on them and forecasts further victories of the citizen army 'overspreading Europe'.[22] The armies of France became the bastion of Revolutionary virtue for Williams and for Wordsworth. Wordsworth borrowed from Stone the simile of Hercules strangling the snakes for the conquests of the infant French republic, and had faith in their ultimate, universal victory.[23]

Gary Kelly speaks of this section as 'feminizing' warfare,[24] but to the critical eyes of her contemporaries Williams had broken with such conventions entirely and become an 'unsex'd female'. The domestic affections may be extended to cover the entire nation, but the activity they provoke is far from domestic: 'already is the great family of Frenchmen composing one army'.[25] From her position as a new Revolutionary woman, she can criticise a 'feminine', voyeuristic expedition by the Archduchess of Brunswick to the siege of Lisle:

> As this siege was made according to the usual rules, the exhibition was very brilliant. It drew a number of the curious to behold the spectacle, amongst whom were the Archduchess and her court, who diverted themselves with beholding the effects produced by the various kinds of artillery, an assortment of each of which, for her amusement, was discharged in her presence. She had the courage, it is asserted, to fire some of these tremendous machines herself; but her curiosity proved fatal to some of the engineers, who, willing to show the extent of their art, charged two mortars with bombs of the largest size, which unhappily burst, and killed thirty-five men that were round the battery.[26]

These are not travellers but tourists, drawn by a feminine delight in the brilliant spectacle, unaware of the terrible effect of red-hot cannon balls on the defenders which Williams has described. The Archduchess might have courage, but it is frivolously employed in making war a dangerous amusement. The incident stands out as a mark of confidence that Williams's own account of hostilities cannot be compared with the superficial 'feminine' mentality of the court.

While Williams charted the growth of a unified sensibility, incorporating both feminine and masculine characteristics in the pursuit of national harmony, she also had to chronicle the tragedies of the Revolution. Many of these she sought to diminish (the September Massacres were perpetrated by a mere fifty conspirators); others she explained as the result of the corruption of the old regime; but she also blamed the French national character. In delineating its faults she linked it with the stereotyped female

characteristics which she and the nascent Revolutionary society had transcended. Initially she rebutted the suggestion that the French had taken
up the cause of freedom 'with the same sort of fondness with which they
have taken up many other fashions which are now cast off'. Her subsequent
criticisms, however, seem to follow the same paradigm of feminine faults.
The French are a people of 'quick sensibility: they seem in some sort the
creatures of passion. Ungovernable in their resentment, cruel and ferocious
in their revenge, they yield with no less facility to the impulse of mercy
and the sympathy of compassion'.[27] The latter impulse is equally dangerous
as she imagines French *women* seeking to rescue Louis XVI and causing
civil strife. Even Robespierre and Collot D'Herbois are moved to instigate
terror by a sort of feminine pique at their rejection as lawyer and actor.

It was her contention that the French achieved a greater maturity during
the Revolution which enabled them to assume the sterner virtues without
losing the freedom and gaiety of their manner. The Marseillois are noted
for their adherence to order and opposition to anarchy despite their
'southern' nature as 'children of the sun'. She relates anecdotes of the taking
of the Bastille which show 'that gaiety which never forsakes the French,
even on such occasions as would make any other people on earth serious'.
French gaiety maintained under adverse circumstances ranges from their
acceptance of the poor quality of inns (a perennial complaint of travellers)
to the brilliant spectacle of intellectual sociability in the prisons of the
Terror. There are, however, some dubious ironic juxtapositions. Williams
describes the *don Patriotique* by which French women gave up their jewellery
to help the war effort, sacrificing 'titles, fortune, and even personal orna-
ments, so dear to female vanity, for the common cause'. She then describes
the medallion worn by Mme de Silléry: a polished stone from the Bastille
set with diamonds and emeralds. Men, too, have not lost their taste for a
pretty face as she hints by describing a patriotic festival where the main
attraction is a procession of five hundred young ladies.[28]

She is less sanguine about French gaiety when it becomes the unfeeling
levity of the Revolutionary Tribunals. 'The levity, and even merriment,
with which this horde of assassins disposed of their victims, gives their
barbarity a deeper shade of horror.' If she hoped that the French would
learn from the lessons of the Terror, her description of their childlike
carelessness gives scant encouragement: 'with the careless simplicity of
children who after the rigours of school hasten to their sports; the Parisians,
shaking off the hideous remembrance of the past, fly to the scenes of
pleasure'.[29] This renewed merriment includes queues at the Catholic
churches, the decision to keep both the old and the new holidays, and the
caprice of women, who again immerse themselves in the cares of the toilette.

Vivien Jones has seen this last as a welcome return of female sexuality,[30] but it is difficult to avoid the impression that Williams is not wholly contradicting the satire of Pope's couplet by which she describes it. Only after the opening of the museums and the national library does she assert that Paris 'once more excites the ideas of taste, elegance, refinement, and happiness'.[31]

Williams does not relinquish her hopes that a framework may be found which allows the widest variety of freedom to flourish, but the French character needs more curbs than the constitution of 1793 had provided. Another must be worked out 'which should have more restrictions, and consequently be better adapted to the lightness and vehemence of the national character'. In her welcome for the constitution of 1795 the image of the ship of state is again invoked, but it has been 'built with toil and trouble and cemented with blood'. Her own voyage has more in common with the Ancient Mariner's. She looks back over a time in which she had doubted Providence with 'the same sort of melancholy pleasure as the mariner who paints the horrors of the tempest when he has reached the harbour, and sheds a tender tear over his lost companions who have perished in the wreck'. Such crimes were now for her, as for Coleridge, 'the beacons of the revolution' which might safeguard future attempts from complete shipwreck, but they had brought her to the nadir of despair. 'Was it for this?' she lamented, in a threnody that Wordsworth might well have echoed in the famous lines of *The Prelude*: 'Was it for this ye overthrew the towers of the Bastille ... was it for this, ye generous patriots, that with heroic contempt of life ye shed your blood.' Here, as in the treatment of the carnage of battle, Williams and Stone show nothing of the 'masculine' sublime which is able to overcome the impasse of terror by imaginative transcendence. The horror is 'unutterable' both because she cannot find images strong enough to convey it and because the feelings cannot encompass it: 'the feelings become deadened, by the long contemplation of so wide a waste of ruin'. It is close to the negative sublime of mental alienation which afflicts some of the characters in her narratives who have lost all those they lived for in the Terror. If such horror can be surmounted by religious faith it is a faith in Providence working through men's minds and hearts, in the progress of those principles of social harmony which might be obscured but will one day break forth 'like the fresh leaves of spring'. Wordsworth's echo of Williams's cry of despair was also his answer to it as he developed his own idea of the growth of the mind through vicissitude and nature's promptings to a firm trust in Providence and the possible grandeur of the human mind's imaginative empire. His development of subjective and aesthetic 'compensations' for the failure of the Revolution, however, did not exclude a hope like that of Williams for a deferred triumph of the ideals of the early Revolutionary period, as Hazlitt noted in his review of *The Excursion*.[32]

Williams's frank avowal of her disappointment in the progress of the Revolution was not registered by Anti-Jacobin critics. For them she demonstrated too clearly the untrustworthiness of sensibility as a creed that could justify assassination and the Terror. Ignoring the subtle distinctions of Williams's use of the term, they economically imposed on the revolutionary enterprise the brand of unregulated feminine sensibility. In satiric poems and novels Wollstonecraft, Williams, Mary Hays, and Charlotte Smith assumed demonic proportions as they, or figures transparently modelled on them, instigated the destruction of domestic and social order as willing tools of French subversion. The far-reaching consequences of stifling the dangerous 'feminine' in man as well as woman were to dominate the representation of woman in the early nineteenth century. Maria Edgeworth banned sensibility from her schoolroom. Hannah More wished to tame sensibility into the servant of religious duties that buttressed the inequalities of society. Even in Wollstonecraft we see a retreat from the idea of a union of reason and feeling which might challenge traditional moral and social ideas. As Vivien Jones has argued, the change in Wollstonecraft's view of the Poissardes from respectable tradeswomen to women tragically misled by their passions and the instigation of the Duke of Orleans demonises the passions, especially the lustful ambitions of the Duke.[33] Wollstoncraft's startling comparison of the French people to an elephant seeks to ascribe their anarchy to a kind of 'must', a derangement associated with male sexual instability.

In remaining faithful to the wider potentialities of sensibility, Williams accepted both its triumphs and its tragedies. The restricted feminine form prescribed a flight from experience and temptation. Addison had attributed to women an intuitive sense which led them to shun anything potentially harmful to their virtue or reputation.[34] Williams and the Wollstonecraft of the *Vindication of the Rights of Woman* claimed for women the same rights as men to the full gamut of experience as a necessary condition of authentic growth. This uncloistered condition had tragic potential. The passions may direct the reason to plans of individual and social amelioration. If the forms of society which react upon them or the reason have not developed commensurably they may lead to disaster.

Wordsworth and Wollstonecraft both seem to respond to a passage in Williams's *Letters* in order to differentiate their positions. In seeking a representative image of the possibilities of the Revolution Wordsworth picks out the Magdalen of Lebrun. This seems to echo Williams's strong response to the portrait of Louise de La Vallière, mistress of Louis XIV, in the Carmelite dress of her later years. Both are pictures of erring womanhood brought to repentance, suggesting the reformation of manners which the Revolution was achieving. Wordsworth's image derives greater moral force from its position in *The Prelude*. The previous elevation of the feminine as mother, sister, and guardian of domestic moral values, and his horror at the shameless women of the town in Cambridge and London lends the image a Blakean capacity to reflect on society the responsibility of the harlot's curse. The picture echoes his utopian hopes that the Revolution will do away with the oldest profession and become a support for the genuine domestic feelings of woman. But his casting out of the fallen woman, splitting the race of man in twain, can be seen as a rejection of the passionate and sexual nature of woman.[35]

Williams's reaction to La Vallière is less judgmental and utopian. She appreciates a genuine if misguided passion, neither the prostitute's suppression of sensibility nor the factitious sensibility which shows what man has made of woman:

> I lamented that sensibility which led into the most fatal errors a mind that seems to have been formed for virtue, and which, even in the bosom of pleasure, bewailed its own weakness ... How can one forbear regretting, that the capricious, inconstant monarch to whom she gave her heart, should have inspired a passion of which he was so unworthy; a passion which appears to have been wholly unmixed with interest, vanity, or ambition.[36]

The monarch here has the 'feminine' characteristics of caprice and inconstancy which are associated with his position in society. Williams writes with some knowledge of her subject. La Vallière was a private, unacknowledged mistress before she was brought into the glare of Versailles (though by all accounts she made considerable interest out of her position). Williams is certainly reacting against the courtly 'mistress-system' as Kelly observes,[37] yet its tragic proportions – it was 'the only picture in Paris which has cost me any tears' – affirms the nobility of such a passion. Williams is willing to see in this immoral situation, deformed by unnatural social distinctions, the genuine passion of a mind 'formed for virtue'.

Williams acknowledges the arrest in her narrative after contemplating the picture and goes on to describe the Palais Royale as if it were wholly unconnected with the portrait. In fact the Palais Royale was noted for prostitution, something which her description suppresses but which was later emphasised by Wollstonecraft. For Williams 'nothing is heard but the voice of mirth; nothing is seen but cheerful faces: and I have no doubt that the Palais Royale is, upon the whole, one of the merriest scenes under the sun'.[38] This was the domain of the Duke of Orléans that Wollstonecraft (who must have read Williams's account) described four years later as the last place 'in which any person of delicacy, not to mention decorum, or morality, would choose to reside', a square occupied by 'the most shameless girls of the town, their hectoring protectors, gamesters, and sharpers of every description'. Over this den of iniquity the Duke ruled as a 'great sultan'.[39] Williams can appreciate the potentialities of the *quartier louche* in the unrestricted, joyous expression of the social passions, despite the dubious conditions in which they are manifested – her 'upon the whole' is a significant reservation in the context of the unqualified fervour of her first letters. It was in the experience of suffering *necessarily* incurred by following the passions that personal growth occurred, according to Wollstonecraft, whose *Vindication* held that the passions should unfold the faculties, including the reason.[40] The cost might be the guilt of a La Vallière for a woman, for a nation, the guilt of the Terror, that 'convulsion of the passions'.[41] Wollstonecraft and Wordsworth grew less inclined to acknowledge such suffering as 'upon the whole' a healthy, educative experience, especially as the conservative reaction gathered strength during the 1790s.

The conscious and rationalised sensibility which Williams championed had one paramount, inherent discipline, that of ministering to the welfare of the community. For the period during which an enlightened patriotism seemed to dominate French life this discipline was maintained, but it became increasingly obvious that a permanent transformation of French life and the French national character could not be looked for. Hazlitt, who drew on Williams's *Letters* in his *Life of Napoleon*, came to the same conclusion: the French Revolution had been wasted on the womanish French.[42] Hazlitt was writing in competition with Scott's *Life of Napoleon*, but his (debatably ironic) assertions that the love of established power always defeats a feminised, Romantic altruism of revolutionary feeling reflects Scott's association of romance with a bygone history of violent change. Ian Duncan gives an impressive account of Scott's version of the 'end of history', seeing him as a successor of Radcliffe in the development of 'Romantic ideology' in the novel.[43] Distance lends enchantment, and the great enchanters of the early nineteenth century were anxious to establish a distance from historical upheavals which had raised more energetic feelings in some of their contemporaries. The 'historical' romances of writers like Helen Maria Williams were an oppositional stimulus for Scott's project. As the record of a traveller into the half-realised, half-imagined future, Williams takes her place in the brief line of 'sentimental travellers', including Wordsworth, Wollstonecraft, and later, Owenson, who looked to France for the freer expression of the passions in a political and social organisation yet to be discovered but tantalisingly glimpsed.

Notes

1 Helen Maria Williams, *Letters Written in France* (London, 1790), 66–7. This volume, published by Cadell, is the first of two series of *Letters from France*, each of four volumes, the remainder published by Robinson. The second volume of the first series was published in 1792, the third and fourth in 1793. The first three volumes of the second set were published in 1795, the fourth in 1796. Subsequent references are to series, volume, and page number. All eight volumes are collected in Janet Todd's facsimile reprint (New York, 1975).

2 Chris Jones, *Radical Sensibility: Literature and Ideas in the 1790s* (London, 1993).

3 Gary Kelly, *Women, Writing, and Revolution, 1790–1827* (Oxford, 1993), 177–8.

4 Vivien Jones, 'Women Writing Revolution: Narratives of History and Sexuality in Wollstonecraft and Williams', in Stephen Copley and John Whale, eds, *Beyond Romanticism: New Approaches to Texts and Contexts 1780–1832* (London, 1992), 190.

5 *Ibid.*, 194.

6 Kelly, *Women, Writing, and Revolution*, 193; Anne K. Mellor, *Romanticism and Gender* (London and New York, 1993), 212–13.

7 Nicola Watson, *Revolution and the Form of the British Novel, 1790–1825* (Oxford, 1994), 33.

8 Mary A. Favret, *Romantic Correspondence: Women, Politics, and the Fiction of Letters* (Cambridge, 1993). See especially 62, 79, 94.

9 Mary A. Favret, 'Spectatrice as Spectacle: Helen Maria Williams at Home in the Revolution', *Studies in Romanticism* 32 (Summer 1993), 280, 292.

10 See Roland Mortier, *Le Coeur et la raison* (Paris, 1990), 427–40.

11 *Letters*, 1st ser. 1: 196–7; 1st ser. 1: 13–14.

12 *Gentleman's Magazine*, 65: 2 (December 1798), 1030.

13 *Analytical Review* 17 (October 1793), 127. Kelly gives a different account of the effect of this division of labour (*Women, Writing, and Revolution*, 50).

14 *Letters*, 1st ser. 2: 116.

15 *Ibid.*, 1st ser. 4: 77; 1: 66; 1: 68.

16 *Ibid.*, 1st ser. 1: 222.

17 *Ibid.*, 1st ser. 1: 46; 3: 221; 3: 223.

18 *Ibid.*, 1st ser. 2: 80.

19 *Ibid.*, 1st ser. 3: 150.

20 Wordsworth, *The Prelude*, eds Jonathan Wordsworth, M. H. Abrams and Stephen Gill (New York, 1979), 1805 version, bk 9, ll. 319–20.

21 *Letters*, 1st ser. 3: 150.

22 *Ibid.*, 1st ser. 4: 134–5.

23 *Ibid.*, 1st ser. 3: 182.

24 *Women, Writing, and Revolution,* 68–9.
25 *Letters,* 1st ser. 4: 130.
26 *Ibid.,* 1st ser. 3: 215–16.
27 *Ibid.,* 1st ser. 2: 150; 4: 35–6.
28 *Ibid.,* 1st ser. 4: 19; 1: 28; 1: 37; 1: 63.
29 *Ibid.,* 2nd ser. 4: 42; 3: 7.
30 'Women Writing Revolution', 196.
31 *Letters,* 2nd ser. 3: 10.
32 *Ibid.,* 2nd ser. 4: 156; 3: 192; 1: 3; 4: 159; 1st ser. 3: 5; 2nd ser. 3: 50; 1st ser. 2: 155.
33 'Women Writing Revolution,' 197.
34 J. Addison, *Spectator* 231 (London, 1711), 7. It is the first illustration in the *OED* of 'sensibility' used in its eighteenth-century sense of quickness and acuteness of feeling.
35 Mary Jacobus, 'Splitting the Race of Man in Twain: Prostitution, Personification and *The Prelude*', in Cynthia Chase, ed., *Romanticism* (London, 1993), 116.
36 *Letters,* 1st ser. 1: 77.
37 *Women, Writing, and Revolution,* 37.
38 *Letters,* 1st ser. 1: 77–8.
39 Mary Wollstonecraft, *The Works of Mary Wollstonecraft,* eds Marilyn Butler and Janet Todd (London, 1989), 6: 207.
40 Mary Wollstonecraft, *A Vindication of the Rights of Woman,* ed. Miriam Kramnick (London, 1975), 212.
41 *Letters,* 2nd ser. 1: 117.
42 Seamus Deane, *The French Revolution and Enlightenment in England 1789–1832* (Cambridge, Mass., 1988), 153–4. See also Chris Jones, 'Hazlitt's Termagant Wife: Gendering the French Revolution', *Prose Studies* 18:1 (1995), 59–73.
43 Ian Duncan, *Modern Romance and Transformations of the Novel* (Cambridge, 1992).

Women who transmute into tourist attractions: spectator and spectacle on the Grand Tour

Chloe Chard

Sites of enthralment

Travel writings of the late eighteenth and early nineteenth centuries register an enormous fascination with travellers who transmute into tourist attractions – who become sights for other travellers to gaze at with wonder or curiosity. Such travellers are usually women – or, alternatively, men who can in some way be defined as feminised (such as Edward Wortley Montagu, described in Venice by John Moore, carefully perfuming his beard in the Turkish manner, and so marking himself out as an instance of effeminate luxuriousness).[1] Two women in particular, who define themselves as travellers on the Grand Tour by arriving in Italy from the other side of the Alps, are accorded great attention: Emma Hamilton and Paolina Borghese. The Earl of Minto, in a letter of 1796, describes Lady Hamilton as 'the most extraordinary compound I ever beheld'; he remarks on her 'monstrous' size, and comments: 'With men her language and conversation are exaggerations of anything I ever heard anywhere; and I was wonderfully struck with these inveterate remains of her origin, though the impression was very much weakened by seeing the other ladies of Naples.' Viewing her famous 'attitudes' (Figure 2), however – in which she presents herself to a select audience in postures derived, in some cases, from classical sculpture – he declares: 'they come up to my expectations fully, which is saying everything'.[2]

Charlotte Eaton, commenting on 'the Principessa Borghese', describes her transmutation into a sight that is all the more intriguing for being shrouded from view:

> Some years ago, Canova sculptured a Statue of this Lady, as Venus, and it is esteemed by himself one of the very best of his works. No one else can have an opportunity of judging of it, for the Prince,

who certainly is not jealous of his wife's person, is so jealous of her statue, that he keeps it locked up in a room of the Borghese Palace at Rome, of which he keeps the key, and not a human being, not even Canova himself, can get access to it.[3]

James Galiffe defines Paolina's readiness to transform herself into spectacle as entertainingly scandalous: 'One of Canova's best statues is said to be that of Buonaparte's youngest sister, Princess Borghese, who sat naked for

2 Engraving of Emma Hamilton. From Frederick Rehberg, *Drawings, Faithfully Copied from Nature at Naples, and with Permission Dedicated to the Right Honourable William Hamilton* (London, 1794).

it; and who replied to an English lady who asked how she could bear to do so, that "there was a very good fire in the room!" ' [4]

The fascination with women who transmute into tourist attractions extends to fictional figures. In Germaine de Staël's novel *Corinne; ou, l'Italie* (1807), the eponymous heroine is introduced as one of the sights of Rome, encountered by Oswald, Lord Nelvil, a Scotsman on the Grand Tour; she performs in public as an *improvvisatrice*, and is first glimpsed by Lord Nelvil as she is crowned with laurel on the Capitol in recognition of her abilities. In the course of the narrative, however, it is revealed that Corinne herself has experience of travel: she has spent her adolescence in England, as the daughter of an Englishman, and is well able to exert the traveller's characteristic power of comparison, having decided to live in Italy because the confined domestic life that women are expected to lead in Britain prevents her from making any public display of her talents.[5]

Another such fictional tourist attraction, frequently cited in other writings of the period, and portrayed in a great many paintings and engravings, is Laurence Sterne's Maria. In *A Sentimental Journey through France and Italy* (1768), the traveller-narrator, Yorick, at Moulines, on his way to Italy, is drawn into an intense emotional identification with a 'disorder'd maid' who has already appeared in Sterne's *Tristram Shandy* (1757–65), and has been driven to despair by the faithlessness of her lover (and also afflicted by the death of her father and the desertion of her pet goat). He finds her 'sitting under a poplar – she was sitting with her elbow in her lap, and her head leaning on one side within her hand.' Her attitude echoes that of the *Weeping Dacia* (Figure 3), in the classical bas-relief, in Rome, and so aligns her with one of the sights of the very city that constitutes the most important point on the itinerary of the Grand Tour. One of Joseph Wright's paintings of Maria (Figure 4) emphasises the resemblance to the *Dacia* especially strongly. The allusion to this classical fragment is reinforced by Yorick's preoccupation with the fact that Maria is herself weeping: he enlarges on his 'undescribable emotions' when she allows him to wipe her tears away with his handkerchief.[6]

Just after this, Maria, like Corinne, reveals that she too is a traveller: she has completed her own version of the Grand Tour – a version yet more unorthodox than Yorick's 'sentimental' journey, but, like his, following a fairly conventional itinerary: 'She had ... she told me, stray'd as far as Rome, and walk'd round St Peter's once – and return'd back – that she found her way alone across the Apennines – had travell'd over all Lombardy without money – and through the flinty roads of Savoy without shoes.'[7]

3 The *Weeping Dacia*. Detail from the engraving 'Rome Triomphante', in Bernard de Montfaucon, *L'Antiquité expliquée et representée en figures, Supplément*, 5 vols (Paris, 1724), plate 72.

4 Joseph Wright of Derby, *Maria, from Sterne* (1777). In a private collection.

Spectator and spectacle: resisting enquiry

The power to enthral that is attributed to these figures is, I shall argue, dependent on their equivocal role within a model of the encounter with the foreign in which the traveller confronts the topography as a distanced pictorial spectacle, to be viewed in the same manner that a work of art might be. The pictorial model of travelling is expounded by Yorick at one point in *A Sentimental Journey*, when he explains to a French count that his curiosity about the female heart is equivalent to the curiosity that other travellers feel about works of art and architecture:

> It is for this reason, Monsieur le Compte, continued I, that I have not seen the Palais royal – nor the Luxembourg – nor the Façade of the Louvre – or have attempted to swell the catalogues we have of pictures, statues, and churches – I conceive every fair being as a temple, and would rather enter in, and see the original drawings and loose sketches hung up in it, than the transfiguration of Raphael itself.[8]

In adopting the viewing of works of art as a metaphor for the encounter with the foreign, travel writings of this period often register an assumption that the objects of observation which possess the greatest power to enthral the spectator are those that in some way present obstacles to scrutiny and enquiry: travellers express particular interest in those objects of commentary that resist investigation especially strongly, and can therefore be deployed as metaphors for difference, unfamiliarity, and mysterious otherness – the very qualities that, in all travel writings, are expected and demanded of foreign places. One of the categories of objects most frequently defined as resistant to enquiry is that of antiquities and ancient ruins – presented as intriguingly mysterious by virtue of their role as fragmentary relics of an ancient, remote past.[9]

The other main category of such objects is women – beings regularly invested with an intriguing inaccessability; Yorick's claim that his curiosity about the female heart distinguishes him from more orthodox travellers is belied by the eagerness with which travel writings of the late eighteenth and early nineteenth centuries launch into elaborate speculations about female desires and female behaviour.[10] Within the setting of the convent, for example, a series of stock features of the mise-en-scène – imprisoning walls, the bars of the parlatory grate, concealing costume – supply obstacles to the traveller's gaze, and so serve to prevent too easy an effort of enquiry. (The harem, in orientalist writings, obviously supplies a similar site of mystery.[11]) Patrick Brydone, in his *Tour through Sicily and Malta* (1773), notes that several nuns in a Sicilian convent that he visits are 'extremely handsome', and comments: 'but, indeed, I think they always appear so; and I am very certain, from frequent experience, that there is no artificial ornament, or studied embellishment whatever, that can produce half so strong an effect, as the modest and simple attire of a pretty young nun, *placed behind a double iron grate*' (emphasis added).[12]

Where the two categories of the antique and the feminine merge, especially intriguing sites of enthralment are produced – as, for example, in Emma Hamilton's attitudes, in which she reproduces some of the poses of classical sculptures, Paolina Borghese's transmutation into a neoclassical statue of Venus, Maria's adoption of the pose of the *Dacia*, and Corinne's appearance on the Capitol infused with a beauty which resembles that of Greek sculpted figures: she is 'grande, mais un peu forte, à la manière des statues grecques'.[13]

Travellers make spectacles of themselves

One way of explaining why women transmute into sites of enthralment more often than men, therefore, might be to invoke the power of the feminine to reinforce the effect of antiquity, in marking out a particular human attraction as a point of resistance to enquiry and appropriation. The fascinations of women such as Emma Hamilton, Paolina Borghese, Corinne and Maria can be explored further, however, with reference to their intriguing anomalousness, as figures who, unlike ruins and antiquities, fall not only into the category of spectacle but also into that of spectator: the fact that they are all travellers ineluctably raises the expectation that they might function as subjects as well as objects of observation.[14] As Mary Douglas argues, our reaction to disorder – for example, the disordering of carefully separated categories that is entailed in anomaly and ambiguity – is not simply one of condemnation: 'We recognise that it is destructive to existing patterns; also that it has potentiality. It symbolises both danger and power.'[15]

These four women are all anomalous in more than one way. The affiliations with antiquity that have just been listed entail, in each case, an affiliation with ancient sculpture – and so with the aloof immobility associated with that art: each of these figures, therefore, constitutes a 'moving statue', confusing and disturbing the boundaries between the inanimate and the animate.[16] In the case of Emma and Corinne, who both give quasi-theatrical performances, the primary boundary disturbed is that between sculpture and theatre; in the case of Paolina and Maria, the main equivocation is between sculpture and life. Emma and Corinne, moreover, are anomalous in that they devise – or play a part in devising – the spectacles in which they appear, and can therefore be classifed both as creative artists, on the one hand, and, on the other, as performers and interpreters.[17]

My main concern here, however, is to analyse the specific attraction of the first of these forms of anomaly: the anomaly of the traveller who becomes part of the spectacle that he or she sets out to view. An early – and very famous – example of a traveller accomplishing this slide into spectacle in a piece of travel writing is found in one of Lady Mary Wortley Montagu's letters from Turkey. At Sophia – then part of the Ottoman Empire, and therefore a place where women could be assumed to be veiled and heavily secluded – she visits the women's baths, where 'the ladies' and 'their slaves' are 'in plain English, stark naked, without any beauty or defect concealed'. By conjuring up a male artist who would be prevented from viewing such a roomful of naked women, Montagu not only positions herself as an authoritative, pictorial spectator but claims an additional authority by virtue of her gender – the authority conferred by a privileged opportunity for behind-the-scenes observation: 'To tell you the truth, I had wickedness enough to wish secretly that Mr. Jervas could have been there invisible. I fancy it would have very much improved his art, to see so many fine women naked.'[18]

The traveller-narrator herself, however, slides, temporarily, from the position of spectator to that of spectacle. Just before an extended account of the naked beauty of the women, Mary Wortley Montagu expresses her conviction that these women must be looking at her with a curiosity that, like hers, is sharpened by a strong sense of cultural difference: 'I was in my travelling habit, which is a riding dress, and certainly appeared very extraordinary to them.'[19] As spectators, these women turn out to demand more of their spectacle than Montagu has anticipated:

> The lady that seemed the most considerable among them entreated me to sit by her, and would fain have undressed me for the bath. I excused myself with some difficulty. They being, however, all so earnest in persuading me, I was at last forced to open my shirt, and show them my stays; which satisfied them very well; for, I saw, they believed I was locked up in that machine, and that it was not in my own power to open it; which contrivance they attributed to my husband.[20]

Naked (and clothed) vulnerability

In allowing herself to transmute into spectacle in this narrative, Mary Wortley Montagu might seem to be taking a major rhetorical risk – to be laying herself open to suspicions of vulnerability or inadequacy. The vulnerability of the traveller who relinquishes the role of detached spectator is charted by Yorick in his 'Preface' to *A Sentimental Journey*, in an elaborate epic simile, which invokes the drunken Noah's self-display:

> The man who first transplanted the grape of Burgundy to the Cape of Good Hope (observe he was a Dutch man) never dreamt of drinking the same wine at the Cape, that the same grape produced upon the French mountains – he was too phlegmatic for that – but undoubtedly he expected to drink some sort of vinous liquor; but whether good, bad, or indifferent he knew enough of this world to know, that it did not depend upon his choice, but that what is generally called *chance* was to decide his success: however, he hoped for the best; and in these hopes, by an intemperate confidence in the fortitude of his head, and the depth of his discretion, *Mynheer* might possibly overset both in his new vineyard; and by discovering his nakedness, become a laughing-stock to his people.
>
> Even so it fares with the poor Traveller, sailing and posting through the politer kingdoms of the globe in pursuit of knowledge and improvements.[21]

Transformation into the object rather than the subject of observation is repeatedly cited as a mark of culpable inadequacy in complaints about dissipated young English travellers who make spectacles of themselves on the Grand Tour – on the model of 'the young Æneas' in the fourth Book of Pope's *Dunciad* (1743), whose transformation is introduced through an effect of sudden bathos: 'Intrepid then, o'er seas and lands he flew: / Europe he saw, and Europe saw him too.'[22]

The role of the inadequate traveller who forgoes the advantages of the spectator is often defined with reference to concepts of gender. The impulse to make a spectacle of oneself is identified as a manifestation of an attraction towards the effeminate luxury of the warm south, as opposed to the manly liberty of the cold north. Clermont Lynmere, in Fanny Burney's *Camilla* (1796), a traveller returned to England, who personifies 'effeminacy in its lowest degradation', has gained an 'acquired luxuriance' from his Grand Tour. Men regard him as 'an unmanly fop', while women display a yet sharper awareness of his predilection for sliding into spectacle: they consider him 'too conceited to admire any thing but himself'.[23]

Anna Jameson's *Diary of an Ennuyée* (1826) describes an acquaintance of the traveller-narrator – 'a young Englishman' named Frattino – who has developed this same 'acquired luxuriance': 'having been abroad since he was twelve years old, and early plunged into active and dissipated life, he is an accomplished man of fashion, and of the world, with as many airs and caprices as a spoiled child'. Frattino's lack of English manliness is further emphasised first by noting his resemblance to the *Belvedere Antinous*, the classical sculpture regularly cited as an instance of smooth-limbed effeminacy, and, secondly, by explicitly defining him as a traveller who has crossed over from the side of the spectator to the side of the spectacle: 'He is by far the most beautiful creature of his sex, I ever saw; so like the *Antinous*, that at Rome he went by that name. The exquisite regularity of his features, the graceful air of his head, his *antique* curls, the faultless proportions of his elegant figure, make him a *thing* to be gazed on, as one looks at a statue.'[24]

Mary Wollstonecraft, in a reference to male and female attitudes to travel, firmly identifies a consciousness of being an object of observation with an abnegation of manly responsibilities:

> A man, when he undertakes a journey, has, in general, the end in view; a woman thinks more of the incidental occurrences, the strange things that may possibly occur on the road; the impression that she may make on her fellow-travellers; and, above all, she is anxiously intent on the care of the finery that she carries with her, which is more than ever a part of herself, when going to figure on a new scene; when, to use an apt French turn of expression, she is going to produce a sensation. Can dignity of mind exist with such trivial cares?[25]

Retaining authority

Far from disparaging Mary Wortley Montagu's role in the scene in the Turkish baths, however, as all these commentaries might lead us to expect, other travel writings eagerly reproduce the plot of crossing over to the side of the spectacle. Mungo Park, in his *Travels in the Interior Districts of Africa* (1799), describes his 'surprise' when, as a prisoner in a remote village, he is visited in his hut by a party of women who wish 'to ascertain, by actual inspection, whether the rite of circumcision extended to the Nazarenes (Christians,) as well as to the followers of Mahomet'. ('I thought it best to treat the matter jocularly', he comments.[26]) In 'Mrs. Belzoni's trifling account of the women of Egypt, Nubia, and Syria', appended to the first edition of Giovanni Battista Belzoni's *Narrative of the Operations and Recent Discoveries within the Pyramids, Temples, Tombs, and Excavations, in Egypt and Nubia* (1820), the narrator offers 'behind the scenes' accounts of foreign women who, returning her curiosity, examine and unfasten her clothing, and inspect her corsets with interest.[27]

Wollstonecraft herself, in her *Letters Written During a Short Residence in Sweden, Norway and Denmark* (1796), constructs a less dramatic version of this same plot – less dramatic because, unlike the travellers just cited, and unlike Noah in Sterne's simile, she is never at risk of being revealed in a state of vulnerable nakedness:

> My clothes, in their turn, attracted the attention of the females, and I could not help thinking of the foolish vanity which makes many women so proud of the observations of strangers as to take wonder very gratuitously for admiration. This error they are very apt to fall into; when arrived in a foreign country, the populace stare at them as they pass; yet the make of a cap, or the singularity of a gown, is often the cause of the flattering attention, which afterwards supports a fantastic superstructure of self-conceit.[28]

The traveller, in this account, spells out more explicitly the main rhetorical strategies by which Montagu, Park, and Mrs Belzoni retain their authority. First, she links her awareness of the spectacle staring back to a recognition of cultural difference, and so affirms her own power to claim from the foreign the primary quality expected and demanded of it: a divergence from tame familiarity. In other words, she makes a gesture of authoritative appropriation that compensates for the threat to her authority produced as she transmutes into spectacle.[29] Second, Wollstonecraft carefully differentiates the adequate traveller from the inadequate one by emphasising that she manages to remain a spectator at the same time as she transmutes into spectacle; while the inadequate traveller congratulates herself on being the object of observation, the adequate traveller continues to scrutinise foreigners as they scrutinise her. Mary Wortley Montagu, after her first declaration of an awareness that the women in the baths are observing her, swiftly introduces an analogy with painting, and so re-establishes herself as a detached, pictorial spectator: 'There were', she says, describing the naked women, 'many amongst them as exactly proportioned as ever any goddess was drawn by the pencil of a Guido or Titian.'[30] Mungo Park, following this same strategy, outwits his female visitors by pointedly reclaiming his role as subject of vision: informing them 'that it was not customary in my country to give ocular demonstration in such cases, before so many beautiful women', he selects 'the youngest and handsomest' of the group as the sole observer whom he will allow to 'satisfy her curiosity'. Park notes that 'the ladies enjoyed the jest; and went away laughing heartily'.[31]

The traveller, in all these commentaries, registers a desire to enjoy the pleasures and advantages of both the two positions mapped out by pictorial viewing. The transmutation into spectacle is classified as an experience that is enviable and at the same time dangerous: the perils located within it must, travellers suggest, be kept at bay by ensuring that the position of spectator is always maintained. Figures such as Emma Hamilton and Paolina Borghese, Maria and Corinne, then, can be seen as supplying another way of exploring, vicariously, the gratification and danger of becoming an object as well as a subject of vision, while maintaining an authoritative detachment: travellers identify with them, in their role as spectators who also manage to assume the role of spectacle, but are able to halt or disavow the process of identification once it becomes too alarming.

Absorption

Commentaries on such figures, in fact, constitute variants on a plot of enthralment that is deployed more generally in travel writing of the late eighteenth and early nineteenth centuries as a means of allowing the traveller-spectator to occupy the positions of spectator and spectacle simultaneously. This plot can be seen as a version of the narrative that Michael Fried traces in eighteenth-century art criticism, in his analysis of the concept of absorptive viewing. Two sorts of painting, Fried argues, were defined, in turn, as possessing a praiseworthy ability to draw in the beholder – to seem to remove the beholder from a position in front of the work of art: first, 'the representation of figures absorbed in quintessentially absorptive states and activities' (such as reverie, or reading) and, second, 'the representation of figures absorbed in action or passion (or both)'.[32] The assumption that the traveller confronts the foreign as a pictorial spectacle allows travel writing to transfer the concept of absorptive viewing very easily from works of art to other domains of objects; human figures within the topography (and figures conjured up by the imagination at particular spots) are frequently presented as enthralling and absorbing the spectator when they become caught up in their own thoughts, or in the drama of their own lives.

Within narratives of absorptive viewing, travellers from northern Europe are at pains to keep at bay any suspicion that in identifying with the spectacle before them they are, like Fanny Burney's Clermont Lynmere and Anna Jameson's Frattino, aligning themselves with the effeminacy of the warm south. Hester Piozzi offers a long account of a female penitent 'with a long white dress, and veiled', in a church in Naples, and declares that her heart is 'quite penetrated' by this woman's behaviour. Piozzi none the less concludes by hastily dissociating herself from the penitent's immoderate display of passion – one of the qualities regularly defined as an instance of southern effeminacy: 'Let not this story, however, mislead any one to think that more general decorum or true devotion can be found in churches of the Romish persuasion than in ours – quite the reverse. This burst of penitential piety was in itself an indecorous thing.'[33]

Many narratives of enthralment achieve the disavowal of such excess more obliquely: in emphasising the traveller's heightened sensibilities, as manifested in his or her capacity to be drawn into the spectacle, they implicitly invoke an established opposition between the category of passion and a contrasting category of 'sentiment' (an opposition that is often explicitly mapped out in the Gothic novel, for example).[34] Paradoxically, then, the traveller repudiates effeminate immoderation by proclaiming an emotional responsiveness that is also marked as a feminised quality, but is nevertheless defined as compatible with manly restraint.

At this point, it is possible to suggest a reason why, within writings of this period, women and feminised men are singled out as sites of enthral-ment much more often than men who are defined as unequivocally masculine. In encountering (or fantasising about) female or feminised figures, the traveller can use these figures to negotiate the boundaries between culpable effeminacy and praiseworthy femininity, and so – in a range of different ways – to establish his or her own position as a person who has gained from the Grand Tour the power of comparison that makes it possible to understand the distinction between the two categories, and to choose the authority of restraint over the allurements of excess.

Northern European female painters living in Italy – such as Angelica Kauffman and Elisabeth Vigée-Lebrun – offer instances of figures whom the traveller can safely praise without seeming to express too avid an approval for effeminate excess or self-display; while such women are assigned a role as sights on the itinerary of the Grand Tour, they are readily reclassified as spectators by reference to their profession.[35]

Corinne is not so easily removed from the category of travellers over-inclined to make spectacles of themselves, and align themselves with foreign excesses. She herself expresses a fear that she has, in a fateful moment in her adolescence, carried her love of displaying her abilities too far; in trying too hard to excite the admiration of Lord Nelvil's father, she has lost the power to enthral: 'Je désirai de lui plaire, je le désirai peut-être trop, et je fis, pour y réussir, infiniment plus de frais qu'il n'en falloit: je lui montrai tous mes talents; je chantai, je dansai, j'improvisai pour lui; et mon esprit, long-temps contenu, fut peut-être trop vif en brisant ses chaînes.'[36]

Emma Hamilton and Paolina Borghese are often classified as yet more alarmingly unrestrained. The Earl of Minto, in the description of Emma already quoted, explicitly brackets her with 'the other ladies of Naples' as an instance of excess, and there are many similar accounts of the Princess

Borghese's excesses.[37] References to Emma's increasing size classify her as dramatically immoderate.[38] To make matters worse, these two women not only slide into spectacle but actually present themselves to the world – in Canova's sculpture and in the 'attitudes' that Emma assumes – in a state of nakedness or semi-nakedness: in other words, the very state that supplies Sterne with a metaphor for vulnerable travel, and that Montagu, Mungo Park, and Mrs Belzoni hold out before the reader as a looming threat, and then just manage to avoid. As vehicles for exploring this slide into spectacle in displaced form, the two of them are therefore invested with a particular danger – one that regularly prompts the traveller to disavow any process of identification, through expressions of censure and even of horror. (Galiffe describes Paolina Borghese as 'this abandoned woman; whose reputation is worse than that of almost any other avowed lady of pleasure.')[39]

At the same time, Emma and Paolina are both, by virtue of their ability to transform themselves into works of art (in the 'attitudes' and the Canova statue), marked out as figures who personify the elevated delights of the classical ideal – an ideal explicitly associated with restraint, and set in opposition to excess.[40] The equivocations between horror and pleasure with which they are greeted serves to classify them all the more firmly as fascinating anomalies – and to invest them with all the greater powers of enthralment. Having described Paolina as 'past all excuse', and deplored the manner in which she forces Lady Jersey to kiss her foot in public, the seventeen-year-old Harriet Charlotte Beaujolais Campbell, in Florence in 1817, declares:

> But nevertheless I should be curious to visit a woman who has been and still is so universally celebrated. Publickly it would not be right as at present it would be against the propriety necessary for an English person, but could I go to her privately I should not waver for a moment. Mr Bury has visited her and will do so again … for a man any thing is allowable. He may visit any woman particularly of such a rank and visit her as a curiosity. He is still himself and returns from her the same and his curiosity is satisfied. Propriety is a sad barrier and I am not the first who has sighed to pass it.[41]

The fascination with travellers who transmute themselves into tourist attractions does not come to an end with such spectacular figures. Dean MacCannell, in *The Tourist*, which was first published in 1976, pursues his analysis of the semiotics of tourism with repeated reference to the hippies of San Francisco – figures who were by definition travellers, in flight from somewhere more conventional and constraining, who, leading a life of 'effeminate' indolence, swiftly transmuted themselves into one of the city's tourist attractions, and who, like Emma Hamilton and Paolina Borghese, imbued those who came to stare at them (in mingled pleasure and horror) with a sense that the barriers of propriety were, in various ways, being transgressed.[42]

Notes

1 John Moore, *View of Society and Manners in Italy*, 2nd edn, 2 vols (London, 1781), 1: 31–2. The concerns of this essay are explored further in my book *Pleasure and Guilt on the Grand Tour* (Manchester, 1999). I should like to thank Rosemary Bechler, Helen Langdon, Marcia Pointon and Wendy Wassyng Roworth for comments, criticisms, and discussion of a variety of aspects of this topic. Thanks are also due to Neil Bingham, Tim Knox and Todd Longstaffe-Gowan for their advice over picture research, and to Judy Mead and Vincent Woropay for their help with photography. I am required to acknowledge a research grant from Wimbledon School of Art.

2 Earl of Minto, *Life and Letters of Sir Gilbert Elliott, First Earl of Minto, from 1751 to 1806*, ed. Countess of Minto, 3 vols (London, 1874), 2: 364, 364–5, 365. For a useful account of the 'attitudes', see Kirsten Gram Holmström, *Monodrama, Attitudes, Tableaux Vivants: Studies on Some Trends of Theatrical Attitudes, 1770–1815*, trans. from the Swedish by Richard Cox (Stockholm and Uppsala, 1967), 110–40.

3 Charlotte Eaton, *Rome in the Nineteenth* Century, 3 vols (London, 1820), 3: 47.

4 James Galiffe, *Italy and its Inhabitants: An Account of a Tour in that Country*, 2 vols (London, 1820), 1: 254–5.

5 [Anne Louise Germaine de Staël-Holstein], *Corinne; ou, l'Italie*, ed. Claudine Herrmann, 2 vols (Paris, 1979), 1: 60. In describing Corinne's appearance on the Capitol, the narrator explicitly emphasises her role as a site of enthralment: 'tous ses mouvemens avoient un charme qui excitoit l'intérêt et la curiosité, l'étonnement et l'affection' (1: 46). For the heroine's account of the tedium of English domestic life, see 2: 90–1. Geneviève Gennari argues, with reference to Corinne's career as a performance artist, that 'l'élément le plus important du personnage imaginé par Mme de Staël est certainement lady Hamilton, modèle parfait de la femme du Nord modelée par la facilité du Sud, pourvue de toutes les grâces et de tous les dons' (*Le Premier Voyage de Madame de Staël en Italie, et la genèse de Corinne* (Paris, 1947), 146).

6 Laurence Sterne, *'A Sentimental Journey' with 'The Journal to Eliza' and 'A Political Romance'*, ed. Ian Jack (Oxford, 1984), 113, 114, 114; see *The Life and Opinions of Tristram Shandy, Gentleman*, ed. Graham Petrie (Harmondsworth, 1967), 600–2 (vol. II, chap. 24). I am grateful to Malcolm Baker for pointing out the resemblance between Maria's attitude, both in Sterne's description and in Joseph Wright's paintings of the episode, and the posture of the female figure in the antique bas-relief.

For literary references to Maria, see, for example, Hester Lynch Piozzi, *The Piozzi Letters: Correspondence of Hester Lynch Piozzi, 1784–1821 (formerly Mrs. Thrale)*, eds Edward A. Bloom and Lillian D. Bloom, 5 vols (Newark, 1989–99), 1: 391; Mary Wollstonecraft, *Letters Written During a Short Residence in Sweden, Norway and Denmark* (1796), with William Godwin, *Memoirs of the Author of 'The Rights of Woman'*, ed. Richard Holmes (London, 1987), 111; and John MacCulloch, *On Malaria: An Essay on the Production and Propagation of this Poison, and on the Nature and Localities of the Places by which it is Produced; with an Examination of the Diseases Caused by it, and of the Means of Preventing or Diminishing them, both at Home and in the Naval and Military Service* (London, 1827), 410. Patricia Jaffé, in her exhibition catalogue *Lady Hamilton in Relation to the Art of her Time* (London, 1972), lists as one of the exhibits a piece of embroidery by Emma Hamilton, in which she adapts an illustration to Sterne's *Sentimental Journey*, transmuting Nelson into Yorick and Maria into herself (76)! Other representations of Maria are catalogued by Catherine M. Gordon, in *British Paintings of Subjects from the British Novel 1740–1870* (New York and London, 1988), 263–74 (see also 73–7).

7 *A Sentimental Journey*, 115.

8 *Ibid.*, 84.

9 Yorick, at Calais, describing his curiosity about the appearance and character of a woman whose face he has not yet seen, emphasises, through his use of the metaphor of piecing together an antique statue, the strength of the attraction that antiquities exert, as objects that invite an effort of investigation precisely by their resistance to such an effort: 'long before we had got to the door of the Remise, *Fancy* had finished the whole head, and pleased herself as much with its fitting her goddess, as if she had dived into the TIBER for it' (*Sentimental Journey*, 17).

10 As literary historians and cultural historians have often noted, women are adopted as metaphors for the geographical otherness – and foreign places as metaphors for femininity – in a wide variety of contexts; one of the most famous examples of this metaphorical equivalence is Freud's designation of female sexuality as 'the dark continent' ('The Question of Lay-analysis', *Complete Psychological Works of Sigmund Freud*, trans. under the general editorship of James Strachey, 24 vols (London, 1953–74), 20: 179–258; 212).

11 For an analysis of this aspect of the harem, see Alain Grosrichard, *Structure du sérail: La fiction du despotisme asiatique dans l'Occident classique* (Paris, 1979), 153–8.

12 Patrick Brydone, *Tour through Sicily and Malta*, 2nd edn, 2 vols (London, 1774), 1: 62.

13 *Corinne*, 1: 46; the evocation of a classical figure is intensified, at this point, by the fact that Corinne is dressed to resemble Domenichino's *Sibyl* (1: 45; see also 2: 278).

14 Emma Hamilton, for example, is described by Elisabeth Vigée-Lebrun as a spectator at a religious festival in Naples (*Souvenirs de Madame Vigée Le Brun* (1835–7), 2 vols (Paris, 1891), 1: 220). Corinne, in de Staël's novel, guides Lord

Nelvil around the sights of Rome. Nancy K. Miller's chapter 'Performances of the Gaze: Staël's *Corinne, or Italy*' considers a number of questions related to the concepts of spectator and spectacle deployed in Germaine de Staël's novel (*Subject to Change: Reading Feminist Writing* (New York, 1988), 162–203).

15 Mary Douglas, *Purity and Danger: An Analysis of the Concepts of Pollution and Taboo* (London, 1966), 94.

16 For an extended exploration of the fantasy of a statue that moves or speaks, see Kenneth Gross, *The Dream of the Moving Statue* (Ithaca and London, 1992).

17 As Jerome Christensen points out, Emma Hamilton is also a figure who 'Romantically equivocates the boundaries between literature and life' (*Lord Byron's Strength: Romantic Writing and Commercial Society* (London and Baltimore, 1993), 374n.). The two fictional women are presented as equivocal in other ways as well. As Eve Kosofsky Sedgwick has noted, Yorick, in his musings on Maria, confuses the roles of mistress and daughter (*Between Men: English Literature and Male Homosocial Desire* (New York, 1985), 81). In *Corinne*, Oswald is struck by the fact that the mystery surrounding the heroine is paradoxically combined with fame, and, when Corinne initially appears on the Capitol, notes that she evokes the idea not only of a priestess of Apollo but also of 'une femme parfaitement simple dans les rapports habituels de la vie' (1: 44, 46).

18 *The Works of the Right Honourable Lady Mary Wortley Montagu*, 6th edn, 2 vols (London, 1811), 1: 174, 175; letter dated 'April 1 O. S. 1717', first published (in a collection of Montagu's letters) in 1763. Other female traveller-narrators also, at times, claim additional authority by reference to their privileged opportunities to observe foreign women; see, for example, Hester Piozzi, *Observations and Reflections Made in the Course of a Journey through France, Italy, and Germany*, 2 vols (London, 1789), 1: 100–1.

19 *Ibid.*, 1: 174.

20 *Ibid.*, 1: 175–6.

21 *Sentimental Journey*, 11–12. Piozzi, too, presents the slide into spectacle as a manifestation of vulnerability: observing the signs of everyday life interrupted by sudden death in Herculaneum and Pompeii, she remarks: 'How dreadful are the thoughts which such a sight suggests! how *very* horrible the certainty, that such a scene may be all acted over again to-morrow; and that we, who to-day are spectators, may become spectacles to travellers of a succeeding century' (*Observations and Reflections*, 2: 35). David Marshall considers at a number of points the threat that various eighteenth-century writers associate with becoming a spectacle for others to gaze upon (*The Figure of Theater: Shaftesbury, Defoe, Adam Smith and George Eliot* (Guildford and New York, 1986); see, for example, 191).

22 *The Dunciad*, ed. James Sutherland, *The Poems of Alexander Pope*, vol. 5 (London and New Haven, 1963), 373, ll. 293–4.

23   Fanny Burney, *Camilla; or, A Picture of Youth*, eds Edward A. Bloom and Lillian D. Bloom (Oxford, 1983), 583, 569, 569.

24   Anna Jameson, *Diary of an Ennuyée* (London, 1826), 240, 240–1. The implications of homosexuality established by referring to the sculpture identified as Antinous, the 'favourite' of the Emperor Hadrian, are absorbed into a more general model of 'effeminate' sensuality by an allusion to Frattino's womanising (241).

25   Mary Wollstonecraft, *A Vindication of the Rights of Woman* (1792), ed. Miriam Brody (London, 1985), 151.

26   Mungo Park, *Travels in the Interior Districts of Africa* (London, 1799), 132.

27   Giovanni Battista Belzoni, *Narrative of the Operations and Recent Discoveries within the Pyramids, Temples, Tombs, and Excavations, in Egypt and Nubia* (London, 1820), 446.

28   *A Short Residence*, 97.

29   Travel writings constantly emphasise the need for the traveller to register a sufficient sense of otherness, and reject as inadequate those travellers who fail to do so: Byron comments derisively on an Englishwoman who, 'at Chamouni – in the very eyes of Mont Blanc', exclaims '"did you ever see any thing more *rural*"' – as if it was Highgate or Hampstead – or Brompton – or Hayes' (*Byron's Letters and Journals*, ed. Leslie A. Marchand, 12 vols (London, 1973–82), 5: 97).
     Piozzi, in *Observations and Reflections* repeatedly adopts the device of gazing at the spectacle as it gazes back (see, for example, 1: 105, 355–6, and 2: 196).

30   *Works*, 1: 174–5.

31   *Travels*, 132. For a very different analysis of 'reciprocal vision', see Mary Louise Pratt, *Imperial Eyes: Travel Writing and Transculturation* (London and New York, 1992), 81–5.

32   *Absorption and Theatricality: Painting and Beholder in the Age of Diderot* (Berkeley, 1980), 107.

33   *Observations and Reflections*, 2: 28, 28, 29.

34   Ann Radcliffe's *Mysteries of Udolpho* (1794) establishes a crisp opposition between the 'fierce and terrible passions' that 'so often agitated the inhabitants' of the Castle of Udolpho and, on the other hand, the heroine's own 'silent anguish, weeping, yet enduring' (*The Mysteries of Udolpho*, ed. Bonamy Dobrée (Oxford, 1980), 329).

35   For descriptions of Kauffman as one of the sights of Italy, see Piozzi, *Observations and Reflections*, 1: 178 and 2: 140–1, and *Souvenirs de Madame Vigée Le Brun*, 1: 149–50 and 156. Vigée-Lebrun is herself described in Rome, in 1790, by Charlotte Louise Éléonore Adélaïde le Borgne, comtesse de Boigne (*Mémoires de la comtesse de Boigne*, ed. Charles Nicoullaud, 4 vols (Paris, 1907), 1: 109–10).

36   *Corinne*, 2: 96. Corinne's Italian admirer, the Prince Castel-Forte, none the less emphasises that she is not merely a performer, for others to gaze at, but a creative artist, 'capable de s'observer elle-même' (1: 60).

37   Anna Jameson comments cheerfully on 'the Princess Pauline': 'she is rather

more famous for her gallantries, than for her bon-goût in the choice of her favourites' (*Diary of an Ennuyée*, 273).

38 Apart from the Earl of Minto's comment, quoted above, see, for example, Vigée-Lebrun, *Souvenirs*, 1: 198.

39 *Italy and its Inhabitants*, 1: 254.

40 The affiliation of the nakedness of classical sculpture with restraint, and the construction of oppositions between the classical ideal and the immoderation regularly identified as characteristic of contemporary Italy, are discussed in my article 'Nakedness and Tourism: Classical Sculpture and the Imaginative Geography of the Grand Tour', *Oxford Art Journal* 18: 1 (1995), 14–28.

41 Harriet Charlotte Beaujolais Campbell, *A Journey to Florence in 1817*, ed. G. R. de Beer (London, 1951), 125–6.

42 Dean MacCannell, *The Tourist: A New Theory of the Leisure Class* (New York, 1976); see especially: 'hippies are tourists and, at home in the Haight Ashbury, they are also sights that tourists come to see, or at least they used to be' (41).

Part III

Pathologies of travel

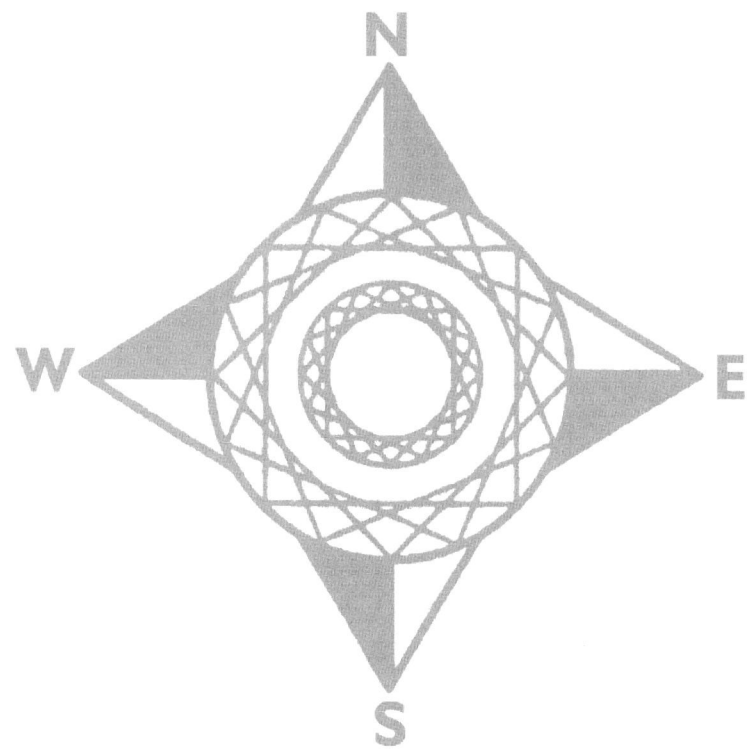

Climates of gender

Clare Brant

In 1775 Sir Nathaniel Wraxall published *Cursory Remarks*, an account of his travels the previous year.[1] Enquiring into the manners, customs, institutions and antiquities of Scandinavia and Russia, what makes Wraxall's letters unusual is the attention given to women. As one commentator put it, they provided 'a minute detail of the regular approaches to the lips of the northern damsels; no doubt, for the instruction of those of his countrymen who may visit Scandinavia'.[2] In Wraxall's encounters, romantic hopes in the sense of erotic yearnings are interestingly related to Romantic desires in the sense of aesthetic fantasies. This brings together the dual senses of romanticism as sexual sublimation and as poeticised subjectivity – a young man's fancy turns to fancy. I want to explore the cultural terrain through which Wraxall travels by way of his and several other texts, before returning for a closer look at the significance of women and what they might represent besides themselves.

Eighteenth-century travel writers used encounters with foreign subjects, both male and female, to construct national identities through sexual identities, and vice versa.[3] In the 1770s, their romanticisation of foreign women made possible romantic constructions of masculine subjectivity. I want to look at one discursive pairing – men and women – and suggest that, when put alongside others – north and south, hot and cold, life and death, words and music, speech and silence, the foreign and the familiar – apparently globally secure differences turn out to be a conceptually insecure network. Like Dr Johnson's net, there are as many holes as threads in this reticulation.

To start with north and south. These were not entirely stable categories. For instance, geographical division in Scotland – north of England but south of other northern countries – was mapped on to political affiliations. The local significance of cultural geography was recognised by John Lettice, who reported from the Isle of Bute that 'when the natives are asked, whether they are high, or lowlanders, they answer: "we are neither; but Bute-men"'.[4] This relativity of north and south affected national and personal conceptions of identity. With respect to England, Italy is south and Sweden is north. But when in Sweden, England becomes south, or, when in Italy, north. This made it easier for men from London, or the south of England, to cast themselves as sensual connoisseurs when travelling north. This is nicely illustrated by James Boswell in his *Journal of a Tour to the Hebrides*, recording a remark of Johnson's about the hygienic properties of linen: 'I have often thought, that, if I kept a seraglio, the ladies should all wear linen gowns, – or cotton'. Boswell commented with astonishment,

> To hear the grave Dr. Samuel Johnson, 'that majestick teacher of moral and religious wisdom', while sitting solemn in an arm-chair in the Isle of Sky, talk, ex cathedra, of his keeping a seraglio, and acknowledge that the supposition had often been in his thoughts, struck me so forcibly with ludicrous contrast, that I could not but laugh immoderately.[5]

The 'ludicrous contrast' is between steamy orientalist indulgence and its articulation in a freezing northern setting. Johnson's ferocious reaction, heaping ridicule upon a contrite Boswell, suggests a consciousness of the significance of erotic fantasies kept undisclosed in London. Going north prompted a number of men to reconsider sexual customs: both Wraxall and Edward Topham, who lived in Edinburgh for six months in the 1770s, considered that, unlike themselves, northern men were not sufficiently appreciative of the charms of their countrywomen. Part of the north's reputation for being primitive derived from what southerners saw as its uncivilised attitudes to women.

As over-runners of the Roman Empire, the Goths and other northern tribes offered an ambiguous historical inheritance; they had destroyed classical culture, but they also personified barbarous energy. The elasticity of definitions of the north allowed southerners to select what cultural aspects they claimed kinship with. Scandinavia could unequivocally be defined as northern, though, since peoples living close to the Arctic circle were racially distinct from those further south, degrees of northernness proved useful. William Thomson observed that the Finns were unlike the Russians, Swedes, and Danes in language, religion, and physical build, though their manners were alike.[6] Germany and the United Provinces could count as the south of the northern countries, or the north of Europe as a whole; Poland usually counted as north. Russia was uneasily included in Europe: Muscovy was culturally European, though its affiliated territories also connected it to Asia, and dynastic links related Russians to hellenism and south-eastern Europe.

Thomson's fascination with ethnic diversity may be an academic litany of difference, which solves the armchair travel writer's difficulty in describing things read about but not seen.[7] But he foregrounds an important issue for travellers – whether they submerged national identity by adopting local dress or customs, or whether they preserved native habits – and if so, whether they become not themselves but, ironically, more conspicuously foreign. Thomson starts his book with the sad story of a Russian visitor to London who, thinking the English weather chilly, wore his fur coat on the street, and met with abuse from the locals. In particular, one woman, after spitting on him 'and giving him a box on the ear, told him that "a French son of a bitch like him deserved no better"'.[8] Ironically she mistakes his fur coat as a sign not of northernness but of foreignness nearer home. Thomson claims that Petersburg is an unusual city in that foreigners do not have to go native:

> Besides the variety of nations which compose the Russian empire, in my daily walk through the city I meet with English, Danes, French, Swedes, Italians, Spaniards, Portuguese, Venetians, Poles, Germans, Persians, and Turks: the last, prisoners from Oczakow. This assembly is a natural masquerade, and no city upon earth presents any amusement of this kind in such perfection as Petersburg.[9]

Again, it is hard to tell if Thomson's use of a masquerade trope can be attributed to bookishness; the absence of travel experience might account for the idea of national identity as a kind of theatrical costume. Seasoned travellers such as Eyles Irwin, who wore Arab dress for coolness, convenience, and to prevent curiosity, did claim that Englishmen (and only Englishmen) could ignore local dress codes with impunity,[10] but he also acknowledged that, even with local clothes, beards, and tans, he and his companions still looked European:

> there is a peculiar characteristic in the individuals of every nation, that will distinguish them through the disguise of dress and language. This is exemplified daily amid the neighboring states of Europe, whose habits and manners are nearly the same, and cannot so much excite wonder in our case, where the whole temperature of our minds and bodies was so contrary to that of the people, whom we endeavored to personate.[11]

The concept of mental temperature turns up again in his comment, after repeatedly paying out money with little to show for it, 'The Arabs give us credit for the *sang-froid* which is the principal ingredient in the composition of their own minds.'[12] Other writers from abroad also destabilised simple notions of difference. Jemima Kindersley reported from Allahabad that many local men did not like to be thought of as black, since they defined themselves as pale and Europeans as coloured; the English, being sunburnt, they thought of as red men.[13]

Similar dissolutions fissure the discourses of hot and cold which often partner north and south. Skin colour, after all, does not match latitude to pallor: the Ancient Mariner's brown weather-beaten look is as likely an effect from being in the land of ice and snow as on the burning ocean. The effects of hot and cold were much debated in connection with medical treatments where bathing or ingestion of mineral waters were prescribed; hot, cold, and tepid temperatures each had their champions. Commercial interests in the developments of spas and colonies coincided with the concerns of scientific enquiry to establish the effects of hot and cold on human bodies in general, and European bodies in particular. The eighteenth century saw extensive attention paid to thermal measurement, and how human precision and technological refinement might improve the exactitude of temperature readings using a variety of different scales. Again, local perspectives broke up neat absolutes and opposites. India had what even Europeans living there described as a cold season; polar countries could have sweltering summers. Lands outside of temperate zones could have climates of both extremes: 'The last winter was uncommonly severe, and it is succeeded by a summer extremely hot. The sun-beams are most insufferable ... A captain of a British East India ship, who is just now travelling here, says, "That he never felt himself more incommoded with heat at Bengal, than he does now at Petersburg".'[14] And altitude could make cold contingent on heat. Patrick Brydone, who climbed Mount Etna with a number of experiments concerning measurement of height, temperature, and electrical activity, exclaimed ecstatically on the view: 'All Nature lies expanded below your feet, in her gayest and most luxuriant dress, and you still behold united under one point of view, all the seasons of the year, and all the climates of the earth, with the whole variety of their productions.'[15]

Two sources of heat in cold climates intrigued travel writers: the natural heat of hot springs, and the artifical heat of indoor stoves. Contradiction of natural elements, or hot springs in cold countries, seemed unnatural, though Uno von Troil, exploring the volcanic regions of Iceland, cheerfully boiled his dinner in a hot spring. But local use of the springs was cultural: von Troil reports that, because there were few flowers for lovers to pick, enamoured swains would select and scrub a spring for their intended bride, who favoured them by sitting in it.[16] Other uses of water were seen to express cultural difference which was read back on to the body – particularly the male body – as physical. Distinctions here between the body as site of health – in an important sense ungendered – and source of sexuality –

masculine in terms of hardiness, feminine in terms of self-indulgence – start to collapse.

Uneasy and incomplete distinctions between health and pleasure were tangled up in gender and class considerations – and vice versa. William Thomson and William Hazlitt show that discursive contradictions about national and sexual identities contribute to the ways in which women are represented in travel writing, and indeed to how they are *not* represented. By 1826, when Hazlitt wrote 'Hot and Cold', the discursive gaps had hardened, though Hazlitt seems to have been aware of potential misunderstandings: 'I do not know whether I make myself intelligible.' [17] His essay is as much about categories of clean and dirty as hot and cold, and projects them stereotypically on to north and south, Protestant and Catholic nationalities in Europe. Thus Italians are said to detest water, whereas the Swiss, who live amongst damp mountains, delight in it:

> Northern people are clean and Southern people dirty as a general rule, because where the principle of life is more cold, weak, and impoverished, there is a greater shyness and aversion to come in contact with external matter (with which it does not so easily amalgamate) ... The Southern temperament is (so to speak) more sociable with matter. [18]

But a simple alliance between north and cold and clean and Protestant breaks down; in turn, Hazlitt is hesitant about advancing alternatives: 'Yet how shall we reconcile to this theory the constant ablutions (five times a day) of the Eastern nations, and the squalid customs of some Northern people, the dirtiness of the Russians and of the Scotch? Superstition may perhaps account for the one, and poverty and barbarism for the other.' [19] A discussion of general national preference in hygiene then slides into a highly gendered equivalent map of morals, in which women are no longer silently included as citizens but explicitly distinguished as females:

> It would be too much to say, that if there is anything of which a genuine Italian has a horror, it is of cleanliness; or that if there is any thing which seems ridiculous to a thorough-bred Italian woman, it is modesty: but certainly the degree to which nicety is carried by some people is a *bore* to an Italian imagination, as the excess of delicacy which is pretended or practised by some women is quite incomprehensible to the females of the South. [20]

Despite the disclaimer – 'It would be too much to say' – Hazlitt seems to want an argument which at least parallels bodily hygiene on a national scale with moral hygiene inflected by sexual difference. And yet it becomes unsustainable: at the end he throws in an odd note which retreats from this discursive entanglement. The foreignness of women, once they are recognised as speaking subjects, dislocates reason from universal practice and universalising patterns: 'Women abroad (generally speaking) are more like men in the tone of their conversation and habits of thinking, so that from the same premises you cannot draw the same conclusions as in England.' [21]

William Thomson comparably reorganises discourse to accommodate cultural difference. He tries extending climatic logic so that bodies, inside and out, enact elemental extremes: 'The rapid change from summer to winter, the only seasons they know, they rehearse upon their bodies, by plunging from the hot to the cold baths ... The quick transitions of the northern climate form themselves a natural bath.' [22] Thomson puzzles over how animals and insects survive these extremes, and over the paradox of – to him – unnatural swings of temperature, demonstrated in Russian enthusiasm for hot and cold baths. He solves the problem, rhetorically, of explaining how there can be unnatural experiences of nature, by a slide from bodily functions to unreliable feminine moral hygiene:

> A few months use to those [children] who pass the ordeal, reconciles them to it: a few years use renders the bath necessary to their existence; and at last it becomes their greatest luxury – as among the higher classes of men to eat and drink substances of the hottest nature, and then to swallow ice creams to cool their burning stomachs. Nature at first rejects these poisons; but at last yields, and even grows fond of her destroyer. [23]

His generalising of class-based custom distinguishes this from Hazlitt's discursive moves a generation later; and he more openly tropes femininity through personification, rather than projecting it on to real women as Hazlitt does. But in both cases, the supposed sexual incontinence of women is used to represent climatic inconstancy or cultural exceptionality.

Both Thomson and Wraxall invoke the stereotype of eastern voluptuousness to stigmatise the Russian custom of mixed bathing, though with a significant difference. Wraxall thinks that the men look more Asiatic than European and the women look hideous – large and saggy. Remembering Lady Mary Wortley Montagu's account of Turkish baths, he deaestheticises the scene: 'this was a sight rather excitive of disgust than desire, and to which only curiosity could ever have led me'. This may be because he is given to eroticising water, rather than bodies in it – 'I am more charmed with the river Neva itself, than with any thing I see here' – or because mixed bathing dissolved class, gender, and national distinctions: a naked body in water is a figure from which many cultural associations are washed away.[24] In other words, Wraxall turns away precisely because difference is floating around unfixed. Thomson, who may well be drawing on Wraxall's account rather than an actual viewing experience, is less fluid. He fixes sexual difference by means of Eastern sensuality connected to degrees of heat: 'The eyes of a Russian gladden with rapture when he speaks of the bagnio; it is his *ne plus ultra* of mortal bliss. In the hot bath they are treated nearly in the same voluptuous manner as in the baths of Asia, from which quarter, indeed, all their customs seem to originate.' He then stereotypically connects heat, easternness, excess, femininity, and immorality: too many baths 'makes the bulk of Russians sickly' and leads them to 'nurture lascivious inclinations, and early prostitution', a stereotypical elision between physical sickliness and moral unhealthiness.[25]

Feminised arts of face-painting were sometimes strategically differentiated from tribal body-art, and ethnic entertainments. Thomson suggested that European masquerades might originate from Tartar masked ceremonies, but he distinguishes this inheritance from a feminine cultural community created by the universal sexuality of women:

> These customs [masquerades] are common to many tribes, and in their dances the women affect the most amorous gestures; in which particular there is a resemblance between them and the Russian females, as there is between both and the balladieres, or dancing girls, in India. Their manner of dancing is exactly the same as that of the women of the islands of the Indian Ocean, represented in the plates of Captain Cook's Voyage.[26]

Again the bookish note suggests that this discourse is literary rather than experiential, but it has the power to animate static illustration. Interestingly, Jemima Kindersley, who did see Indian female dancers, did not reach for global parallels as obvious ones, even though she conceded that it was difficult to give an idea of their performance.[27] One might compare Thomson's sense of similarity between dancing women to that of Hollywood movies, from the golden age onwards, where women from South Sea islands, gypsy tribes, the Asian steppes, or Arabian nights – anywhere that a European or white North American could class as a dark-skinned or hot-blooded culture – show a uniform dance style of 'native' wiggling.

In cold climates, the artificial heat of stoves was a necessity. Masculine hardiness was often separated from the debilitating comfort of indoor heating. Thomson approvingly cites Pallas on the Kalmucs: '"They cannot endure hot rooms, and are very healthy."'[28] Women could be kept out of this indoor picture if heat could be racially exoticised, connected to the warmth of passion, or to luxury. 'The luxury of a Laplander is, to be wrapped in furs during winter, to scorch some favourite part of his body at the fire, to eat bears' flesh, and to drink whale oil', reported Thomson in a distinctly gendered depiction (it is adjacent to a discussion of how religions in this part of the world do not accord souls to women). As a form of personal and national extravagance, luxury involved both sexes; as a form of self-love, it was ungendered, though Thomson points to masculine narcissism in Englishmen's refusal to wear fur coats lest it spoil the display of their elegant persons and fine clothes.[29] The pairing of heat and amorousness, and its opposition to cold and chastity, made the cold a traditional figure for non-consumption of various kinds, even literary productions. As Edward Topham put it, in Scotland

> You are pestered with none of those weekly, daily, and almost hourly pamphlets, which every where meet one's eye in London, under the names of Nuptial Elegies, Sentimental Scruples, Juvenile Poems, Amorous Epistles, and a thousand others of the same ingenious and tender natures. Such delicate productions would expire in this cold climate, as they owe their birth to idle hours and mild skies.[30]

But hot interiors in cold climates made even this opposition unstable. Topham suggested that central heating made women forward, like plants made to flower early in hothouses; since sexual awareness could not be naturally part of female nature, it must be artificially forced, by heat. He argued that the heat-induced forwardness of Scottish women was comparable to the sexual precosity of Indian girls, which could be explained as the natural effect of the hot climate they lived in.[31] Thomson similarly blamed the allegedly amorous disposition of Russians on their hot houses and hot baths, but applied it to both sexes. He tries to spin out an explanation of national difference compatible with sexual, political, and economic specificity:

> The Germans, Danes, Swedes, and Norwegians, having likewise the stove, preserve the summer heat in the bleak months, and are fond husbands and gallants all the year. Britons are moulded by other causes: without stoves, without clothing, no nation suffers so much from cold. It is surprising, then, that we are not as famous for our chastity as for our courage. Liberty is the stove which warms us! Liberty gives commerce – commerce, wealth – wealth, luxury – and luxury, an amorous complexion.[32]

By an astonishing – and ludicrous! – rhetorical flourish, Thomson makes being British politically, economically, and sexually desirable.

In these discursive contexts, in which femininity is used as a sign of national continence or moral hygiene, the representation of women is curiously blank. A number of travel writers agreed that similarities between women were greater than their differences: gender erased national, religious, political, linguistic, even ethnic identity. As Edward Topham put it, observing women drinking one evening in an oyster-cellar in Edinburgh, 'let local customs operate as they may, a truly polite woman is every where the same'.[33] For Topham, class and language use could differentiate between women; for Thomson, women were a global tribe. His opinions show a resolute embodiment of women which none the less enables them to be perversely expressive:

> Whatever disputes may arise about the origin of men, the origin of women affords no grounds for any: it is perfectly distinct: they are all of the same race and family – whether they tread bare-footed the deserts of Tartary, or lead the dance in the gayest Parisian assemblies, they shew themselves to be of the same genuine stock in customs and manners. The Parisian lady pillages every toy-shop to ornament her person: the Tartarian damsel, for the same end, is equally eager in exploring the shores of every lake, every hill, and plain, and wood: in order to set off her charms, she picks up every pebble and shell: they all agree in one pursuit – man. Their language and oratory are the same: the same their eyes – their tears. They allow men to conquer Asia, Africa, Europe, and America; and, when men have done, they lay hold of the victors.[34]

Thomson later suggests, rather more rationally, that the supposed uniformity of women can be attributed to their being 'more uniformly occupied in one pursuit, that of household oeconomy and the care of their children'.[35] His association of them with the arts of seduction is none the less unable to avoid associating them with seductive arts such as poetry, oratory, dance, and music. In part this brings together straightforwardly a long-standing feminisation of dance and music (arts which involve the body or effects upon the body), conjoined with mistrust of sensibility's language of tears and a misogynist reading of femininity as heterosexual entrapment. But it connects directly with a late eighteenth-century aesthetic development which is crucial to Romanticism: the silencing of women in order to make femininity an object or sign expressive of a poetic masculine subject. In describing women around the world, and in suggesting women were impervious to cultural difference, travel writers played a key part in helping to clear the way, symbolically, for the elevation of a mute feminine muse over the politely and spiritedly conversational women of a rational eighteenth-century world.[36]

New discussion of northern parts of the world in late eighteenth-century travel writing offered a fresh space to map ideologies of gender. If women exemplified cultural difference least because they were alike around the globe, if women were defined not by national traits but by sexual ones, then women could represent the possibility of pure communication. In other words, women's universal identity could disclose a universal language – either one untrammelled by the particularity of a foreign tongue, or one which bypassed potential unintelligibility by privileging song and dance, which are universally recognised as expressive regardless of national origin. Hence the significance in travel writing of moments in which writers meet women they cannot speak with, or women who sing to them. Wraxall's narrative illustrates this extensively. But before turning to this, and to what follows from it with regard to Romanticism, I want to sketch in some sense of how wordlessness came to be powerful.

Burke's enquiry into the sublime and beautiful mingled influentially concepts of gender, language, and aesthetics.[37] In part five, Burke discusses how words can affect the mind without raising images. He observes that poetry and rhetoric are not as concerned with description as painting is: 'their business is to affect rather by sympathy than imitation; to display rather the effect of things on the mind of the speaker, or of others, than to present a clear idea of the things themselves'. This aligns poetry with signification and the receptive subject, which although itself ostensibly gender-neutral, allows for gendering. In strong expressions, passion can convey meaning regardless of the words used: 'We yield to sympathy, what we refuse to description.' Passion touches and moves us and can kindle fires; discursive energy is detached from its object. For Burke, the French language illustrates clarity and lack of strength: 'Whereas the oriental tongues, and in general the languages of most unpolished people, have a great force and energy of expression; and this is but natural.'[38] Here is a glimpse of that discursive pattern which becomes distinctive in later texts: language which acquires meaning from the power of expression rather than the sense of its words, associated with orientalism, heat, and the natural. Although the supposed inferior physical strength of women made it possible to trope the French language as effeminate, this pattern could be gendered by associations between women and heat, the natural, and the potentially exotic.

One familiar example shows how naturalised this pattern became. In Coleridge's poem *Christabel*, Geraldine drinks reviving wine, and begins to speak clearly and directly:

> And from the floor whereon she sank,
> The lofty lady stood upright:

> She was most beautiful to see,
> Like a lady of a far countree.

The spectacle of an exoticised woman is fused with a figure for the powers of speech. The trope appears inside-out – exotic linguistic power made available through sexuality – in a story told by John Lettice of a visit in Scotland to the famous traveller to Abyssinia, James Bruce. Viewing his curiosities, Lettice and his party hear that Bruce had wanted a translation of the Song of Solomon into a collection of different African languages:

> This was executed for him in ten of them, beautifully written in Æthiopic characters; and each in a different-coloured ink, to prevent a confusion of tongues; which, in this instance, had certainly not been miraculous. To spare the ears of the unlearned, and perhaps, at some moments, his own recollection, he calls these languages, with some humour, the red, blue, green, or yellow languages, &c. Upon Mr. Bruce's shewing these manuscripts to a lady distinguished for the vivacity of her remarks, and informing her, that the word *kiss*, which occurs in Solomon's song, is to be met with, expressing the same idea, in some passages of his rain-bow of languages, she pleasantly observed to him – 'I always told you, Mr. Bruce, that kissing is the same all the world over'.[39]

In reality, communication for male travellers could be uncontrollably polyglot. As William Coxe wrote from Switzerland:

> I cannot describe how much I am perplexed with a variety of languages. I speak Italian or French with the principal gentry, and sometimes am obliged to hold a conversation in Latin. I talk a smattering of German with my servant, who understands no other language, and, with my guide and the common people, a kind of corrupt Italian, like the Milanese. I write my notes in English, and during my progress through Engadina, was employed in collecting a vocabulary of the Romansh. I must therefore warn you not to be surprised, should you find a confusion of tongues in my Letters.[40]

For the less linguistically adept, unable to understand a local language and silent from necessity, the mute expressiveness of women could be appealing as a poetic analogue of their own inarticulacy. The language of the heart, or of music, or both together, did away with difficulties of communication. This trope simultaneously reinforced the idea that women were alike, regardless of cultural difference, and aestheticised the relation between a universal language and poetry, especially as mediated or performed by feminine figures. Ironically this may well have reduced the value put on actual women's self-expression. A symbolic relation between femininity and the arts is hardly a new idea, but I would suggest that the importance of foreignness in the equation has been underestimated. So the exoticism of Coleridge's damsel with a dulcimer in *Kubla Khan*, the Abyssinian maid who sings of Mount Abora, symbolises not simply cultural difference but linguistic diversity made intelligible by art. After all, how could one know of what she was singing, if her words were in her own language, which might be the equivalent of any colour in or beyond Bruce's chromatic scheme? Place names need least translation between languages: hence they stand as signs of what might translate best between different places.

Wraxall's representation of the interchanges between women, wordlessness, expression, and desire is also important because he illustrates the most symbolically powerful types of wordless women – musical women, imprisoned women, and dead women. His consciousness of their charms is closely connected to aestheticised moments of self-reflection. The first woman he is smitten by is a fair Norwegian, the daughter of his landlord.[41]

> I have bowed the knee to her from the first moment I saw her, and have talked to her continually; nay, even said all that the sight of innocent beauty may be supposed to dictate, to a heart not unsusceptible of its soft impressions. – How I said them, I leave you to judge from your own feelings, since language constitutes no part of our interchange of ideas, as I am unhappy enough not to speak Danish, and she can converse in no other. But the most animated expression of admiration may be conveyed without the aid of words or sounds; and there is a language, and that an eloquent one too, which is given by bounteous nature in common to the inhabitants of England and of Norway.[42]

Cultural difference is mediated through this woman – he is intensely aware that they come from different lands – but is also erased by her: her music creates harmony between them. In their 'dumb tete-a-tete', Wraxall's Englishness becomes invisible or irrelevant, displaced by his gendered identity as a man with a pretty woman who just happens to come from another country. Her national identity is also erased in favour of a gendered identity – the fair Norwegian becomes a pretty woman – but she takes on a further symbolic role as the sign of language. Unable to speak the same language, they communicate wordlessly, but at her silent dictation. She becomes the sign not of language but of sign language. They use a discourse of the heart which passes over cultural barriers, but only on condition that gender boundaries stay in place. Though Wraxall has similar language problems with Scandinavian men, he does not solve them by gazing into their eyes or listening to them sing.

Wraxall was drawn to a number of imprisoned women, who are tantalisingly out of view. Northern Europe had a plentiful supply of deposed princesses, like Queen Matilda, of whom Wraxall eagerly heard details from a former fellow prisoner, or the Princess Royal of Russia, of whom he laments, 'In the bloom of her age, she is immured in a frightful old castle'. This allows for a kind of Gothic voyeurism, a peeping tourism, when Wraxall spies on the Princess Royal taking a walk. The spectacle of virtue in distress, however, takes on new aesthetic implications, since these women are differentiated from others in that Wraxall cannot hold a conversation with them. In this text, women are repeatedly associated with the arts, especially music and with powers of speech – not the powers of female speech but the power of women to move men to eloquence, and to silence them by arousing emotions too powerful to articulate. In this respect, women become both the inspiration for and opposite of poetry. At Königsberg, Wraxall meets a woman who, though not the most beautiful he has met, possesses subtly and irresistably what he calls sympathy. His analysis of it takes up Burke's vocabulary to observe that love is not allied with loquacity: 'The passions of the heart depend not on the deductions of the understanding, and admiration may be experienced without defining it.' [43] This woman, the one who leaves him most tongue-tied, offers to teach him German by reading poetry. His choked enthusiasm anticipates the psychic numbness which a number of male Romantic poets saw as the precondition to composition – as Keats put it, 'the feel of not to feel it'.

The pleasures and pains of wordlessness prompt Wraxall to reflect not only on his inability to articulate feelings of desire to the women who arouse them, but also on the limits of his powers of description. The most intense encounter Wraxall has is with a dead woman. In a crypt in Bremen which holds five strangely preserved bodies, he investigates them with dispassionate curiosity. But in the case of one, a young woman said to be an English countess two hundred and fifty years old, he hangs longingly over her body, touching her, lifting her up from her oak coffer by her hair, still glossy and brown, of which he cuts a lock. This bizarre episode, in the last week of his travels, brings strikingly together the tensions between gender, class, nationality, language, spectacle, and story which make Wraxall's gallantries expressive of the power of unspeaking female icons.

The gendered dynamics of this discourse are interestingly shown up by a comparison between Wraxall's *Cursory Remarks* and Mary Wollstonecraft's *Letters Written During a Short Residence in Sweden, Norway and Denmark*. Where he eroticises, she looks rather to class to stabilise cultural difference.

For instance, contemplating with reluctance enbalmed bodies in a church in Tonsberg, she presents them as ungendered, to be sexualised privately and through previous attachment, and otherwise distinguished only by their absence of distinction:

> For worlds, I would not see a form I loved – enbalmed in my heart – thus sacrilegiously handled! – Pugh! – my stomach turns. – Is this all the distinction of the rich in the grave? They had better quietly allow the scythe of equality to mow them down with the common mass, than struggle to become a monument of the instability of human greatness.[44]

Like Wraxall, moved by the fate of Queen Matilda – 'Poor Matilda! thou has haunted me ever since my arrival' – Wollstonecraft otherwise reflects on women as agents of the arts for class rather than sexual reasons: 'The women seem to take the lead in polishing the manners everywhere, that being the only way to better their condition.' And yet even Wollstonecraft remarks on the coquettishness of country girls in Denmark, and in a letter from Norway she discusses singing and dancing in connection with an evening spent in the company of pretty women. Moved, as Wraxall was, by the sight of beauty, she too responds to a wordless attraction: 'They gathered round me – sung to me – and one of the prettiest, to whom I gave my hand, with some degree of cordiality, to meet the glance of her eyes, kissed me very affectionately.' [45] It is not clear whether the kiss was on hand or cheek – a significant distinction locally. Wraxall spent an evening plotting stratagems to plant a kiss, 'in the English style' on one beautiful but all too respectable woman's cheek; at the last minute he was foiled, and publicly embarrassed.[46] For Wollstonecraft, there might as well be no distinction because she has no interest in seduction; though conscious of physical intimacy, she recognises the other woman as a subject, because she sees in their reciprocity herself as an object. The glance she meets makes her a spectacle, no longer only a spectator, but the warmth of touch dissolves any hierarchy. Throughout dinner, the women sing and keep up with Wollstonecraft 'a sort of conversation of gestures':

> As their minds were totally uncultivated, I did not lose much, perhaps gained, by not being able to understand them; for fancy probably filled up, more to their advantage, the void in the picture. Be that as it may, they excited my sympathy; and I was very much flattered when I was told, the next day, that they said it was a pleasure to look at me, I appeared so goodnatured.[47]

Though Burkean concepts are in play here, Wollstonecraft neither romanticises nor sexualises the appeal of wordlessness. The will to attribute meaning is not condemned, any more than the narcissistic pleasure she takes in their compliments, but it is recognised as self-interested.

A less disturbing variation of Wraxall's interest in the aesthetic appeal of dead northern women is found among a number of writers who took an interest in Mary Queen of Scots. Here history lent respectability. John Lettice, who rhapsodised over a number of her portraits and places with which she was associated, treats her straightforwardly as an example of virtue in distress, but he noted with satisfaction 'those achievements of literary chivalry, which have lately been displayed in defence of her honour'. But even when she can be thought of as a writer rather than a subject of poetry, she requires the assistance of her admirers' fancies: 'Here, it is imagined, she composed, and sung, to the lute, some of those little effusions of lyric poetry, which tradition has attributed to her pen.'[48] The invisibility of the singing female figure allowed the imagination to project its own shapes of desire. So Eyles Irwin, safely arrived at last in Cairo, heard an invisible woman play the guitar and sing, 'a damsel, whom my imagination had pictured out in all the graces of beauty and youth'.[49] Sir Richard Sulivan, travelling jauntily through Scotland, passed Loch Tay by moonlight and was held spellbound by a woman singing serenely: 'The sight was bewitching! innocence taught her not to be afraid; she continued her song, and seemed to be inspired the more she saw that we were pleased with her exertions: native goodness is wonderfully winning and attractive.'[50] 'Native goodness' here becomes both the moral propriety supposed to be innate to females, and indigenous ethnicity. Sight could reinforce the fantasies conjured up by sound: William Thomson describes approvingly the music of an orchestra hidden from view among trees, but conceded, 'Any one who has seen and heard a beautiful woman sing, will confess that the sight gives new pleasure to the hearing'.[51] For male Romantic writers, the eroticisation of female singers prevented their encroachment on masculine poetic territiories. Another figure for poetry, the nightingale, is also symbolically placed, but made absent, at the site of production – famously in Keats's 'Ode to a Nightingale' (1820). The woman who has to be seen, the bird who cannot be seen – both become objects of the poetic gaze, the subject for poetry rather than the poetic subject.

A comparative study of how this discourse features in a text written by a woman shows up its gendered aspects. This is not to suggest that women writers were anxious or able to resist it, but rather that it was enabling and constricting in different ways. The central section of *Frankenstein*, concerning the relationship between the creature and the de Laceys, makes significant use of the discourse connecting women, music, language, climate, and culture. Safie and her story are most relevant to my argument, though, since the creature himself is also a traveller, she is not the only exotic.

When Safie and Felix first meet they cannot speak each other's language. They 'conversed with one another through the means of an interpreter and sometimes with the interpretation of looks; and Safie sang to him the divine airs of her native country'.[52] The fair Arabian, like the fair Norwegian, uses the language of looks and music; with the help of an old servant, she is able to express herself to Felix in letters in French. When she arrives at the cottage, the creature notes, 'Her voice was musical, but unlike that of either of my friends'.[53] That night, Felix gives Safie her first English lesson. The next day, when Felix has left and his sister Agatha's work is done,

> the Arabian sat at the feet of the old man, and, taking his guitar, played some airs so entrancingly beautiful, that they at once drew tears from my eyes. She sang, and her voice flowed in a rich cadence, swelling or dying away, like a nightingale of the woods.
>
> When she had finished, she gave the guitar to Agatha, who at first declined it. She played a simple air, and her voice accompanied it in sweet accents, but unlike the wondrous strain of the stranger. The old man appeared enraptured, and said some words, which Agatha endeavoured to explain to Safie, and by which he appeared to wish to express that she bestowed on him the greatest delight by her music.[54]

Although Safie's music is more beautiful than Agatha's, both women do play. There are not only two female singers but an audience of two males who are also complementary, in that the creature is primarily a spectator and the old man an auditor. The old man is blind, and the creature in one sense deaf, deaf to the meaning of the spoken conversations between the de Laceys ('I ardently desired to understand them, and bent every faculty towards that purpose, but found it utterly impossible').[55] Safie, like the creature, cannot understand what the de Laceys say, making her and the creature aliens alike, linguistically estranged. So the creature's tribute of tears to her fluid songs – a tribute which she cannot see – is no less effectively communicative than the awkward translation of the old man's verbal appreciation. The traces of magic – the creature is entranced, the old man enraptured – reinscribe the seizure and paralysis evoked by earlier male writers listening to foreign women sing, although its double inscription curiously destabilises it. Why have two women sing, two males listen, two students of a language new to them? Is there more to this than Shelley's predilection for iconographic doublings, or Gothic duality, or the over-determinism of a woman writing in a masculine voice?

One aspect of this scene is, I think, different. The creature and Safie are learning a language. For the creature, it will be his mother tongue, in that it is his first language; for Safie, it will be her second (at least). The lessons she has learnt from her mother are not specifically linguistic, but generally cultural: it is later said that she taught Safie to be a Christian, and 'to aspire to higher powers of intellect, and an independence of spirit, forbidden to the female followers of Mahomet'. When Safie arrives, the old man is playing his guitar, and the mime-language which follows – of tears, sighs, smiles, blushes, kisses – embodies Felix as much as her. The episode of Safie playing takes place when both she and the creature are unable to continue learning because Felix has gone out: with their instructor absent, the common language pursued is the wordless one of music. But after this, they make progress: 'Safie was always gay and happy; she and I improved rapidly in the knowledge of language.' But as spring comes, the creature makes faster progress than Safie in learning to speak and read. She, re-racialised as 'the Arabian', is associated with a Lacanian incompletion or lack. The creature declares 'I may boast that I improved more rapidly than the Arabian, who understood very little, and conversed in broken accents'. His progress in the science of letters comes from understanding Volney's *Ruins of Empires*, and he attributes this to Felix: 'I should not have understood the purport of this book, had not Felix, in reading it, given very minute explanations.' [56] This text crucially teaches the creature three things: the skill of letters, cultural difference, and sexual difference. Though this episode is not reducible to a single reading, in the light of its musical introduction a gendered reading of access to language becomes apparent. There is both a cultural and a sexual dynamic here, in that the foreign musical woman is a trope for both cultural and sexual difference expressed symbolically through language. The creature learns through Felix's instruction: the assimilation of the colonial subject is accomplished through masculinity. Despite the proliferation of European languages in the story (Walton is English, Frankenstein German, the de Laceys French), the communicative skills which teach the creature the knowledge of his own difference, which is crucial, are termed simply 'language'. Hence the very specific blankness which other travellers face – for Wraxall or Wollstonecraft, for instance, their inability to speak Norwegian – becomes in *Frankenstein* an inability to comprehend culture in general without the preliminary intervention of gender. Felix is absent so the creature cannot continue with his language lessons, but Safie's playing enables him to express himself. Women singing teach the creature something wordless, without which his acquisition of language cannot take place, nor his comprehension of gender and culture difference. It is tempting to read Safie as a maternal figure in a Kristevan sense.

It is also tempting to take this track because of the text's treatment of the acquisition of language in relation to pleasure. Following Safie's playing – a term meaning both musical performance and pleasurable activity – the creature notes 'The days now passed as peaceably as before, with the sole alteration that joy had taken the place of sadness in the countenances of my friends.' This makes Safie more teachable: 'Safie was always gay and happy; she and I improved rapidly in the knowledge of language.' Yet, a few lines on, Safie becomes again the Arabian who can speak only in broken accents. It is as if the intervention of race means she must serve as the trope of imperfect language after all. Safie is both the foreign woman whose medium of music offers Europeans the dream of a global language, and the Arabian whose inability to speak a European language fluently condemns her to feminised subservience, in comparison to the creature's cultural mastery. This story is psychoanalytic: Safie and the creature have gendered relations to the acquisition of language, where music may represent the semiotic, as a signifying system which is prelinguistic, not necessarily wordless or meaningless, but not employing fully linguistic notation. And the story is racial, in that both represent types of social and national relations. The two come together in concepts of a mother country and a mother tongue. Safie has no family and lives in exile; the creature faces a tragic tribal singularity: 'I saw and heard of none like me.'[57]

'She sang, and her voice flowed in a rich cadence'; she speaks, and her accents are broken. Shelley's characterisation of Safie illustrates how strategically Romantic writers treated the fluency of women as foreign subjects. That fluency troped language as liquid, and increased its associations with temperature. The discursive connections between warm and cool climates, hot and cold waters, words and music, and north and south, were accomplished through the symbolic agency of women, as simultaneously foreign and familiar, a race united and apart.

Notes

1 Nathaniel Wraxall, *Cursory Remarks made in a Tour Through Some of the Northern Parts of Europe, particularly Copenhagen, Stockholm, and Petersburgh* (London, 1775).

2 William Thomson, *Letters from Scandinavia, on the Past and Present State of the Northern Nations of Europe*, 2 vols (London, 1796), 1: 269. Thomson's words are actually about William Coxe's *Travels into Poland, Russia, Sweden and Denmark*, 2 vols (London, 1794), which he compares with Wraxall's book. But he seems to have confused them, since it is Wraxall who is notably interested in women. Thomson cites Wraxall as lamenting 'that in his journey of 4000 miles, he could not obtain a single kiss from any of the

ladies near the pole, unless from an old Swedish duchess wanting teeth' (1: 268–9).

3   This chapter was prepared before the publication of Felicity Nussbaum's *Torrid Zones: Maternity, Sexuality and Empire in Eighteenth-Century English Narratives* (Baltimore and London, 1995); for further discussion of climate, see 8–11. Nussbaum's stimulating analyses share my concerns here with the sexualisation of 'exotic' women, but she maps them on to postcolonialism rather than masculinity.

4   John Lettice, *Letters on a Tour through Various Parts of Scotland, in the year 1792* (London, 1794), 161.

5   James Boswell, *Journal of a Tour to the Hebrides*, ed. R. W. Chapman (1924; Oxford, 1978), 303–4 (Thursday 16 September).

6   *Letters from Scandinavia*, 1: 133.

7   It is possible that Thomson did not actually go to Scandinavia. Travel writing as a category cuts across fiction and non-fiction, for instance in Ann Radcliffe's descriptions of scenery she had never seen.

8   *Letters from Scandinavia*, 1: 4.

9   *Ibid.*, 1: 86–7.

10 Eyles Irwin, *A Series of Adventures in the Course of a Voyage up the Red-Sea … in the year 1777* (London, 1780), 335. As a variation on this theme, he also tells an anecdote about an English friend who 'went to the house of the bey here in a shaul turban. This is strictly prohibited to Christians of all denominations; but was nevertheless overlooked in him, because he was an Englishman' (335).

11 *Ibid.*, 152.

12 *Ibid.*

13 Jemima Kindersley, *Letters from the Island of Teneriffe, Brazil, the Cape of Good Hope and the East Indies* (London, 1777), 250: 'They usually call the Europeans *lol addama*, which means red men; and, indeed, it is no very improper appellation for a sun-burnt English-man'.

14 Thomson, *Letters from Scandinavia*, 1: 174–7.

15 Patrick Brydone, *A Tour Through Sicily and Malta*, 2 vols (London, 1773), 200.

16 Uno von Troil, *Letters on Iceland* (London, 1780), 10, 9.

17 William Hazlitt, 'Hot and Cold', Essay 16 in *The Plain Speaker: Opinions on Books, Men and Things*, in *The Complete Works of William Hazlitt*, ed. P. P. Howe, 21 vols (London and Toronto, 1931), 12: 175. I am grateful to John Woolford for alerting me to this essay.

18 *Ibid.*, 170.

19 *Ibid.*, 175.

20 *Ibid.*, 170.

21 *Ibid.*

22 *Letters from Scandinavia*, 1: 307–8.

23 *Ibid.*, 1: 310. This suggests there were class inflections to Keats's experiments with putting claret and cayenne in sequence on his tongue.

24 *Cursory Remarks*, 252, 247.

25 Thomson, *Letters from Scandinavia*, 1: 310, 313–14.

26 *Ibid.*, 1: 136–7.

27 *Letters from … Teneriffe*, 231. Discussing the 'notch', or performance of the dancing girls, Kindersley keeps an economic dimension in mind – the entertainment demonstrates the wealth of the men who pay for it. And she stresses cross-cultural similarities, especially amongst men: this spectacle is 'very delightful, not only to black men, but to many Europeans'.

28 *Letters from Scandinavia*, 1: 158. He confuses the paradigm when he moves south: 'The Germans are generally described as a grave, phlegmatic people; but, reversing the order of animal nature, they revive in the cold season of the year' (2: 242).

29 *Ibid.*, 1: 436, 418–20.

30 Edward Topham, *Letters from Edinburgh Written in the Years 1774 and 1775* (London, 1776), 186.

31 Scotch women could pass on these amorous heats: 'in spite of the coldness of their atmosphere and northern blasts, [they] light up as consuming fires in the hearts of their admirers, as the dames of Italy' (Topham, *Letters from Edinburgh*, 84–5).

32 *Letters from Scandinavia*, 1: 271.

33 *Letters from Edinburgh*, 131.

34 *Letters from Scandinavia*, 1: 143–4.

35 *Ibid.*, 1: 423.

36 This is not to deny the existence of feminised tropes of a poetic muse available earlier in the eighteenth century. But I think it could more comfortably co-exist with real women's conversation. When Felicia Hemans visited the Wordsworths in the 1830s, she was thought to talk too much. This seems symptomatic of a new incompatibility since the time when a poetry of wit allowed women to speak cleverly in prose.

37 Edmund Burke, *A Philosophical Enquiry into the Origin of our Ideas of the Sublime and Beautiful*, ed. Adam Philips (1757; Oxford, 1990), 105.

38 *Ibid.*, 157, 160, 160.

39 *Letters on a Tour*, 496–7.

40 William Coxe, *Travels in Switzerland*, 3 vols (London, 1789), 3: 89.

41 *Cursory Remarks*, Letter 2 (25 April 1774).

42 *Ibid.*, 18.

43 *Cursory Remarks*, 387–8, 318.

44 Mary Wollstonecraft, *Letters Written During a Short Residence in Sweden, Norway and Denmark* (1796; Fontwell, Sussex, 1970), 91.

45 *Ibid.*, 203, 243, 100.

46 *Cursory Remarks*, 150–3.

47 *Short Residence*, 101.

48 *Letters on a Tour*, 460, 458.

49 *Adventures*, 332.

50 Sir Richard Sulivan (*sic*), *Observations Made During a Tour through Parts of England, Scotland and Wales* (London, 1780), 211.

51 *Letters from Scandinavia*, 1: 184.

52 Mary Shelley, *Frankenstein, or the Modern Prometheus* (1818; Oxford, 1989), 124. The episode with which my discussion is most concerned takes place in chapter 13. The creature shares some characteristics with northern peoples: for instance, he can endure extremes of hot and cold, as Lettice thought the Scots could.

53 *Ibid.*, 116.

54 *Ibid.*, 118.

55 *Ibid.*

56 *Ibid.*, 124, 118, 118–19, 119.

57 *Ibid.*, 118, 118, 120.

Politics and the occupation of a nurse in Mariana Starke's *Letters from Italy*

Jeanne Moskal

Literary history has not been kind to Mariana Starke (?1762–1838), playwright, translator, poet, and travel writer. Though her reputation flourished only in the genre of travel writing, the work she did there was recognised and appreciated by her contemporaries, only to fall into obscurity well before our own day. In this chapter and in its companions I restore for present-day attention the historical and literary record of Starke's achievement in the hope that such restoration will illuminate our sense of gender and politics in the Romantic period.[1] I shall demonstrate that Starke's work, especially the travel memoir, *Letters from Italy* (1800), richly exemplifies the complicated position of women writing politics in the reactionary 1790s, a position Gary Kelly has analysed under the rubric of 'anti-Jacobin feminism'. This feminism is a collection of attempts to maintain some of the public visibility for women advocated by Jacobins like Mary Wollstonecraft, William Godwin, and Mary Hays, but to maintain it in the service of British patriotism, Whig politics, Protestantism, and their sometime corollaries of Francophobia, anti-catholicism, and misogyny. Starke and others like her challenge present-day literary scholars to confront the political conservatism of women writers of past eras – not to mention their occasional outright xenophobia and/or complicity in patriarchal systems.[2] The paradox of these 'conservative' women is that they found a voice by speaking for a system that professed its desire to silence them and women like them. Kelly argues that a woman writer's safest refuge was the role of '"domestic woman" as professionalized custodian of "national" conscience, culture, and destiny'.[3] In this chapter, I shall be examining Starke's manipulation of the role of 'nurse' to achieve a version of the intricate refuge Kelly describes. In Starke's crafty, quirky memoir, 'the occupation of a nurse' becomes the guarantor of Starke's membership in a conservative ideology and of her domestic propriety in defining her fulfilment of duty. At the same time, 'the occupation of a nurse' authorises public advice-giving, the pronouncement of what is clean and dirty, what figures in public heath – in short, the role of national custodian that Kelly has theorised. Finally, 'the occupation of a nurse' provides a cover story for Starke's professional ambition as a writer.

For the reader unfamiliar with Starke, a sketch of her life, works, and reputation may be in order. Starke grew up in India, where her father, Richard Starke, served as governor of the British East India Company's colony at Fort St George in Madras for several years. When she returned to England, she launched her literary career with two plays, *The Sword of Peace* (1788) and *The Widow of Malabar* (1791), both set in India, and meeting with a little success. She then accompanied 'an invalid relative' (the exact relationship is never mentioned) to Italy for seven years, where she witnessed much of the French Revolutionary army's invasion of Italy. She shaped her account of this event to form the travel memoir *Letters from Italy*, supplementing the volume with a compendium of advice for the British traveller to Italy. This book met with some success, being translated into German and going into a second English edition.[4] During the rest of the war, while travel was difficult, Starke worked as a translator and an imitator, writing *The Tournament* (1800), an imitation of a German play, and producing the hybrid volume *The Beauties of Carlo-Maria Maggi, Paraphrased: to which are added Sonnets: by Mariana Starke* in 1811. After the war, Starke returned to the Continent, finding her literary voice in travel books for a British public eager to travel. Her *Information and Directions for Travellers on the Continent* (1820) follows the guidebook format, omitting the kind of personal memoir that introduced *Letters from Italy*. Starke's guidebooks were reissued in various forms throughout the nineteenth century. She died in 1838 in Milan, en route from Naples to England, probably in the company of her nephew, Richard John Hughes Starke, who died that same year.[5]

Starke's literary importance lies in her creation of the genre of the travel guidebook as contrasted with the travel memoir. She industriously compiled for the traveller all the pertinent information about a given destination. Stylistically, we can trace the beginnings of the guidebook to her choices, such as organising her advice for the traveller to Rome into day-long excursions, anticipating the layout of some present-day guidebooks with itineraries for 'First Day in Rome', 'Second Day in Rome', and so forth. Moreover, she writes these sections in imperatives for the tourist, rather than the memoirist's past tense: 'Set out at nine in the morning; drive to the Colosseum; go to the house within the walls, where there lives a Monk, who conducts Travellers safely through the whole building – Give him three or four pauls.'[6] This technique proved foundational for the creation of travel guidebooks by removing the memoirist from the picture (and from the sentence) and allowing the reader-tourist mentally to write himself or herself into that impersonal formula. A further innovation, apparently Starke's own creation, is a quantified rating system, the earliest version of our now-conventional formula 'four-star hotel' or 'five-star restaurant'.[7] In listing the works of art in a particular gallery, Starke ranks the most noteworthy by exclamation points – one, two, or three, according to their value. In the Pitti Palace, for example, she catalogues all the paintings and sculptures according to the twenty-odd rooms in which they are exhibited, but only seven items earn Starke's three-exclamation-point rating.[8] Starke simplifies the tourist's task by noting only those few paintings really worth her or his limited attention. She thus met the needs of the new breed of British tourists with limited time abroad, the middle-class men and their families who flocked to the Continent following Waterloo.

Starke earned respect as a guidebook writer. In 1844, Mary Shelley praised her account of Sorrento as 'both accurate and well-written', adding that, 'for this part of Italy she is an excellent guide'.[9] And Starke's guidebooks provided much of the information used by her publisher, John Murray III, when in 1836 he issued *Handbook for Travellers on the Continent*, a book that inaugurated Murray's Handbook series, imitated by Karl Baedeker in Germany and growing by 1848 to a list of over sixty 'Works for Travellers' published by Murray alone.[10] Indeed, Murray himself acknowledged the importance of Starke's work:

> At that time [1829] such a thing as a Guide-book for Germany, France, or Spain did not exist. The only Guides deserving the name were: Ebel, for Switzerland; Boyce, for Belgium; and Mrs. Starke for Italy. Hers was a work of real utility, because, amidst a singular medley of classical lore, borrowed from Lemprière's dictionary, interwoven with details regulating the charges in washing-bills at Sorrento and Naples, and an elaborate theory on the origin of Devonshire Cream, in which she proves that it was brought by Phoenician colonists from Asia Minor into the West of England, it contained much practical information gathered on the spot.[11]

Murray's tribute to Starke stands out in this essay, which mostly defends Murray's claim that he himself is 'the author, inventor, and originator' of travel handbooks.[12] Murray's testimonial to Starke's utility – by virtue of her absolute comprehensiveness – is echoed in a bit of anonymous doggerel verse from the early nineteenth century, preserved in a copy of Mrs Starke's *Continental Guide*:

Young Gentlemen, going abroad in their raw age,
Have need of a decent *compagnon-de-voyage* ...
Mrs. Starke, that most learned old matron, will save a
Youth's turn, or they misrepresent her,
Will chatter of flannel and thread, like Minerva,
And spout crabbed Greek, like old Mentor.

Cyclopean walls, and Gorgona Anchovies,
Westphalian hams, and proconsular Trophies,
Swiss chalets, Dutch Inns, and Sicilian cloisters,
Danube, Silarus, Tiber, or Po,
Quails, ortolans, sparrows, Marsala, Port, oysters,
For her nought's too high, or too low.

Weird Woman, indeed! human things and divine,
She crams in one page, nay, and oft in a line;
Like a poet in phrenzy her vision can glance
In a twinkling creation all o'er.[13]

More misogynist and grudging than Murray, this poet too praises Starke's inclusion of things high and low, 'Gorgona Anchovies' and 'proconsular Trophies', things human and divine, in her guidebook. The testimonies of Mary Shelley, John Murray, and one anonymous poet hint at Starke's importance in the nineteenth century. Yet the transmutation of her creation, the genre of the guidebook, into Murray's immensely popular series contains the key to our forgetting her name. Paradoxically, Starke made her success by creating a genre that erased the writer's self, and, when the genre proved lucrative for Murray, Baedeker, and others, Starke herself almost vanished. The eclipse of Starke's reputation may also provide a clue about the success of such self-staging strategies as 'the occupation of a nurse' – strategies which gained Starke a hearing in her own time but in the long run fixed her firmly in the ranks of amateurs unworthy of posterity's attention.

Women writers and the politics of the 1790s

Starke's situation as a traveller in wartime Italy and as the author of a travel book certainly would have demanded, in the late 1790s, for some fig leaf of propriety to justify and excuse it, propriety such as 'the occupation of a nurse' might offer. Critics of women travel writers have identified a set of taboos – some external, some profoundly internalised – specific to the genre. Some of the taboo relates to the act of a woman's travelling. Eric J. Leed and Karen R. Lawrence have demonstrated that women travellers in most historical periods face the massive cultural prejudice that equates masculinity with mobility, typified in the figure of Odysseus, and that equates femininity with place, typified in Penelope.[14] From a materialist point of view, Georges Van Den Abbeele and Janet Wolff have astutely classified travel as one of the 'technologies of gender'.[15] And when women travellers craft their experiences into writing, new taboos and restrictions emerge in the language. For example, as Elizabeth A. Bohls argues, women travel writers struggle to subvert a masculinist aesthetic vocabulary in their descriptions of landscape, and, Sara Mills has shown, Victorian women's travel writings become entangled in 'the conflicting demands of the discourse of femininity and that of imperialism'.[16] The intertwined acts of travelling and of writing one's travels are thus inescapably gendered and gendering.

In the Romantic period, the gendered currents of travelling and travel writing had a specific historical shape, in which the tradition of the Grand Tour held strong, overtly serving as the capstone of an English gentleman's education and covertly allowing him an opportunity for sexual adventures before assuming his adult duties.[17] As Kelly has noted, the English political reaction against the French due to the September Massacres of 1793 and the Reign of Terror of July 1794 entailed a cultural reaction against women writing politics. For example, this cultural reaction saw new editions of James Fordyce's influential 1766 conduct book, which held that war, commerce, politics, abstract philosophy, 'and all the abstruser sciences, are most properly the province of men'.[18] The cultural reaction was manifested also in Richard Polwhele's 1798 poem *The Unsex'd Females*, which denounces Helen Maria Williams, author of the widely read political commentary *Letters from France*, for being 'a politician'. Polwhele's use of this term is worth noting, for, since women could not stand for election and so be 'politicians' in our present-day sense, what Polwhele means is a political commentator, 'an intemperate advocate for Gallic licentiousness'.[19] As an 'advocate' for a political position, Williams has become a 'politician'. These pressures exerted by conservative reaction impacted particularly on women travel writers both because the genre had been associated with the French sympathisers Williams and Wollstonecraft, freshly infamous owing to the publication of Godwin's *Memoirs*, and also because travel books conventionally took up the topic of 'national manners', meditations often political in nature. Within this set of pressures, the cause of 'the family' remained ideologically unexceptionable. Many women thought their own status and safety and those of their families were threatened by the French Revolutionaries, who had destroyed Marie Antoinette and her family, along with Louis XVI, and who had guillotined numerous female and not just male victims.[20] To be pro-family was to be patriotic, anti-French.

Thus, invoking explicit domestic roles opened a way to comment safely on politics. Wollstonecraft astutely delineates the dangers of failing to invoke such domestic roles. Travelling to Scandinavia in 1795, she records that, after a discussion of the French Revolution, her Norwegian host 'told me bluntly that I was a woman of observation, for I asked him *men's questions*' (Wollstonecraft's emphasis). She minimises this danger in her enterprise as a whole by foregrounding her domestic role as Fanny's mother, creating a persona of sensibility that encompasses both politics and family.[21] Similarly, novelist Charlotte Smith asserts women's right to discourse on politics by virtue of their domestic relationships to the men who, she seems to concede, were most deeply affected: 'Women, it is said, have no business with politics ... Have they no interest in the scenes acting around them, in which they have fathers, brothers, husbands, sons, or friends engaged?'[22] In Smith's formulation, women do have political standing, but only under the aegis of the domestic – that is, they have standing as daughters, sisters, wives, mothers, or friends, but not as 'women', a category that is domestically unmarked. Finally, travel writer Lady Morgan proposed a domesticated version of politics that women can legitimately claim, even in an ideologically conservative system: 'Politics can never be a woman's science, but patriotism must naturally be a woman's sentiment.'[23] By splitting these hairs between 'politics' and 'patriotism', Morgan redefines a slice of political response 'properly' located within the feminine realm of 'sentiment'. Thus, skilful invocation of their conformity to domestic roles enabled women to gain a hearing for their political views.

The occupation of a nurse

The full title of Starke's travel book is florid in a manner typical of the day: *Letters from Italy, between the years 1792 and 1798, containing a view of the Revolutions in that Country, from the Capture of Nice by the French Republic to the Expulsion of Pius VI from the Ecclesiastical State: Likewise pointing out the matchless Works of Art which still embellish Pisa, Florence, Siena, Rome, Naples, Bologna, Venice, &c. with Instructions for the Use of Invalids and Families who may not choose to incur the Expence attendant upon travelling with a Courier.* The fluctuations of the title reveal Starke's fecundity in proposing justifications for her efforts: it is worthwhile because of its eyewitness journalism ('containing a view of the Revolutions in that Country'), because of its up-to-date gallery catalogues ('pointing out the matchless Works of Art'), and because it offers the advice and example of the nurse who wrote it ('with Instructions for the Use of Invalids and Families'). The book itself delivers the wide repertoire of roles the title promises. It is a two-decker, comprising an epistolary memoir of eye-witness journalism about 200 pages long, recounting Starke's activities during Napoleon's Italian campaign from 1792 to 1797. The memoir is followed by a guidebook, about 200 pages of which fill the rest of the first volume and 400 pages that make up the second, full of advice in the imperative mood that removes the travel writer from the scene. Starke's *Letters*, like Williams's, bear few traces of a personal correspondence to a friend; instead, they read like journalistic dispatches, spaced at intervals of about one year.[24] Although the roles of journalist, art critic, and nurse seem merely accretive in the title, I shall show here the interdependence of 'nurse' and 'politician' in Polwhele's sense (leaving aside the role of art critic), showing that Starke weaves the two roles together in order that the domestic propriety of the occupation of a nurse can blunt the transgressive potential of a 'politician'.

It was such great journalistic material that, at first glance, one would not think Starke needed any justification for her telling it other than the fact she was there. Starke observed in person or knew by first-hand report the details of one of the most exciting (and, for Britons, alarming) historical events of her time: the French Directory's Army of Italy, led by Napoleon, won a stunning series of victories in the First Italian campaign, from March 1796 until October 1797, culminating in the Treaty of Campo Formio (October 1797) by which Napoleon forced Austria to cede Belgium to France, to allow French occupation of the Rhine, and to recognise the French satellite republics in Italy, the Ligurian and the Cisalpine Republics. Starke calls these events 'the most rapid and brilliant conquests ever gained in so short a period, either by ancient or modern Warriors'.[25] Increasing the value of Starke's scoop, by the time she published *Letters from Italy* in 1800, Napoleon's star had risen even further, as he returned from Egypt to Paris in November of 1799 to declare himself First Consul and solidified his power in Italy during the rapid Second Italian Campaign, crowned by his victory at Marengo, June 1800, that led to further concessions from the Austrians and thus to the collapse of the Second Coalition and William Pitt's resignation as Prime Minister. Starke's experiences in Italy gave her with a journalistic 'scoop', a close-up look at the man who, in 1800, dominated much of Europe and the world. And given this extraordinary opportunity, Starke does indeed preface her material by playing the 'eye-witness' card:

> Having witnessed the first entrance of the French into Italy, resided in Tuscany when they seized Leghorn and endeavoured to revolutionize Florence, and having been at Rome in March 1797, when they threatened to overthrow the Papal Government, and in February

1798, when that threat was realized, I am tempted to give such a short account of these transactions as Persons on the spot only are capable of describing.[26]

The word 'tempted' is revealing here in terms of Starke's positioning herself properly in response to the extraordinary luck of being 'on the spot' at these momentous events. Starke's self-positioning as a nurse to a sick relative, devoting '[her] time and thoughts … [to] endeavours to mitigate the sufferings of those most dear to [her]' justified her being on the scene for Napoleon's Italian campaign.[27] For public consumption, at least, Starke speaks of the role of 'politician' as a 'temptation' against decorum and silence. At this tricky juncture, Starke counters the appearance of failing in her duty to silence by invoking the 'higher' duty, that of a nurse, to which she has been faithful:

> I presume not to imagine myself correct in every thing which I have advanced. The occupation of a Nurse has often prevented me from obtaining accurate knowledge on points worthy of minute investigation. Nevertheless, general outlines will sometimes convey tolerably just ideas of a country, even though the picture be not shaded by a Master's hand.[28]

'The occupation of a nurse' here does multiple service. Starke's travels themselves – a potentially transgressive activity in the light of the Grand Tour – are justified by her invalid relative's needs and so become authorised by the higher duty of nursing and domestic obligation. Starke's *writing* about her travels is justified by her demoting the endeavour itself as merely 'general outlines' and not the work of a 'Master'. Starke then brilliantly makes a virtue out of any faults the reader might find. Nursing has prevented her from 'obtaining accurate information on points worthy of minute investigation'. Thus, if the reader sees a factual error, at the same time that the error proves Starke faulty as a journalist it simultaneously proves her virtuous as a nurse. In this way Starke has used the occupation of a nurse to perform a virtuosic variation on the double bind so frequently hindering women writers, crafting in 'nurse' the role by which all strengths *and all weaknesses* of the writing redound to her credit.

Even more creatively, Starke justifies her undertaking of *writing* about her travels by expanding the role of nurse to the role of *adviser* to nurses of other invalids. Starke writes, 'hence, I trust, that the little knowledge I have been able to collect may so far inform Travellers, as to guard them against those serious inconveniences which too generally retard, and unfrequently prevent, the recovery of consumptive persons', continuing in this vein: 'I am likewise encouraged by a hope of being serviceable to those of my Countrymen, who, in consequence of pulmonary complaints, are compelled to exchange their native soil for the renovating sun of Italy.'[29] Once again, Starke invokes patriotic duty, the 'hope of being serviceable to ... my Countrymen', though this time as a nurse, not as an eyewitness, as overriding the convention of feminine self-effacement.

Starke's itinerary and what we can infer about the health regimen of her relative confirm her sense that her experience is authoritative because it is typical. Her itinerary includes destinations associated with travel for health (Nice on the Riviera and the Bay of Naples).[30] Starke's family's residence at Nice registers its new importance among invalid British travellers. Although Tobias Smollett provides an early account of numerous tubercular and asthmatic patients at Nice in the 1760s,[31] locations on the Riviera did not replace Spa and Aachen in popularity until the 1780s, when the civil wars in the Netherlands and Belgium made access to Germany difficult. Nice soon afterwards surpassed Montpellier in its cachet for Britons.[32] Starke's sojourn there, in 1792, thus occurred just after the fashion had definitively changed in Nice's favour.

Similarly, Starke's family situation reflects the current state of treatment of 'consumption', a general term used in the 1790s mostly for pulmonary complaints of various causes, but sometimes for any disease that seemed to 'consume' or 'devour' the patient, such as diabetes or cancer.[33] Since consumption was thought to be hereditary, not infectious (until Robert Koch discovered the tubercular bacilli in the 1880s), quarantine was not used to shield family members. Physicians stressed change of climate as a treatment, prescribing sea air as especially salubrious. A warmer climate, too, was a standard prescription (as the more famous example of Keats attests). All in all, Starke had considerable reason for thinking her experience as a nurse normative for such cases and for concluding that her advice might be valuable.

The metaphoric power of Starke's positioning herself in the occupation of a nurse saturates other parts of the travel book beyond the Preface, endowing Starke's political and religious concerns with the urgency of matters of public health. The binary opposition 'clean/dirty' and its variant, 'healthy/sick', thus informs Starke's political commentary, making her a nurse of national morals – much like Kelly's professional champion of national destiny – as well as the nurse of a consumptive relative. Throughout the book, Starke has been placed in a religious/political dilemma. As a staunch Anglican, she despises the Italian Catholics because of their 'superstition' and 'bigotry', while hating the atheist French for their immoral, freethinking views. Thus any military confrontation between the French and the Italians leaves Starke to judge which side she dislikes the least.[34] This tension is finally brought to a metaphoric resolution, if not a conceptual one, in the section most explicitly concerned with health, the conclusion to Starke's memoir, the disturbing letters datelined from Rome.

The anti-catholicism in Starke's religious and political persuasion prompts her to warn her readers of the dangers of Rome, in her role as nurse, by an extended comparison of Rome to a sewer. She laments that 'Rome has suffered so much from the frequent ravages of Barbarians' and continues:

> The stupendous common-sewers, through which the offal of Rome was conveyed into the Cloaca-maxima, are many of them choaked up, and even the Cloaca-maxima itself is in bad order; this causes pestilential air; and workmen who, by digging deep, have opened apertures to the above-mentioned common-sewers, not unfrequently have lost their lives from the putrid effluvia.[35]

She describes the sewers for nearly four pages (!), concluding the 'approach to Rome' section by conceding, without much conviction, that Rome is 'the most magnificent city of Europe'.[36] Starke's literal role as nurse emerges here, as she notes that the 'putrid effluvia' endanger the Italian workmen and the 'pestilential air' puts the invalid British traveller at risk. But the powerful emotional investment suggests that here Starke expands the role of nurse to a moral meaning as well, using the British idea of dirty Italy to symbolise the corruption of the Papacy that Napoleon is about to conquer. This idea of dirty Italy varied in intensity, sometimes evoking only earthen dirt and sometimes, as in Smollett and Starke, evoking faeces. Charlotte Eaton, in *Rome in the Nineteenth Century* (1821), wrote that 'wherever the Catholic religion is established, I have uniformly observed indolence, with its concomitants, dirt and beggary, to prevail; and the more Catholic is the place, the more they abound', thus using earthen dirt to suggest poverty.[37] This stereotype served British nationalism, Colley argues, because characterising 'Catholic countries as poverty-ridden was also a way of claiming that only Protestants could enjoy a true and lasting prosperity'.[38] In a travel anecdote from the early eighteenth century, a Briton implicitly equates Roman Catholicism with faeces: the traveller defaecates in a cathedral to pull a practical joke. He takes his faeces to the priest as a sign that the cathedral's patron saint had cured him from a constipation, and the reader is intended to be regaled by the credulity of the superstitious priests who take him at his word.[39] While the trope of Italian dirt is frequently invoked, the intenser, faecal version is rarer. Starke's warning against literal sewers in her purview as a nurse takes on metaphoric and ideological

significance as the Protestant Briton's response to poor, dirty Catholic Italy
and corrupt, dirty Roman Catholicism.

Most travel books on Italy treat the approach to Rome rapturously, with
excitement and reverence. Goethe, travelling in 1783, exemplifies this idea-
lising trend in *Italian Journey*:

> for the last few years this was becoming an illness, which could only
> be cured by the sight and presence of Rome ... Yes, I have finally
> arrived in this city, the capital of the world ... Now I am here and
> calm – calmed, it would seem, for the rest of my life. For it may
> well be said that a new life begins when something previously known
> inside and out, but still only in parts, is beheld in its entirety.[40]

Here the over-valuing tendency of the idealised split is evident: for Goethe,
arrival in Rome cures illness, endows new life, and reveals complete
knowledge – all metaphors which compare it to conversion in Christian
tradition. In a similarly rapturous vein Samuel Rogers (popular author of
Italy and *The Pleasures of Memory*, who was offered the laureateship in 1850)
writes:

> I am in Rome! Oft as the morning-ray
> Visits these eyes, waking at once I cry,
> Whence this excess of joy? What has befallen me?
> And from within a thrilling voice replies,
> Thou art in Rome![41]

The almost religious ecstasy in approaching Rome exemplified in Goethe
and Rogers tells only half the story of a split response to Rome. The
repressed negative of the rapture also has literary precedent. Dante
denounced the 'usurper', Pope Boniface VIII, as one who has made the
burial-ground of St Peter (i.e. Rome) a 'cloaca' or sewer.[42] And Smollett
mentions the dirt and sewers of Rome in his *Travels through France and
Italy* (1766). Though the Roman fountains '[pour] forth prodigious quan-
tities of cool, delicious water', 'Their streets, and even their palaces, are
disgraced with filth'.[43] In addition to this revulsion to contemporary Italians,
Smollett recounts an equally revolting fact about classical Rome, that its
inhabitants threw the bodies of criminals and suicides into the Cloaca
Maxima.[44] Smollett's version of the 'filth of Rome' encompasses both
classical and contemporary elements. Thus literary history provided precedent for both rapture and revulsion in the approach to Rome.

The cultural precedents of portraying Rome as ideal and as filthy attest
to the extremity that usually accompanies the projection of otherness.
Starke's choice of the darker of these two alternatives – Italy as sewer –

suggests that, even under the pressure of the immediate events of the 1790s, British convictions remained unshaken about the fundamentally Protestant nature of their own nation and about the outlandishness of Catholicism and its 'superstition'. Starke, speaking in her persona as the public-health nurse of British nationhood in the 1790s, makes clear that the more serious threat to her nation is embodied in the Italians' religion than in the French republic's new brand of politics. Present-day critics may conclude, in part from this retrieval of Starke's effort, that the 'conservative' politics practised by some British women allocated a more important role to religion than we have yet granted it.[45]

Notes

1 See Jeanne Moskal, 'Napoleon, Nationalism, and the Politics of Religion in Mariana Starke's *Letters from Italy*', in Kari Lokke and Adriana Craciun, eds, *Rebellious Hearts: Women Writers and the French Revolution* (Albany, forthcoming); and 'English National Identity in Mariana Starke's "The Sword of Peace": India, Abolition, and the Rights of Women', in Catherine B. Burroughs, ed., *Women in British Romantic Theatre: Drama, Performance, and Society* (Cambridge, forthcoming).

2 See Gary Kelly, *Women, Writing, and Revolution, 1790–1827* (Oxford, 1993). Beth Kowaleski-Wallace, *Their Fathers' Daughters: Hannah More, Maria Edgeworth, and Patriarchal Complicity* (London and New York, 1991), and Margaret J. M. Ezell, *Writing Women's Literary History* (Baltimore, 1993), provide examples of scholarship that faces this problem. On nationalism, see especially Gerald Newman, *The Rise of English Nationalism* (New York, 1987), and Linda Colley, *Britons: Forging the Nation 1707–1837* (New Haven, 1992).

3 *Women, Writing, and Revolution*, 21.

4 Cf. J. D. Reuss, *Alphabetical Register of all the Authors actually living in Great Britain ...* (Berlin, 1804), part 2, 350. For Starke's publication history in French, see J.-M. Querard, *La France littéraire*, 12 vols (Paris, 1838), 9: 257.

5 See *DNB* s.v. 'Starke'; and Syvanus Urban, *The Gentleman's Magazine* n.s. 10 (July–Dec. 1838), 111. The four present-day discussions of Starke occur in Jane Robinson, *Wayward Women: A Guide to Women Travellers* (Oxford, 1990), 194–5; Francis Haskell, *Rediscoveries in Art* (Ithaca, 1976), 107–8; Claire Richter Sherman and Adele M. Holcomb, eds, *Women as Interpreters of the Visual Arts, 1820–1979* (Westport, 1981), 10–17; and Shirley Foster, *Across New Worlds: Nineteenth-Century Women Travellers and Their Writings* (New York, 1990), *passim*.

6 Mariana Starke, *Letters from Italy, between the years 1792 and 1798, containing a view of the Revolutions in that Country, from the Capture of Nice by the French Republic to the Expulsion of Pius VI*, 2 vols (London, 1800), 1: 338. I have used the texts *The Sword of Peace; or, a Voyage of Love; a Comedy in Five Acts* (London, 1789); *The Widow of Malabar*, 3rd edn (London, 1791); *The Tour-*

nament, a tragedy; imitated from the celebrated German drama, entitled Agnes Bernauer (New York, 1803); and *The Beauties of Carlo-Maria Maggi Paraphrased* (Exeter, 1811). For Starke's other works, I have retained Starke's punctuation but not her capitalisation and italics.

7 I had reached my conclusion about Starke's priority independently when I discovered the same conclusion in Francis Haskell's *Rediscoveries in Art*.

8 *Letters*, 1: 252–8.

9 Mary Shelley, *Rambles in Germany and Italy*, in Jeanne Moskal, ed., *Travel Writing*, vol. 8 of *The Novels and Selected Works of Mary Shelley*, general ed. Nora Crook, with Pamela Clemit (London, 1996), 370n.

10 This number includes both handbooks and travellers' phrase-books, according to James Buzard, *The Beaten Track: European Tourism, Literature, and the Ways to 'Culture', 1800–1918* (Oxford, 1993), 72.

11 John Murray III, 'The Origin and History of Murray's Handbooks for Travellers', reprinted as chapter 2 in John Murray IV, *John Murray III, 1808–1892: A Brief Memoir* (London, 1919), 41. The copy I have consulted bears the printed reference '*Murray's Magazine* 1887' for the first appearance of this article, which date has been corrected in an unknown hand to 'Nov 1889'. Since the copy I consulted was the publisher's file copy of the John Murray Company, now owned by the Rare Book Collection of the University of North Carolina at Chapel Hill, this handwritten note may be authoritative, but at this writing I have not been able to verify the date.

12 *Ibid.*, 40.

13 *Notes and Queries*, 2nd series, 3 (1857), 87.

14 See Eric J. Leed, *The Mind of the Traveler: From Gilgamesh to Global Tourism* (New York, 1991); and Karen R. Lawrence, *Penelope Voyages: Women and Travel in the British Literary Tradition* (London and Ithaca, 1994). More general feminist works underlying this approach are: Mary Poovey, *The Proper Lady and the Woman Writer: Style as Ideology in Mary Wollstonecraft, Jane Austen, and Mary Shelley* (Baltimore, 1984); and Sandra M. Gilbert and Susan Gubar, *The Madwoman in the Attic: The Woman Writer and the Nineteenth-Century Literary Imagination* (London and New Haven, 1979).

15 Georges Van Den Abbeele, *Travel as Metaphor: From Montaigne to Rousseau* (Minneapolis, 1992), xxv–xxvi; and Janet Wolff, *Resident Alien: Feminist Cultural Criticism* (New Haven, 1995), 115–34. The phrase 'technologies of gender' was coined by Teresa de Lauretis in her book by that name (Bloomington, 1987).

16 Elizabeth A. Bohls, *Women Travel Writers and the Language of Aesthetics, 1716–1818* (Cambridge, 1995); Sara Mills, *Discourses of Difference: An Analysis of Women's Travel Writing and Colonialism* (London and New York, 1991), 21.

17 Jeremy Black, *The British and the Grand Tour* (London and Sydney, 1985), 246.

18 James Fordyce, *Sermons to Young Women*, 2 vols (London, 1766), 1: 271–2.

19 Richard Polwhele, *The Unsex'd Females* (London, 1798), 19n.

20 Colley, *Britons*, 255.

21 Mary Wollstonecraft, *Letters from Norway*, in Janet Todd and Marilyn Butler, eds, *The Works of Mary Wollstonecraft*, 7 vols (London, 1989), 4: 248. See Jeanne Moskal, 'The Picturesque and the Affectionate in Wollstonecraft's *Letters from Norway*', *Modern Language Quarterly* 52: 3 (1991), 263–94.

22 Charlotte Turner Smith, *Desmond, a Novel*, 3 vols (London, 1792), 1: iii–iv.

23 Sydney Owenson, Lady Morgan, quoted in William Fitzpatrick, *The Friends, Foes, and Adventures of Lady Morgan* (Dublin, 1959), 49. On this matter I am indebted to conversations with Ina Ferris and to her paper 'Writing on the Border: The National Tale, Female Writing, and the Public Sphere', delivered at the North American Society for the Study of Romanticism conference in August 1993. See also Jeanne Moskal, 'Gender, Nationality, and Textual Authority in Lady Morgan's Travel Books', in Paula R. Feldman and Theresa M. Kelley, eds, *Romantic Women Writers: Voices and Countervoices* (Hanover, 1994), 256–86 and 298–302.

24 For the political implications of epistolary genres in the Romantic period, see Mary A. Favret, *Romantic Correspondence: Women, Politics, and the Fiction of Letters* (Cambridge, 1993).

25 *Letters*, 1: 153.

26 *Ibid.*, 1: iii.

27 *Ibid.*, 1: v.

28 *Ibid.*, 1: vi.

29 *Ibid.*, 1: vi, v.

30 Black, *The British and the Grand Tour*, 128.

31 Tobias Smollett, *Travels through France and Italy* (1766), ed. Frank Felsenstein (London and New York, 1979), 195–6.

32 Black, *The British and the Grand Tour*, 127.

33 René and Jean Dubos, *The White Plague: Tuberculosis, Man, and Society* (New Brunswick, 1987), 20–3, 72.

34 I develop this analysis in 'Napoleon, Nationalism, and the Politics of Religion'.

35 *Letters*, 1: 330–1.

36 *Ibid.*, 1: 335.

37 Charlotte Waldie Eaton, *Rome in the Nineteenth Century* (1821), 4th edn, 3 vols (Edinburgh, 1826), 3: 294. See Mary Shelley's rejoinder in *Rambles*, 353.

38 *Britons*, 35.

39 Quoted in Black, *The British and the Grand Tour*, 193–4, and in Colley, *Britons*, 36.

40 Johann Wolfgang von Goethe, *Italienische Reise* (1816), trans. as *Italian Journey* by Robert R. Heitner, ed. Thomas P. Saine (New York, 1990), 103–4.

41 Samuel Rogers, 'Rome', in *Italy, A Poem* (London, 1836), 141–2.

42 Dante, *Paradiso*, canto 27, l. 25.

43 Smollett, *Travels*, 253.

44 *Ibid.*, 255 and 280.

45 The author thanks Terry Bowers, Catherine Burroughs, Stuart Curran, Paola Frascari, Madelyn Gutwirth, Gary Handwerk, William Keach, Gary Kelly,

Victoria Kirkham, Melissa Moorehead, Marjean Purinton and Michele Strong-Irwin for their comments on earlier versions of this chapter; Christine Bowes, RN, Watson Bowes, MD, and Keith Wailoo for medical information; Sharon L. Jowell for translating from the French; and Tamara Graham-Voelker, Tim Sadenwasser and Shelley Wunder Smith for their research assistance. Thanks also to the Rare Book Collection of the University of North Carolina at Chapel Hill.

Spas and salutary landscapes: the geography of health in Mary Shelley's *Rambles in Germany and Italy*

Beth Dolan Kautz

> Though absent long,
> These forms of beauty have not been to me,
> As is a landscape to a blind man's eye:
> But oft, in lonely rooms, and mid the din
> Of towns and cities, I have owed to them,
> In hours of weariness, sensations sweet,
> Felt in the blood, and felt along the heart,
> And passing even into my purer mind
> With tranquil restoration.

In this familiar passage from 'Tintern Abbey', William Wordsworth describes a remembered landscape's influence on the body and mind.[1] Recreating the landscape inspires 'sensations sweet', felt quite physically 'in the blood', and 'along the heart'. The organ and substance Wordsworth names – heart and blood – have rich metaphorical significance. If we momentarily ignore the metaphors and interpret the words literally, though, Wordsworth implies that the landscape can act on the body for physical and mental healing. In this chapter, I explore the last work of the second-generation Romantic writer Mary Wollstonecraft Shelley, who explicitly describes the healing power she finds in the interplay between the body and the landscape. Like Wordsworth, Mary Shelley posits a correlation between what the eye consumes and how the healthy mind functions, a kind of salutary aesthetics. Though Mary Shelley's epistolary travel narrative, *Rambles in Germany and Italy, in 1840, 1842 and 1843* (1844), addresses many topics – including politics, Continental art, manners, history, and the details of travel – I focus on her search for health.[2]

In *Rambles*, Mary Shelley describes two trips to the Continent, both taken to further her son's education and to recover from her own illness.

Mary Shelley hoped to restore her health in Germany's spas and in Italy's salubrious climate. She includes in *Rambles* accounts of the two types of treatment that she explored on these trips – the institutional medicine she encountered in her visits to Germany's spas and the salutary landscape she enjoyed both at the spas and while travelling. Ultimately, Mary Shelley champions the balm derived from viewing picturesque landscape over the prescriptive spa regimen. Her position as a late Romantic writer and female patient cultivates both her disenchantment with the German spas and her desire to heal herself in the picturesque landscape.

The 1840 and 1842 trips both began in the midst of emotional strain and illness. Prior to her 1840 trip, Mary Shelley had suffered from depression, her condition exacerbated by editing Percy Bysshe Shelley's complete works. On 12 February 1839, while editing Volume II of the *Works*, and while also receiving criticism for her revisions of *Queen Mab* in Volume I, she speculated: 'I almost think that my present occupation will end in a fit of illness.'[3] Later in the spring of 1839, a particularly bad bout of a recurring nervous illness characterised by 'weakness and languor' prevented her from writing at all.[4] As she prepared to leave on the 1840 journey, Mary Shelley described herself during the preceding sixteen months as 'long oppressed by care, disappointment & ill health – which all have combined to depress and irritate me'.[5] The 1842 journey followed a similar period of depression and chronic headaches. In addition, she received disappointing news about her much-reduced inheritance from Shelley shortly before leaving.[6] In the first letter of *Rambles*, Mary Shelley expressed the hope that 'travelling will cure all', more specifically that her 'mind will ... renew the outworn and tattered garments in which it has long been clothed'.[7] Given her condition, Mary Shelley sought spas that specialised in nervous illness.

German spas

Although Continental travel and visits to health resorts were practices common to the Shelley circle, Mary Shelley had never before visited a German spa.[8] She notes that Dr A. B. Granville's 1837 travel guide, *The Spas of Germany*, inspired her first visit: 'Doctor Granville's book extended our acquaintance with the spas of Germany; and, in particular, gave reputation to those situated in Bavaria.'[9] Mary Shelley seems to have chosen spas based in part on Dr Granville's advice. In 1842 she visited two spas – Brukenau and Brocklet – whose waters Granville claimed would 'restore lost vigour, or impart a new one to a diseased constitution'.[10] According to Granville, the waters at the Kissingen spa, where Mary Shelley also visited in 1842, were useful in the treatment of chronic rather than acute or febrile illness, and were particularly helpful for 'female complaints'. Although she relied on Granville's advice initially, Mary Shelley's assessment of the spa experience differs radically from his account of spa healing. This variation arises not only from generic differences but also from differing constructions of medical authority, or, more specifically, opposing responses to the value of physician regulation of patients' behaviour.

The surface structures of Granville's guide and Mary Shelley's narrative reveal where each writer locates authority. Granville's text exudes a Victorian regard for order, political authority, and careful documentation. He shows respect for Germany's regional rulers by organising the spas in his guide-book into four 'geographical groups', composed of states in the German Confederacy, established by the 1815 Congress of Vienna: the Baden and Württemberg spas, the Salzburghian spas (Tyrol), the Bohemian spas, and the Bavarian and Nassau spas. He advises his reader that he could have organised the book by the illnesses treated at each spa, but chose instead to focus on regions. His deference to the political anatomy of German geography anticipates his recommendation that spa-goers should submit themselves to the medical 'map' that spa doctors impose on their patients' bodies.

In characteristically Romantic fashion, Mary Shelley structures her text in deference to what might be called an internal authority. She presents her narrative as an informal and subjective account of her 'rambles' on the Continent. The text, based on letters to her stepsister Claire Clairmont, is arranged chronologically to recreate her journey. The itinerary itself is shaped by personal relationships. Some cities visited fulfil her desire for Percy Florence Shelley to experience a version of the Grand Tour, while others teem with memories of the deceased – Percy Bysshe Shelley, and the other Shelley children Clara and William. While Granville surveys the German spas through a masculinised national and institutional lens, Mary Shelley views them through the lens of a Romantic ideology of organicism and individual authority.

Granville endorses the spa physician's authority by repeatedly empha-sising the dangers of taking the waters without correct medical supervision. In the preface he discusses English doctors' ignorance of and prejudice against the German spas, outlining the inaccuracies of their recommen-dations. He describes the complexities of choosing a spa appropriate for a specific illness, distinguishes among a dizzying variety of mineral waters based on chemical composition, and asserts that individual patients may react differently to the waters. In short, without the doctor's guidance through this maze of geographical, chemical, and medical factors, taking the waters is a risky proposition: 'It scarcely need be stated ... that mineral waters should be used not only in accordance with the advice (and only with it) of a physician well acquainted with their nature and effect; but also agreeably to the long-established rules that exist at all the Spas (both of diet and regimen) for their administration or application.'[11] The spa doctor's authority is broad and deep – reaching into all aspects of the patient's daily life, and rooted in 'long-established' traditions at the spas.

As Granville indicates in his preface, the spa physicians believed the spa regimen's success depended on minute regulation of behaviour: 'Mineral water should be drunk like other liquids; not gulped down in a hurry, for the sake of the gas or any other reason ... The warm water should be sipped out of the glass – the cold water should be drunk slowly, and at several draughts.' Though extraodinarily detailed and prescriptive, Granville's recommendations contain confusing, conflicting absolutes. For example, he asserts that 'gentle exercise between each glass of water is *necessary*', yet, he adds, patients who do not usually walk before breakfast do not have to follow this rule, 'for fatigue is the very *worst* concomitant of water-drinking'.[12] One clearly needs a doctor's guidance to navigate the complexities of spa life.

Entering the care of one of the Kissingen spa physicians in June 1842, Mary Shelley finds Granville's model of authoritarian medical supervision confirmed.[13] At first she expresses hope for the spa's healing waters. Echoing Granville's preface and its warnings, she believes the mineral waters 'to be very conducive to the restoration of health; but they must only be taken under a physician's superintendence, as it is dangerous to play with them'. Even when the cure is most disagreeable, she voices her 'great faith in the advantages that accrue'.[14] In her initial portrayal of the spa treatment, Mary Shelley enthusiastically accepts the medical authority endorsed by Granville.

After three weeks at Kissingen, though, she grows frustrated with the spa physicians' regulation of her daily life. She reports that the Kissingen doctors closely monitor their patients' environment to regulate the influences on both mind and body: 'the physicians here discountenance every sort of excitement, and their *malades* are very obedient'. Mary Shelley notices that no one dances in the ballroom: 'The cause is the despotic decree of the triumvirate of doctors ... who maintain dancing to be absolutely incompatible with drinking the waters'. The doctors' authority also reaches into the family structure: 'This is another decree of the physicians: children are prohibited, because the mind must enjoy perfect repose, and children are apt to create disturbance in the hearts of tender parents.'[15] The physicians ignore the diversions and delight of being with children, taking into account only their potential disruptiveness. Time and space, usually seen as private, are subject to medical control.

The regulation of diet is perhaps the most striking example of the spa doctors' control over their patients' lives. Granville concludes his preface with an 'alphabetical list of articles of food proper and improper for the patients' undergoing spa treatment.[16] Mary Shelley expresses frustration with the limited diet: 'So many things are supposed to disagree with the waters, that not only everything substantial, but also butter, fruit, tea, coffee and milk are prohibited.'[17] In the spa, negations and denials of certain foods help to generate one's identity as a 'good' patient, as a productive spa-goer. Again, though, the patient is dependent on the doctor for the rules. Although Granville asserts that dietary regulations are a 'long-established' tradition, the specific rules seem to change daily, requiring a sign to be posted in the Kissingen dining hall listing 'the articles of forbidden diet'.[18]

Some of the restrictions the doctors placed on spa-goers reflect medical theories about the influence of various stimulants on an individual's health. For example, the physician John Brown asserts that either an excess or a lack of excitability causes illness, with stimulants affecting individuals in response to their baseline tendency toward excitability.[19] Stimulants include heat, exercise, electricity, opium, alcohol, various kinds of food, and 'violent passions of the mind'.[20] In part, the spa doctors regulate the activity of their ill patients to restore in them a healthy balance between the individual's physical system and the environment. None the less, many of the spa rules seem to exceed medical justification, reflecting instead the influence of politics.

In anticipation of Foucault's argument that modern institutional control is implicitly state control, Mary Shelley explains the apparent arbitrariness of the spa rules by establishing their connection to political authority: 'The King of Bavaria is so afraid that his medicinal waters may fall into disrepute if the drinkers should eat what disagrees with them, that we only eat what he, in conjunction with a triumvirate of doctors, is pleased to allow us'.[21] With the word 'triumvirate', Mary Shelley recalls one of the most powerful political structures in Western history – the Roman Empire. Far from obscuring the connection between medical and state authority, Granville boasts in the second edition of *The German Spas* that the first edition was praised both by spa doctors and by the sovereigns of several German states. As a practising physician at Kissingen, Granville augments his power by aligning himself with state authority. In stark contrast, Mary Shelley resists what she began to see as the tyranny of the state over the individual.

She is particularly critical of state intrusion into medical treatment and private life. The doctors seem to act as tentacles of the Bavarian King's patriarchal rule, issuing 'decrees' that exclude children and control diet, thus usurping two domains generally supervised by women. Mary Shelley wonders that the doctors do not behave even more like dictators: 'It is surprising that, to forward the cure, all letters are not opened first by the doctors, and not delivered if they contain any disagreeable news ... Kissingen will not be perfect, until the post is put under medical *surveillance.*' [22] Mary Shelley's speculation gains significance in light of her own experience with postal surveillance. On the previous trip in 1840, she was delayed in Milan waiting for letters containing necessary travel money; the letters were probably being held for inspection by local government authorities. [23] In the narrative, only a few pages separate her 1840 account of postal surveillance and the comparison between the spa doctors and the despotic government at Kissingen in 1842. Mary Shelley's statement, then, may be interpreted as a sharp criticism of the intrusive authority exercised by the spa doctors, a resistance to medicine practised as surveillance.

Mary Shelley uses military images to draw another parallel between state power and medical authority. She observes her fellow patients' deference to the medical regulation of their bodies, using words that connote the minute physical regulation of soldiers. She observes the synchronicity of their movement: 'All the Germans get up at four, and *parade* the gardens to drink the waters till nearly eight; I contrive to get there soon after five.' One meaning of the verb 'parade' is to move as a regulated group, as military troops might parade. This military vocabulary pervades Mary Shelley's descriptions of her fellow spa-goers: 'we are all in the midst of a general cure of a *regiment* of sick people'. [24] As Foucault argues, and Mary Shelley here observes, the modernisation of the state, including military and medical institutions, exerts control over the individual body. Mary Shelley criticises the spa regimen for regulating bodies as if they were machines, repairable by applying a kind of formula. She rejects the industrial age's treatment of the body, relying instead upon a more Romantic understanding of the body as an organically organised entity, structured by internal, or 'natural', power, rather than external institutional power.

Though Granville, like Mary Shelley, relies on a discourse that privileges the 'natural' as the location of healing, his sense of the 'natural' differs greatly from hers. Despite the mechanistic regulation of diet and activity, and the professed need to consult a physician interpreter of the mineral waters, Granville positions the German spas as authentic, natural healing sites. He promises his readers that, upon visiting the German spas, 'you will have reason to rejoice that you exchanged art for nature'. [25] Granville seeks to naturalise the structures of authority in which he is so deeply invested. In Granville's view, medical and political authority are naturally appropriate, even necessary, for transmitting the power of the earth through the human body.

Healing in the landscape

Like Granville, Mary Shelley is interested in deploying the earth's power for human healing. Characteristically though, she depends on her own trained perception, rather than on medical regimen. While Mary Shelley resists the doctors' efforts to protect their patients from every possible stimulus, the same concept of excitability, discussed above, underlies her belief in the therapeutic effect of aesthetic scenes. In other words, Mary Shelley suggests that the stimulation derived from viewing picturesque scenes can positively influence an individual's health. In her account of the 1840 visit to Baden-Baden, Mary Shelley portrays the picturesque excursions often available at spas as more crucial to health than the official spa treatments. However, she notes that most of her fellow spa-goers seem uninterested in exploring the countryside: 'to wander, and ramble, and discover new scenes does not form a portion of their amusements; and yet this is the only real one to be found in such a place'.[26] The words 'ramble' and 'wander' connote a less purposeful, less predictable, more leisurely progression than the step-by-step spa regimen. Mary Shelley suggests that healing at the spas may result not just from a formula for healing but from the holistic effect of the spa setting.

Granville discounts holistic possibilities, noting that travel, a vacation from work and a change of air, are not responsible for one-tenth of the cure.[27] However, medical authors continued to raise the issue throughout the nineteenth century. Dr Julius Braun argues in 1875 that the successful spa *cur* resulted from multiple causes, including 'travelling, country and mountain life, air, and bodily exercise'.[28] Although travel to the spa, walking excursions, landscape viewing, and mountain air were not the focus of the spa regimen, these activities may have contributed to the spa-goers' recovery. In her search for health Mary Shelley certainly finds that the official spa treatment alone is not effective.

Distressed by the powerlessness she feels as a patient and disappointed with her worsening health at the end of the spa regimen in Kissingen, Mary Shelley longs for a change of location. The spa regimen encourages walks, but Mary Shelley misses the healing scenery she has encountered earlier in the trip: 'I am heartily tired of the waters ... and the surrounding scenery is by no means interesting enough to *compensate* for our disagreeable style of life.' Mary Shelley's portrayal of the scenery as 'compensation' for her boredom and frustration with the treatment sets up a contrast between spa healing and picturesque healing. Thus, she begins to emphasise the picturesque setting of spas – formerly a kind of 'added attraction' – as the most crucial element of healing. She compares the baths of Brukenau, the spa the group visits next, with Kissingen in terms of the picturesque setting: 'above all, the country around was, without being striking from crag and precipice, far more picturesque than at Kissingen'.[29] By comparing the two spas only in terms of their picturesque landscape, Mary Shelley links their healing capacity with their geographical location, and implies that the landscape may have a more positive effect on her health than does the spa regimen. While the spa regimen puts the patient's health under the often arbitrary control of doctors and politicians, the healing Shelley derives from an aesthetic appreciation of picturesque scenes seems to rest more in her own hands.

Mary Shelley's interest in a salutary picturesque emerged from a cultural context that included a number of related theories about the interaction of the human mind with the 'natural' world. Turn-of-the-century art theorists argued for the positive influence of aesthetic scenes on the viewer's virtue. In essays written in 1802, the artist Edward Dayes asserts that drawing the external world trains the mind to think clearly by educating visual perception: 'It is not too much to say', he insists, 'that drawing opens the mind more than years devoted to the acquiring of languages, or the mere learning of words: it teaches [one] to think.'[30] He suggests further that drawing influences moral conduct because it requires the study of order in nature. Training the eye, then, can improve both mind and morality. Mary Shelley's presentation of the salutary picturesque adds health to the aesthetic's realm of influence. Her assertion that the aesthetic landscape will positively influence health implies that she sees the healthy body as a response to nature's order.

The chemist Sir Humphry Davy, whose works Mary Shelley first read in 1816, articulates a similar late eighteenth-century confidence in the intrinsic healing power of nature's logic:

> The study of nature ... must always be more or less connected with the love of the beautiful and the sublime: and, in consequence of the extent and indefiniteness of the views it presents to us, it is eminently calculated to gratify and to keep alive the more powerful passions and ambitions of the soul.[31]

The 'contemplation of various phenomena in the external world' through a double lens – both scientific and aesthetic – 'may be a source of consolation and of happiness in those moments of solitude when the common actions and passions of the world are considered with indifference. *It may destroy diseases of the imagination,* owing to too deep a sensibility.' [32] By diseases of the imagination, Davy probably meant melancholia. A contemporary of Davy's, the German medical theorist Dr Wilhelm Friedrich Dreyssig (1770–1819), suggested that an imbalance between the power of judgement and the power of the imagination caused melancholia.[33] In the above passage, Davy implies that observing nature's logical order might restore this balance, alleviating the discord in one's mind.

Davy's attempt to find healing in the landscape is on Mary Shelley's mind as she travels. In a letter describing a visit to the Lake of Gmünden during the 1842 tour, she refers to Davy's *Salmonia: or Days of Fly Fishing*: 'You may remember that this was the spot that poor Sir Humphry Davy visited during his last painful illness: many hours he beguiled fishing in the streams that fall into the lake.' Inspired by Davy's attempt to alleviate his pain in the outdoors, Shelley vows to return to the location: 'Happy, or in sorrow, I hope to return, and spend a summer in this neighbourhood: joy would be more than doubled, and grief softened into resignation, amidst scenes which … exercised a power over my imagination I never felt before.' In this passage Mary Shelley echoes Davy's language in the *Discourses*; the scenes will soothe her imagination, replacing grief with joy. Her description of Davy's search for comfort in the landscape prepares the reader to understand Mary Shelley's own search. Furthermore, Mary Shelley explicitly contrasts this healing scene with the spa at Kissingen: 'How deeply I regret not having spent the season here instead of at Kissingen.' [34] Mary Shelley feels a more powerful kind of healing in the scenery at the Lake of Gmünden than she did in Kissingen's baths.

Mary Shelley embraces Davy's belief in salutary aesthetics, but directs her interest towards the picturesque, probably for its explicit dependence on the viewer's participation. The aesthetic healing that Mary Shelley discovers depends on what the most influential promoter of the picturesque, William Gilpin, calls 'the picturesque eye'. The trained eye is capable of identifying and then actually augmenting a scene's picturesque quality in a sketch. Gilpin asserts that 'nature … must be a little assisted … I take up a tree here, and plant it there. I pare a knoll, or make an addition to it. I remove a piece of paling – a cottage – a wall – or any removeable object, which I dislike.' [35] Gilpin's 'paring', adding, and removing all emphasise human involvement in the composition process. Composing a picturesque scene requires the sense of agency or control that Mary Shelley seeks in her healing process.

Malcolm Andrews, Ann Bermingham and Jonathan Wordsworth have described modulations in usage of the term 'picturesque' from 1750 to 1850, revealing that 'picturesqueness' was reinvented several times to help negotiate various political, aesthetic, nationalistic and class anxieties.[36] Textual evidence suggests that Mary Shelley uses the term to indicate a healing interaction between specific landscapes and the viewer. More specifically, Mary Shelley's brand of the picturesque depends upon travel. In a November 1842 letter written to her aunt from Florence, Mary Shelley gives credit to the experience of travelling for her improved health.[37] In her own period, Mary Shelley's desire to recover through travel was not uncommon, the tradition of travel books which focus on the search for health dating back at least to Mariana Starke's *Letters from Italy* (1800). Mary Shelley, though, explicitly connects travelling in pursuit of health with travelling in pursuit of picturesque scenery. In her travel narrative, Mary Shelley embraces some aspects of picturesque convention and revises others in order to formulate a theory of self-healing. For the purposes of this argument I will reduce some of the historical complexities of the term 'picturesque', structuring the discussion around William Gilpin's definition of the three primary pleasures of the picturesque – the pursuit of novelty and variety, 'high delight', and judgement.[38]

First, appreciation for the picturesque requires what Gilpin terms the pleasurable 'pursuit' of novelty and variety in a scene: 'Under this circumstance the mind is kept constantly in an agreeable suspense. The love of novelty is the foundation of this pleasure.'[39] Although Gilpin never argues for the pursuit of novelty's effect on health, in the first letter of *Rambles*, written from Brighton, Mary Shelley expresses in picturesque terms her hope that the journey will dissipate her nervous illness: 'Travelling will cure all: my busy brooding thoughts will be scattered abroad; and ... my mind will, amidst *novel and various scenes*, renew the outworn and tattered garments in which it has long been clothed.' Like the picturesque traveller, Mary Shelley seeks novelty; more specifically, however, she identifies the pursuit of novelty as a balm for her nerves: 'Travelling is occupation as well as amusement, and I firmly believe that renewed health will be the result of *frequent change of place*. Besides what can be so delightful as the perpetual novelty – the exhaustless current of new ideas suggested by travelling?'[40] Implicit in this pursuit of novelty is the viewer's control. Rather than endure medical surveillance, Mary Shelley attempts to renew her health by actively looking. As the person who decides to change locations in the picturesque pursuit of novelty, she takes control of the healing process.

Mary Shelley addresses Gilpin's idea of variety – 'the indescribable *variety* of the landscape, enchant[s] the eye' – by emphasising scenes that contain both feminine and masculine elements. In Salzburg, for example, 'lofty mountains and an extensive plain unite'. Even the mountains are composed of more masculine, 'high and picturesque' forms and of more feminine, 'softer forms'.[41] Treating the picturesque as a location for revising gendered relationships finds a precedent in Mary Wollstonecraft's *Letters Written During a Short Residence in Sweden, Norway and Denmark* (1796). As Jeanne Moskal argues, Wollstonecraft denies Edmund Burke's sharply gendered aesthetic categories by repeatedly invoking the picturesque, 'in which the sublime merges, in a most un-Burkean way, with the beautiful'.[42] Wollstonecraft replaces Burke's erotically feminised landscape with descriptions of a maternally feminised landscape.[43] The geographer Gillian Rose observes that women have had to challenge masculine visual ideology in order to find 'a feminine position from which to perceive the land'.[44] Although Mary Shelley, like her mother, embraces the picturesque as a way to challenge this visual ideology, she does not necessarily see the picturesque landscape as maternal. Mary Shelley's position as an active viewer, which she terms her 'gaze', is as varied as the landscape she seeks.

At times Mary Shelley celebrates a powerful gaze that inspires picturesque pleasure. This second pleasure of the picturesque, Gilpin's 'high delight', occurs when 'some grand scene, tho perhaps of incorrect composition, rising before the eye, strikes us beyond the power of thought ... and every mental operation is suspended'.[45] She describes her delight in gazing as the group travels down the Rhine from Cologne to Koblenz: 'We *gazed* ... with eager curiosity, as at each succeeding mile the river became more majestic, its shores more picturesque; and every hour of the day brought its store of *delight* to the eye.'[46] At this moment, Mary Shelley seems to embrace the traditional, masculine pleasure that accompanies high delight, thus appropriating a kind of masculine scopophilia. Here she rejects the woman's traditional role as a component of the landscape – implied in Burke's eroticised aesthetic.

Mary Shelley's picturesque gaze celebrates a female self in active, rather than passive relationship with the world. She accepts the masculine delight inherent in looking, but translates that eroticised delight into a charge for women to look, and to act. In Darmstadt she comments on women's need for action: 'We must act, suffer, or enjoy; or the worst of all torments is ours ... We are not born to be cabbages.'[47] Mary Shelley suggests that women's health depends not only on an intense emotional life – women must 'suffer' and 'enjoy' – but also on action. Read through her spa experience, Mary Shelley's active gaze gives control of health to the female patient. As Anne P. Kahana argues, the Romantic poet's gaze imitates a physician's in its dissecting search for meaning beneath surfaces.[48] Mary Shelley puts herself in the position of gazer and of diagnostician.

The final pleasure of Gilpin's picturesque, 'judgement', follows the 'attainment of the object', and requires the traveller to consider both the whole and parts of a scene, always judging with an eye trained by art.[49] Mary Shelley includes in her list of picturesque travel's benefits a positive effect on one's judgement:

> to fly abroad from the hive, like the bee, and return laden with the sweets of travel – scenes, which haunt the eye – wild adventures, that enliven the imagination – knowledge, to enlighten and *free the mind from clinging, deadening prejudices* – a wider circle of sympathy with our fellow creatures; – these are the uses of travel, for which I am convinced every one is the better and the happier.[50]

While Gilpin is interested in how reconstructing a scene according to a formula can bring pleasure, Mary Shelley is interested in how observing new scenes can free the mind from preconceptions.

Breaking the picturesque frame

In her most radical revision of aesthetic conventions, Mary Shelley acknowledges the limits of the picturesque frame, expressing a desire to walk inside the scene. She has 'seen enough of the Rhine as a *picture*', and would like 'to penetrate the ravines, to scale the heights, to linger among the ruins, to hear still more of its legends'.[51] Here Mary Shelley seems to challenge even the mild prescription of the aesthetic frame. Her motion within the landscape causes the scene to shift repeatedly out of the picturesque frame. By participating in the scene, she transforms a two-dimensional objectified landscape into a three-dimensional world of interaction.

Mary Shelley's desire to 'penetrate' the landscape has masculine, erotic connotations. Elsewhere she asserts: 'Some day I should like much to establish myself for a summer on the banks of this river [the Rhine], and *explore its recesses.*' As I have suggested before, the gendered nature of Mary Shelley's subject position is not easily categorised, however. She explains her desire 'to explore its recesses' in terms that sound more traditionally feminine: 'One longs to make a familiar friend of such sublime scenery, and refer, in after years, to one's intimate acquaintance with it, as one of the most valued among the treasures of recollection which time may have bestowed.'[52] Mary Shelley expresses a desire to cultivate a relationship with the landscape, the relationship of a familiar friend. Gillian Rose characterises this kind of appreciation of the landscape as 'the rearticulation of traditional space so that it ceases to function primarily as the space of sight for a mastering gaze, but becomes the locus of relationships'.[53] Mary Shelley's gaze does not seem wholly to exclude eroticisation, yet it does not completely objectify the landscape either. She wishes for a kind of complex intercourse with the scenes that she encounters.

Mary Shelley, then, breaks through the picturesque frame, disrupting the subject/object relationship between landscape and viewer. Disgusted with a young Englishman who seems to travel only to collect visual souvenirs, Mary Shelley insists, 'We must become a part of the scenes around us, and they must mingle and become a portion of us, or we see without seeing and study without learning.'[54] Indeed, one of her reviewers praises Mary Shelley's description of Lake Como for its potential power to reform crass tourists 'who take a glance at a country, and then away, and who seem to go not because they enjoy the sight, but that afterwards they may say that they have seen'.[55] Mary Shelley encourages her readers and fellow travellers to break the frame they look through, to interact with the picturesque scenery.

Why does Mary Shelley prefer picturesque scenes to a spa regimen and then attempt to revise even this aesthetic frame? The twentieth-century medical historian Mary C. Rawlinson's work on the discourse of medicine offers a possible explanation. Medicine's discourse, Rawlinson argues, 'recognises the body only as a physical object, rather than as a structure of possibility for being and doing in the world which must be appropriated in an individual existence'.[56] To escape medical surveillance, Mary Shelley adopts the role of viewer in the picturesque landscape. Even viewing the landscape through a picturesque frame, though, prescribes a subject/object relationship. Mary Shelley's move to break the frame insists on the mingling of the subject, or body, with the object, or landscape. Movement within the landscape allows her the agency to be and do. Mary Shelley seems to feel closest to health when she escapes the medical eye that sees only her body, only a set of symptoms that require regimented treatment. Instead, she finds relief in action.

I have organised this chapter into a progression from prescriptive medicine to self-healing, though, as the title *Rambles* suggests, Mary Shelley creates no linear progression. In fact, the narrative of her search for health reflects picturesque conventions; the epistolary form creates an irregular, non-linear, and varied story of the search for health. In the Preface to *Rambles*, Mary Shelley says of the work, 'I give fragments – not a whole'. Explicitly, the statement serves as a kind of apology for referring to Italy's politics without creating a full 'political history'.[57] I argue that the statement can be interpreted to refer also to Mary Shelley's theory of health. Indeed, etymologically, the word 'health' derives from the Old English 'hal', translated as 'whole'. Offering 'fragments' and 'not a whole' then, Mary

Shelley acknowledges that her search for health is not finished. In *Rambles*, Mary Shelley explores healing strategies in a recursive manner, returning to both spa and picturesque healing multiple times. While I have argued that she prefers to control her own healing process when possible, I do not mean to suggest that she completely discards spa healing. She returns to spas several times in the narrative, and later in life. Diagnosed with neuralgia and nervous rheumatism in 1845, she returned to Baden-Baden in 1846 for treatment of what her doctor called 'things' pressing on her spinal nerves.[58]

Anthropologist Judith Farquhar's discussion of Chinese medicine is helpful for interpreting Mary Shelley's recursive exploration of healing. Farquhar notes that Westerners are predisposed to feel that 'science (a collective undertaking) provides true knowledge and that action (a matter of individual choice) cannot be responsible without this solid foundation'.[59] It would be convenient to argue that Mary Shelley acts from a theory of healing that she developed from established knowledge. In actuality, she seems to develop her theory of self-healing as she experiments with options that she encounters both accidentally and purposefully. Her search for health, then, is a continual exchange between theory and practice.

Although I find her impulse to embrace self-healing inspiring, it is not an uncomplicated desire. It seems that part of Mary Shelley's desire to heal herself emerged from a conviction that she was somehow responsible for her illness. In her time, the medical establishment often did not take women's illness seriously, as the symptoms were regarded as part of being female. Sensibility and emotion were praised in women, then blamed for a variety of nervous illnesses. Emily Sunstein notes: 'She [Mary Shelley] would be a courageous, resilient patient, who herself believed, too long, unfortunately, that much of her trouble was emotionally induced.'[60] In 1850, she was diagnosed with the brain tumour that caused her death. In *Rambles*, Mary Shelley records her relationship to a culture that implicitly blamed her for her illness, and yet, ironically resisted her desire for agency in the healing process. Mary Shelley's attempts to design a theory of self-healing in her spa visits and interactions with the landscape, then, both reflect and challenge nineteenth-century medical and aesthetic discourse.[61]

Notes

1 William Wordsworth, *Lyrical Ballads and Other Poems, 1797–1800*, eds James Butler and Karen Green, *The Cornell Wordsworth*, gen. ed. Stephen Parrish (Ithaca, 1992), 116–20, ll. 23–31.

2 Mary Shelley, *Rambles in Germany and Italy*, in Jeanne Moskal, ed., *Travel*

Writing, vol. 8 of *The Novels and Selected Works of Mary Shelley*, gen. ed. Nora Crook, with Pamela Clemit (London, 1996).

3   *The Journals of Mary Shelley: 1814–1844*, eds Paula R. Feldman and Diana Scott-Kilvert (Baltimore, 1987), 559.

4   *Ibid.*, 563.

5   *Ibid.*, 564. At the turn of the nineteenth century, medical writers such as Buchan, Cullen, Dreyssig and Esquirol began to distil from melancholia a description of what we now call depression. Although Mary Shelley's understanding of depression's origins surely differs from our biochemical explanation of the illness, her description of the symptoms is similar to today's clinical description of depression.

6   Emily W. Sunstein, *Mary Shelley: Romance and Reality* (Baltimore, 1989), 356.

7   *Rambles*, 2.

8   After her husband's death, Mary Shelley visited Brighton in 1826 and 1827. She returned in November of 1836 and again a few months before the first journey described in *Rambles* (*Journals*, 549, 564).

9   *Rambles*, 170. Granville's travel guide was first printed in two volumes in 1837. The textual references in this chapter are drawn from his second, single-volume edition: Augustus Bozzi Granville, *The Spas of Germany*, 2nd edn (London, 1838).

10 Granville, *Spas of Germany*, xxix.

11 *Ibid.*

12 *Ibid.*, xxxii (emphasis added).

13 Dr Granville was practising at Kissingen when Mary Shelley underwent her cure in 1842 (*Rambles*, 174).

14 *Rambles*, 170, 172.

15 *Ibid.*, 172–3, 176.

16 *Spas of Germany*, xxxvi–xxxviii.

17 *Rambles*, 170.

18 *Spas of Germany*, 382.

19 John Brown, *The Elements of Medicine of John Brown, M.D. Translated from the Latin, with Comments and Illustrations, By the Author 1786. A New Edition, Revised and Corrected with a Biographical Preface by Thomas Beddoes, M.D.* (London, 1795), clxiii.

20 *Ibid.*, 'Table of Excitement and Excitability' (unpaginated).

21 *Rambles*, 170.

22 *Rambles*, 176 (emphasis in original).

23 One reviewer explains that Mary Shelley's letters were probably retained because she wrote to a friend that she wanted to meet a member of the Carbonari (review of *Rambles in Germany and Italy in 1840, 1842, and 1843*, *The Literary Examiner* (27 July 1844), 468).

24 *Rambles*, 170, 169 (emphasis added).

25 *Spas of Germany*, xxxv.

26 *Rambles*, 96.

27 *Spas of Germany*, xxvii.

28 Julius Braun M.D., *On the Curative Effects of Baths and Waters, Being a Handbook to the Spas of Europe*, ed. Hermann Weber, M.D. (London, 1875), 10.

29 *Rambles*, 172 (emphasis added), 178.

30 Edward Dayes, *The Works of the Late Edward Dayes* (London, 1805), 258.

31 Humphry Davy, *A Discourse, Introductory to a Course of Lectures on Chemistry, Delivered to the Theatre of the Royal Institution* (London, 1802), 24–6.

32 *Ibid.*, 23, 24–6 (emphasis added).

33 Aubrey J. Lewis, 'Melancholia: A Historical Review', *The Journal of Mental Science* 80: 328 (1934), 6.

34 *Rambles*, 242.

35 William Gilpin, *Three Essays: On Picturesque Beauty: On Picturesque Travel: And on Sketching Landscape: With a Poem, on Landscape Painting*, 3rd edn (London, 1808), 67–8.

36 Malcolm Andrews, *In Search of the Picturesque* (Stanford, 1989), 40–65. Ann Bermingham, 'System, Order, and Abstraction: The Politics of English Landscape Drawing around 1795', in W. J. T. Mitchell, ed., *Landscape and Power* (Chicago, 1994), 77–101. Jonathan Wordsworth, Michael C. Jaye and Robert Woof, *William Wordsworth and the Age of English Romanticism* (New Brunswick, 1987), 87–92.

37 *Selected Letters of Mary Wollstonecraft Shelley*, ed. Betty T. Bennett (Baltimore, 1995), 318–19.

38 *Three Essays*, 47–50.

39 *Ibid.*, 47–8.

40 *Rambles*, 76, 157 (emphasis added).

41 *Ibid.*, 245 (emphasis added), 244, 244.

42 Jeanne Moskal, 'The Picturesque and the Affectionate in Wollstonecraft's *Letters from Norway*', *Modern Language Quarterly* 52: 3 (1991), 276.

43 *Ibid.*, 277.

44 Gillian Rose, *Feminism and Geography: The Limits of Geographical Knowledge* (London and Minneapolis, 1993), 111.

45 *Three Essays*, 49–50.

46 *Rambles*, 161 (emphasis added).

47 *Ibid.*, 91.

48 Anne P. Kahana, 'Illness, Health, and the Romantic Subject' (diss., SUNY Stonybrook, 1991).

49 *Three Essays*, 49.

50 *Rambles*, 157 (emphasis added).

51 *Ibid.*, 163 (emphasis in original).

52 *Ibid.*, 89 (emphasis added).

53 *Feminism and Geography*, 112.

54 *Rambles*, 213.

55 Review of *Rambles in Germany and Italy in 1840, 1842, and 1843*, *The Critic* (2 September 1844), 37.

56   Mary C. Rawlinson, 'Medicine's Discourse and the Practice of Medicine', in Victor Kestenbaum, ed., *The Humanity of the Ill* (Knoxville, 1982), 83.

57   *Rambles*, 70.

58   Sunstein, *Mary Shelley*, 374.

59   Judith Farquhar, 'Multiplicity, Point of View, and Responsibility in Traditional Chinese Healing', in Angela Zito and Tani E. Barlow, eds, *Body, Subject and Power in China* (Chicago, 1994), 89.

60   *Mary Shelley*, 374.

61   My thanks to Jeanne Moskal, Marya DeVoto, Holloway Sparks and Mark Kautz for their comments on previous drafts of this chapter.

Part IV

Colonial and imperial cartographies

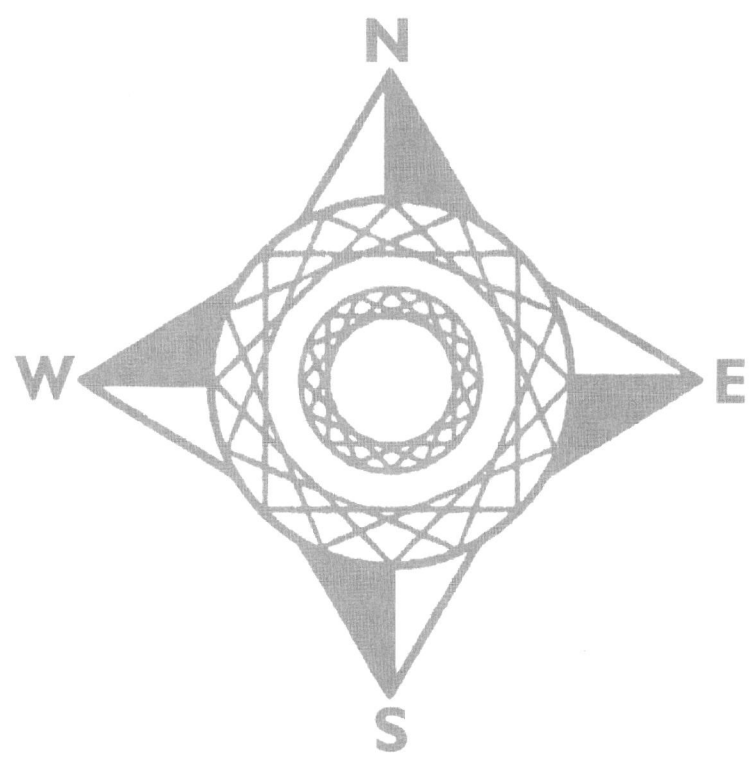

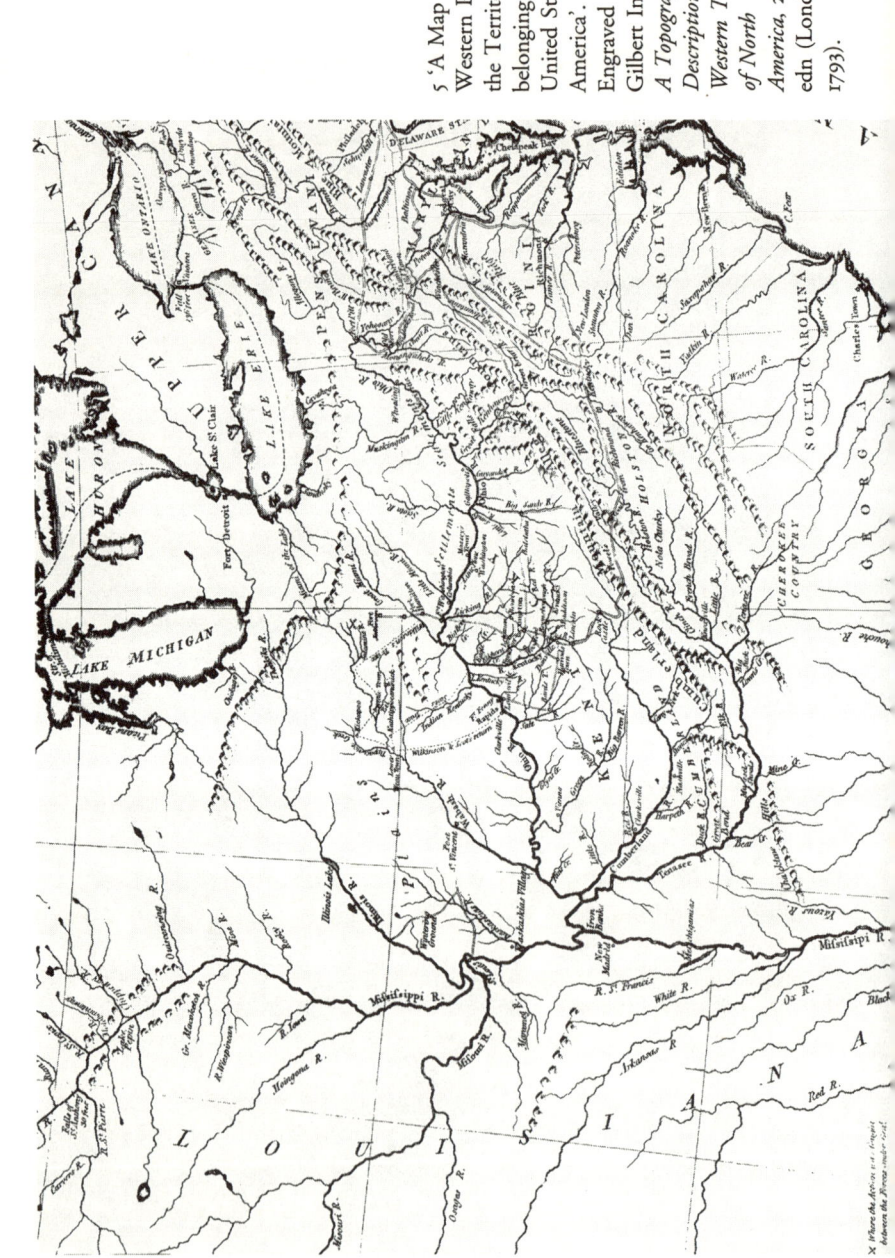

5 'A Map of the Western Part of the Territories belonging to the United States of America'. Engraved for Gilbert Imlay's *A Topographical Description of the Western Territory of North America*, 2nd edn (London, 1793).

Land-jobbing in the western territories: radicalism, transatlantic emigration, and the 1790s American travel narrative

W. M. Verhoeven

> Printing and navigation have compleately changed the complexion of Europe; they must change that of the whole GLOBE. (Gilbert Imlay, *The Emigrants*)

The genre of the Romantic travel narrative has traditionally been associated primarily with journeys to the south – notably the Mediterranean – and the east – notably Turkey and the Levant. In this chapter I want to look at another popular, though less widely debated destination, namely the west, and in particular North America. The idea of America as a modern Atlantis in the west is, of course, an old one – the product of the age of the great explorations and circumnavigations of the globe. But it was especially in the course of the eighteenth century that America began to fascinate European writers and thinkers, and, in ever-increasing numbers, travellers of one kind or another – tourists, scientists, traders, missionaries, adventurers – crossed the mountains and traversed the plains of the New World. Inspired by the ideas of the *philosophes*, many travellers from Britain and France struck out for the western wilderness on the trail the Noble Savage, trying to catch a glimpse of the real-life specimen of the image that had occupied European minds and imaginations for so long. When their accounts reached audiences in Europe, many recognised in their representations of the American landscape, its wildlife, and its natural inhabitants the idealist-positivist belief in the perfectibility of life in a pristine environment.[1] Travel books like Captain Jonathan Carver's 1778 *Travels Through America* – the first popular American travel account and an international bestseller – inspired back-to-nature cultists to construct the notion of an American Golden Age. During the Revolutionary War

185

and the early years of the Republic, America became for many French radicals – and, after the Peace of Paris (1783), also for their English counterparts – an envied experiment in social and ideological change, and a whole string of travellers produced accounts of their visits – including the Marquis de Chastellux (1780–82), Francisco de Miranda (1783–84), Brissot de Warville (1788), and Chateaubriand (1791). We will also recall that Thomas Jefferson's *Notes on the State of Virginia* (1787) was written in direct response to the desire of the French authorities to amass a body of detailed and reliable information concerning the American states, with whose fortunes the French were becoming increasingly involved in the course of the uprising against the British.

Yet, curiously enough, given the mass of American travel narratives produced in the course of the 1780s, there was a growing feeling amongst post-Revolutionary travellers that the true America was still largely a *terra incognita*. Thus W. Matthews boldly states in his 1789 book, *Historical Review of North America*, that America 'is a country hitherto little known', and he also professes to know who is to be blamed for this: 'The perfidious French while they retained any power in North America, took every method to keep the English in ignorance, even by publishing false maps with false names and false accounts annexed to them; probably (says Carver) the greatest part [of North America] is entirely unexplored.'[2] In the same vein (and the same year) the American geographer Jedidiah Morse opened his well-known book *The American Geography; or, A View of the Present Situation of the United States of America*, with the remark,

> So imperfect are all the accounts of America hitherto published, even by those who once exclusively possessed the best means of information, that from them very little knowledge of this country can be acquired. Europeans have been the sole writers of American Geography, and have too often suffered fancy to supply the place of facts, and thus have led their readers into errors, while they professed to aim at removing their ignorance.[3]

'Fancy' and the 'perfidious French', however, were not the only, nor the main, reasons why so many travel narratives presented a distorted picture of America. Just as there are no totally disinterested writers, there are no totally disinterested travellers – and, it follows, no totally disinterested travel writers. The traveller sees and finds what he or she can make sense of – that is, what he or she has seen and found – or *imagined* – before. Every travel narrative is to varying degrees an autobiographical portrait of the traveller. It is therefore not surprising to find that the narrative of a traveller like the Encyclopedist and *philosophe* Chastellux, a child of the

Enlightenment and a staunch believer in the progress of humankind, should present – in the words of Jefferson – 'the most flattering account of America that had ever been written';[4] written in the mid-1780s, Chastellux's *Travels in North America* presents not so much an account of contemporary America as a glorified vision of the future state of France *after* the revolution that had still to take place. Nor does it come as a surprise, given their theories of geographic pessimism and evolutionary degeneration regarding the future of the New World in general, that writers like Comte de Buffon, De Pauw and Abbé Raynal should produce such dismissive accounts of America and such gloomy forecasts of its unavoidable demise: they *could* only depict the American Indian as a degenerate mongrel instead of the Noble Savage others had raved about because, as cultural pessimists, they felt concerned for the future of European civilisation and were therefore keen to prove its *a priori* superiority over all other civilisations and forms of human existence. But even travellers and writers whose powers of observation might be expected to be less clouded by prejudice and ideological false consciousness, such as trained geographers and topographers, could not avoid distorting, and misrepresenting America in their travel narratives – whether for reasons of self-aggrandisement, promoting book sales, flattering their patrons or political backers; or simply because they had not actually seen and experienced what they described, more often than not because they never visited the country in the first place and were merely rehashing what other travel writers had written before them.[5]

Distortion, or misrepresentation of the object, then, appears to be an inherent aspect of the travel narrative, but what is perhaps more interesting is that that very same distortion can indirectly be credited with having given the genre its vitality and diversity of textual format. Since all travellers' powers of observation, as well as their pens, are directed by the *motives* that brought them to the country they are visiting, there are as many textual formats of the travel narrative as there are motives to travel: constantly negotiating between fact and fiction, the known and the unknown, narrative styles vary from virtually unedited notes and impressions written more or less 'to the moment' – for instance, going down the Ohio River in a canoe (as in the case of the Reverend David Jones in the early 1770s)[6] – to carefully edited and worked-over travel memoirs written long after the actual journey took place (such as Chateaubriand's *Travels in America*, which was written thirty-five years after the actual trip).

In the radical years of the early 1790s an interesting new format was added by especially British travellers, as exaggerated praise for America – that naive, virtuous, democratic country far beyond the horizons of European vice, corruption, injustice, and oppression – began to translate itself into a medium for criticism of Europe, which most typically chose the format of the semi-fictional genre of the 'Letters of a Foreign Visitor'.[7] In this chapter I want to look at two examples of this type of narrative, Gilbert Imlay's 1792 text *A Topographical Description of the Western Territory of North America* – subtitled 'a Series of Letters to a Friend in England' – and Thomas Cooper's 1794 *Some Information Respecting America* – subtitled 'Letters from America, to a Friend in England'. What interests me in particular in these texts are the ways in which *narrative format* – an epistolary travel account – and *motive* – to persuade people to emigrate to America for ideological reasons – interrelate to form an intriguing species of radical prose writing of the 1790s: a generic blend of the promotional tract on the advantages of emigration and the travel narrative proper. I will be arguing also that the success of this brand of 1790s travel narrative was as short-lived as the spirit of radicalism that produced it and whose medium it was.

Radical writers in the 1790s generally believed that they lived in an age in which the future of humankind was being decided; radical *travel writers* such as Imlay and Cooper were absolutely convinced that an increase in the knowledge of other countries and cultures, and in particular of the socio-political experiment that had just been started in America, could function as a rhetorical *and* an ideological weapon in the fight for greater justice and liberty.[8] Not surprisingly, Imlay's and Cooper's books made a strong impact on all those radical minds in Britain who considered their society to be hopelessly corrupt and their civil rights under serious threat from an outdated and despotic government. First published at a time when tensions were rising between the French and the British (with war between them eventually breaking out in February 1793) and when British opinion was becoming rapidly less favourable (not to say violently opposed) to revolution, Imlay's book was seized upon by many as the promise of a Rousseauesque return to nature in the pristine wilderness of the New World.[9] The decision of the radical, scientist, and philosopher Joseph Priestley (1733–1804) to settle in America and build an agrarian utopia there not too long after a reactionary mob had burned down his house and laboratory in July 1791, initiated a widespread American emigration movement in the 1790s among progressive idealists, many of whom were thrilled by Imlay's description of the Kentucky paradise. One of the best known of these utopian emigration schemes is no doubt Samuel Coleridge's Pantisocracy – an experiment of human perfectibility which was to be created in pastoral seclusion, and which would be run on the principle of sharing property, labour, and self-government equally among all of its adult members, both men and women. It is known that Coleridge thoroughly researched the possibilities of an American Pantisocracy, and enthusiastically read several of the recent reports on the country's topography, including Brissot de Warville's *New Travels in the United States* (1792), Imlay's *Topographical Description* and Cooper's *Some Information Respecting America*.[10] It is probably not a coincidence that Kentucky was the first prospective site for Coleridge's Pantisocracy, only some time later to be superseded by the site that most people nowadays tend to associate with Pantisocracy, the idyllic Pennsylvanian hinterland on the banks of the picturesque Susquehanna River – which was the region Thomas Cooper (a business associate of Priestley's son in the Susquehanna project) recommended to potential emigrants. By the middle of the decade emigration to the New World had become so popular in radical circles that 'America' had become a byword for an asylum for radical emigrants. Thus, in his *A Political Dictionary* Charles Pigott defined the word 'emigrant' as 'one who, like Dr. Priestley or Thomas Cooper, is compelled to fly from persecution, and explore liberty in a far distant land, probably America'; the word 'refugees' Pigott annotated as 'English Patriots, as Dr. Priestley and his family, Mr. Cooper, of Manchester, &c. &c. who ... were obliged to quit a country pregnant with bigotry and persecution'.[11]

Radical travellers like Imlay and Cooper did not travel to *see* things; they travelled to *sell* things: radical ideas, of course, but also, and perhaps more so, *land*. Soon after his arrival in Kentucky in early 1783, Imlay became deeply immersed in land speculation deals, leaving a long and complex trail of legal entanglements, which kept the various county courts busy for years. Even so, he was sworn in as deputy surveyor of Jefferson County, Kentucky, in April 1784. But instead of serving the public interest, lining his own pocket was his main, if not his sole, preoccupation at the time. One of his earliest land deals was with one of Kentucky's most illustrious pioneers, Daniel Boone. In March 1783 Imlay gave a bond for £2000 in payment for 10,000 acres of prime land, which he subsequently disposed of to someone else. Boone was still waiting for the first instalment of the bond to be paid out to him when Imlay quietly absconded from Kentucky in 1786 – never to be seen there again. Because not all land deeds were recorded, it is impossible to estimate how much land Imlay may have owned, but it is likely to have been well over 50,000 acres. Although it is not known whether at that time Imlay himself still held any land rights in Kentucky, land-jobbing was certainly one of the activities that kept him occupied during the six-year interval between the time of his departure from America in December 1786 and the publication of *A Topographical Description* in 1792.

Thomas Cooper, too, had a stake in a considerable chunk of pristine

American wilderness, in his case in Pennsylvania, near the 'forks' or confluence of the north-east and western branches of the Susquehanna River.[12] Along with his business partner, Joseph Priestley, Jr, and some others, Cooper had apparently contracted for an estimated 300,000 acres of land and was now actively encouraging like-minded souls to buy land – at a price starting at a dollar an acre – in what they envisaged to be a large settlement for (in Priestley's phrase) 'the friends of liberty in general'.[13] Though perhaps more for revolutionary than commercial reasons, Cooper's travel narrative was none the less written specifically as a guide for prospective emigrants, or, more accurately, as a sustained argument in favour of emigration to Pennsylvania, rather than Kentucky.[14]

It was apparently common knowledge in the 1790s that Imlay and Cooper were interested in more than the mere sale of their books. Thus, in January 1795 an article appeared in the *British Critic* discussing the activities of American and British land agents in London at the time, in particular the rival emigration schemes for Kentucky and the Susquehanna, which were being promoted by Gilbert Imlay and Thomas Cooper respectively. The article was highly critical of the dealings of both men, referring to 'Messrs. Imlay and Cooper as two rival auctioneers, or rather two show-men, stationed for the allurement of cautious passengers; "Pray ladies and gentlemen, walk in and admire the wonders of Kentucky". – "Pray stop and see the incomparable beauties of the Susquehanna".'[15] Similarly, in the Supplement to its 1794 issue the *Gentleman's Magazine* published what it claimed was an authentic letter from an actual emigrant who had settled in Pennsylvania, hoping that its contents might 'help to check the spirit of emigration so prevalent in [the] country', and that it 'might serve as an antidote to the poison so generally diffused by writers, who scruple not to injure their native country by the grossest misrepresentations'.[16] However, it was generally acknowledged that there was a growing popularity of American emigration schemes among Quakers, Unitarians, and other idealist freethinkers. It has been calculated that some two thousand radicals had set out for America by 1796 – many of whom had returned disillusioned.[17]

Following the example of Crèvecoeur's *Letters from an American Farmer*, published in London in 1782, *A Topographical Description* presents itself as 'a series of letters to a friend in England', but internal evidence suggests that the book was written (at least in part, but probably in its entirety) long after the author had left both Kentucky and America, most probably in England, in the course of 1791–92. Again like Crèvecoeur's *Letters, A Topographical Description* is aimed at a European, particularly British audience, and, as may be concluded from its format (a cross between an epistolary correspondence and a travelogue), it asks to be read as an authentic, eyewitness account of the American social experiment in terms of the 'real-life' application of a long tradition of progressive, utopian Enlightenment thinking, which could be described as radical pastoralism. Thus, the English 'editor' of the letters describes his American friend, 'Imlay', as a 'man who had lived until he was more than five-and-twenty years old, in the back parts of America', where he had become 'accustomed to that simplicity of manners natural to a people in a state of innocence'.[18] Having since travelled to Europe, his friend 'must have been powerfully stricken with the great difference between the simplicity of [the New World], and what is called *etiquette* and good breeding in the [Old]'. Being a man of unspoiled manners and morals, his American friend, the editor believes, 'is better calculated than ourselves to judge our manners'. Besides being an eclectic account of the American Horn of Plenty and a practical 'How-to-emigrate-to-Kentucky' guide, Imlay's *Topographical Description* thus becomes a comparative analysis of, in the words of our Kentuckian Noble Savage, 'the simple manners, and rational life of the Americans, in these back settlements' and 'the distorted and unnatural habits of the Europeans', which, Imlay's voice-over reminds us, 'have flowed no doubt from the universally bad laws which exist [in Europe], and from that pernicious system of blending religion with politics, which has been productive of universal depravity'.[19]

Although it has been claimed in the past that Imlay's *Topographical Description* is closely modelled after (or even concocted from) earlier topographical classics – notably Thomas Hutchins's *A Topographical Description of Virginia, Pennsylvania, Maryland, and North Carolina* (1778); Jonathan Carver's *Travels Through the Interior Parts of North America* (1781); Thomas Jefferson's *Notes on the State of Virginia* (1784–85); Comte de Buffon's *Histoire Naturelle* (1749–1804); Jedidiah Morse's *American Geography* (1789); Brissot de Warville's *New Travels in the United States* (1792); and, especially, John Filson's *The Discovery and Settlement of Kentucke* (1784) – a closer look at Imlay's text reveals that, unlike its predecessors (with the exception of Jefferson's *Notes*), Imlay's book constitutes a sustained geopolitical doctrine, in that it not merely describes the western territories in terms of a New Canaan for the prospective emigrant but also provides the physiocratic *rationale* for the opening up and development of the western territories.

A doctrine of political economists developed in France in the eighteenth century, physiocracy is characterised chiefly by the belief that government policy should not interfere with the operation of natural economic laws and that land is the source of all wealth. In contrast to Enlightenment thought in general, liberty is considered not so much a precondition for universal prosperity as the *consequence* of prosperity. In other words: liberty follows trade and commerce, not the other way around. Accordingly, Imlay's attitude towards the natural environment of the western territories is not that of an idealist Pantisocrat seeking refuge from oppression and persecution or of a vapid 'lover of the meadows and the woods, and the mountains', but that of a staunchly rationalistic, pragmatic Enlightenment real estate developer. Thus, when he describes the area around Lexington, Kentucky, as the 'finest and most luxuriant country, perhaps, on earth',[20] Imlay is not transported by 'aching joys' and 'dizzy raptures', but is rather thinking of the richness of the soil, the navigability of the rivers, and the wholesomeness of the climate. Roughly speaking, Imlay's topographical description of the western territory of the United States, as well as the geopolitical vision based on it, centres on just two natural phenomena: mountains and rivers – more particularly, the Allegheny Mountains and the Ohio and Mississippi Rivers.

The Allegheny Mountains, which until the 1760s caused the colonisation of America to be contained within the relatively confined coastal strip bordering on the Atlantic, have undergone a crucial metamorphosis in Imlay's *Topographical Description*, as well as in his novel *The Emigrants* (1793). Rather than an impregnable obstacle for further westward expansion, the Alleghenies are presented to us in both texts not so much as a physical but as a *moral* watershed, separating the pastoral innocence of the western settlements from the social evil, political corruption, and religious blindness that dominated life in the eastern states; as *The Emigrants* has it, the 'chaste regions of innocence and joy' lie to the west of the mountains, while vice runs rife in Bristol and the east.[21]

But Imlay knew well enough that even a Promised Land is a worthless land if it is not easily accessible. The northern route to Kentucky – by waggon from either Philadelphia or Baltimore across the Alleghenies to Pittsburgh and then down the Ohio River on flat-bottomed barges – was an onerous one, and no matter how smooth Imlay makes the journey appear, it would (as Filson had already noted in his book) continue to render produce dear in the western settlements (see Figure 5). The key to the back settlements lay in the navigability of the Mississippi and Ohio Rivers, and it is not surprising that in his *Topographical Description* Imlay (following earlier authors like Carver, Filson, and Jefferson) dwells at length on the west's unique transportation potential of interlocking rivers and lakes, which effectively turns the region into a physiocratic paradise:

You will observe, that as far as this immense continent is known, the courses and extent of its rivers are extremely favourable to communication by water; a circumstance which is highly important, whether we regard it in a social or commercial point of view. The intercourse of men has added no inconsiderable lustre to the polish of manners, and, perhaps, commerce has tended more to civilize and embellish the human mind, in two centuries, than war and chivalry would have done in five.[22]

And, once the problem of upstream navigation had been solved with the help of steam (and Imlay is confident that this will only be a matter of time, given that experiments with steam-powered boats were already under way in Virginia), this would enable the dwellers on Kentucky's green and fertile fields to open up communication and trade with the settlements on the Pacific coast and in Canada. Seeing that, 'According to the present system, wealth is the source of power' and that 'the attainment of wealth can only be brought about by a wise and happy attention to commerce', Imlay proudly concludes that the western regions, far from being an outpost of civilisation on the margins of America, were actually at the heart of the North American experiment and mankind's best bet to realise even the wildest, most extreme notions of physiocratic idealism and neoclassical perfectibility.[23]

The Emigrants in many respects simply puts into fictional form the ideological concerns of the earlier text. While downplaying any overt commercial angle, the plot nevertheless emphasises the ease with which emigrants may travel west and how an elaborate infrastructure of roads and waterways will be at their disposal once they arrive there. With its sentimental interest frequently being put to the service of its geopolitics, it is therefore no coincidence that *The Emigrants* at times reads more like a travelogue than a novel. Thus, the opening letters make much of the heroine's insistence to *walk* much of the way across the Allegheny Mountains (in sharp contrast to her lethargic brother, George, who prefers to be moved around on a waggon, along with the old people in the company) – more like a picturesque tourist than a pioneer. But even more significant is Arl—ton's unstoppable wanderlust, which first takes him from Pittsburgh down the Ohio River to Louisville, and later, in what John Seelye calls 'a fit of expansionist pique',[24] further west, via St Vincent's (Vincennes) toward St Anthony's Falls and the sources of the Mississippi, from where he plans to travel down the river to Kaskaskia, then up the Missouri, back again to Kaskaskia, down the Mississippi to New Orleans, and from there back to Baltimore. Even though Caroline's captivity by the Indians forces Arl—ton to abandon his frantic wilderness trip prematurely, the reader gets the distinct impression that moving across vast tracts of the rugged

American landscape is not more arduous, and only slightly more risky, than a journey in rural England or a promenade in London, and certainly much more thrilling – sublime or picturesque sights being available at every twist and turn of the emigrant's tour. As Caroline puts it, 'here is a continual feast for the mind'.[25]

However, Imlay was not merely mindful of the economic, social, and aesthetic significance of the western landscape, especially its elaborate network of waterways: he was also very sensitive to its political significance. Blending the region's rivers with its mountains, soil, climate, and natural resources into a physiocratic, geopolitical doctrine of progress and universal prosperity, Imlay in effect creates a prototype of the doctrine of Manifest Destiny, albeit with at least one significant difference. Crucially, Imlay's physiocratic millennium does not have its origin in the early colonial experiments in Virginia and New England, nor even in the ideological energy released by the American Revolution: instead, Imlay envisages the cradle of his physiocratic utopia to be in the west, more particularly in Kentucky, and the ideological forces that rock it to be generated by the French, rather than by the American Revolution. Indeed, underlying Imlay's dream of America is a fervent plea for a secessionist utopia across the Alleghenies, whereby 'the Mountain' (as he refers to them) creates an ideological dichotomy between two distinct Americas: between the eastern states, which he regards as an outpost of an earlier, Puritan exodus, whose original energy had petered out and had become permeated with the social evils of the Old World, and the 'true', trans-Alleghenian America in the west, which was radically discontinuous with the earlier, European colonisation of North America. Imlay's separatist agenda leads him to reformulate the notion of a federal America as a nation whose political power is centred not in the east – not in the 'federal city' that had just been established in the District of Columbia – but in the West:

> The federal government regulating every thing commercial, must be productive of the greatest harmony, so that while we are likely to live in the regions of perpetual peace, our felicity will receive a zest from the activity and variety of our trade. We shall pass through the Mississippi to the sea – up the Ohio, Monongahala and Cheat rivers, by a small portage, into the Potowmac, which will bring us to the federal city on the line of Virginia and Maryland – through the federal rivers I have mentioned, and the lakes to New York and Quebec – from the northern lakes to the head branches of the rivers which run into Hudson's-bay into the Arctic regions – and from the sources of the Misouri [*sic*] into the Great South Sea. Thus in the centre of the earth, governing by the laws of reason and humanity,

we seem calculated to become at once the emporium and protectors of the world.[26]

Here, transcending the travel narrative proper and sublimating it into a metaphor for utopian radicalism, lies the ultimate significance of Imlay and his *Topographical Description*. Although still remembered almost exclusively as the philandering cad who abandoned Mary Wollstonecraft, Imlay in his 1792 travel narrative in fact prefigures by more than a century Frederick Jackson Turner's well-known concept of the west. Thus, when Turner, aided by the advantage of hindsight, identified the Ohio Valley of the 1780s and 1790s as 'a great highway to the west', and the West itself as 'at bottom ... a form of society, rather than an area',[27] Imlay, like one of Crèvecoeur's 'western pilgrims', had already travelled ahead of him, closing 'the great circle' of physiocratic millennialism on the banks of the Ohio River.[28]

Imlay's physiocratic dream of an independent western state governed by the laws of reason and humanity is fulfilled in the utopian community founded by Arl—ton toward the end of *The Emigrants*. Arl—ton confirms that he turns to the western territory as the site of his new society, named Bellefont, 'as its infancy affords an opportunity to its citizens of establishing a system conformable to reason and humanity' and is thus able to 'extend the blessings of civilization to all orders of men'.[29] No problems are foreseen for the fictional Bellefont, but in the *Topographical Description* Imlay is somewhat more pragmatic: he recognises that if Kentucky had the potential to become the centre of the New World, indeed, the centre of a New World millennium, thanks to its strategic position at the junction of the waterways of the future, this was at the same time what threatened to undermine its position in Imlay's geopolitical masterplan. For he was acutely aware that 'whoever are possessed of this river [the Mississippi], and of the vast tracts of fertile lands upon it, must in time command that continent, and the trade of it, as well as all the natives in it'.[30] In the early pages of the book, Imlay recounts with evident disgust the attempts by the French in the course of the seventeenth and eighteenth centuries to lay a stranglehold on the western settlements by an 'insidious' plan to first occupy the mouths of the St Lawrence and Mississippi Rivers and subsequently to secure the communication between Canada and Louisiana by erecting an elaborate network of fortresses. But this 'colossian plan' is very much attributed to the *ancien régime*, notably to Louis XIV ('that voracious tyrant'), and emphatically *not* to the new, Revolutionary administration in France.[31] Besides, by the time Imlay was composing his *Topographical Description*, the French sphere of influence on the North American continent had been drastically reduced at the close of the French and Indian wars, when, in the Treaty of Paris of 1763, Louisiana and the control over the mouth of the Mississippi had been seceded to Spain. Although the United States, as the inheritors of the Treaty of Paris, had formally retained the navigation rights of the Mississippi, the Spanish had more or less blockaded the river so as to be able to frustrate the westward expansion of the United States. With the federal government showing only little sympathy with the plight of the western settlers, it is not difficult to see why in the early 1790s the rebellious Kentuckians should be ready to make overtures to the French, whose territorial ambitions toward Lousiana and the Mississippi Valley had been rekindled by the Revolution of 1789. Nor is it hard to see how Imlay, as the author of one of the most recent, popular treatises on the western settlements, was about to start rubbing shoulders with prominent Girondist politicians in France and get involved in French foreign affairs.

It is one of those curious coincidences of the Revolutionary period that the very man who first recommended Imlay to the Girondist leader Brissot de Warville in March 1793 was also the man whose American travel narrative was soon to vie with Imlay's *Topographical Description* as the highest popular authority on emigration to America. As one of Britain's foremost radicals, Thomas Cooper was held in high esteem by the Girondists at the time (even holding honorary French citizenship), and he must have recognised in Imlay the expert on the western territories that the Girondists might be wanting to talk to. Nor is this very surprising: before Cooper published his own text on America in 1794, Imlay's book had already been reissued in a much-expanded second edition (now with maps, plans, a mileage chart, an extensive index, the complete text of Filson's account of Kentucky, and more), while reprints had appeared in New York and Dublin, as well as a translation into German – and all this in 1793, the very year in which Cooper was in America trying 'to determine whether [that country], and what part of it, was eligible for a person, like [him]self, with a small fortune, and a large family, to settle in'.[32] That Cooper was aware of the popularity of Imlay's book and of Kentucky in emigrant circles both in Britain and the eastern United States appears from remarks he makes in the very first pages of the book, in which he sets out first to consider, and then to resolutely discard one by one all possible sites for settlement (including Imlay's Kentucky) until only western Pennsylvania remains – allegedly for such 'objective' reasons as its ideal climate, cheapness of land, and richness of the soil.

Cut from the same hybrid fabric as Imlay's text – being a blend of an epistolary travelogue, a radical pamphlet, and a tract on emigration –

Cooper's book is set up in terms of a textual dialectic, not just between traveller and landscape but between traveller and traveller; between travel narrative and travel narrative; and between one radical ideology and another. Appealing to a string of authorities – historical as well as fictional – Cooper explicitly takes on Imlay and his Kentucky scheme. While first quasi-graciously admitting that 'Imlay has told the truth', he immediately adds that he has not told 'the whole truth', subsequently going on to demonstrate that Imlay is actually a blatant liar.[33] In contrast to what Imlay claimed, Cooper argues, Kentucky's climate is in fact hot and damp; the soil too rich and produce too dear; the land is inaccurately surveyed, infested with mosquitoes and hostile Indians, and so on. As each writer tries to set up an intricate genealogy of textual authorities supporting his position (extracting or simply reprinting such texts as the US Constitution; Franklin's 'Information To Those Who Would Remove to America'; currency conversion tables; and surveys of import and export duties), their competing narratives become curiously intertextual to the point where the reader begins to get the impression that the tussle is not so much over an actual landscape as over the *representation* of that landscape: the travelling that is described largely takes place in the *textual* landscape handed down from previous writers on America, rather than in some actual backwoods landscape. In this way, the travel narrative, as well as the 'America' it describes, become part of the rhetoric of early 1790s radical debate, and achieve a significance beyond, and independent of, both the genre and the country.

In the dialectic between Imlay's and Cooper's texts, Cooper's *Some Information Respecting America* was often cited as the winner; for one thing, it was Cooper's book that persuaded the Bristol Pantisocrats, led by Coleridge and Southey, to opt for settlement on the banks of the Susquehanna rather than those of Imlay's Ohio River.[34] It is not difficult to see why Cooper's book had this impact on prospective emigrants. Not only did Cooper, seeing that his book came out two years after Imlay's, have the advantage of being able to respond critically to Imlay's text and correct his mistakes, but, more importantly, he was in a position to present his arguments for emigration to America in the light of the rapidly changing cultural and political climate in Europe. Thus, whereas the arcadian, Rousseauesque flavour of Imlay's *Topographical Description* – borrowing heavily from the language of the sentimental and the picturesque – appealed to many progressive minds during the climate of universal optimism immediately following the French Revolution, the onset of a reactionary, anti-Jacobin movement in Britain and elsewhere in the wake of the outbreak of the Terror rendered it much less effective as an argument in favour of emigration *after* 1793. As the reasons for emigration to America amongst

British radicals were changing from creating a transatlantic utopia to fleeing from oppression at home, there was a growing need for practical, down-to-earth, reliable 'information respecting America' – the timely publication of Cooper's book catered precisely for all those who either by choice or by force needed to make a speedy getaway from Britain.[35]

But it was not merely the counter-revolutionary reaction in Britain that contributed to the success of Cooper's *Some Information*, the waning of the French Revolution as the inspiring example for British radicalism itself worked in its favour. Whereas Imlay in his *Topographical Description* was still staunchly sympathetic towards the ideology of the French Revolution and was actively involved in exporting it to the American west, Cooper is equally adamant in his *dismissal* of the regime in France for having established 'compleat and absolute despotism': 'Highly as I approve of many alterations in the theory and practice of government adopted by the French', Cooper writes with direct reference to the Terror, 'it is impossible for me to approve of the ferocious injustice of many of their practices.' The only benefit of radically egalitarian post-Revolutionary France, according to Cooper, is that the country is unlikely to become an industrialised nation. In contrast again to Imlay, Cooper reveals himself more and more as a convinced Jeffersonian agrarian, and he admits at one point that he 'detest[s] the manufacturing system' because of the 'fallacious prosperity it induces, its instability, and its evil effect on the happiness and the morals of the bulk of the people'. Cooper begins to sound distinctly Luddite when he goes on to attack Alexander Hamilton for his support of a commercial and manufacturing system that will reduce 'a large portion of the people ... into mere machines, ignorant, debauched, and brutal'. By contrast, says Cooper, farming in America will not only be very profitable but will also enhance familial bliss, safeguard an individual's independence and civil rights, and allow 'him' to participate in the running of the country – pointing out that 'nine-tenths of the legislators of America are farmers'.[36]

But even in 1794 the Jeffersonians and their dream of an American Arcadia were beginning to lose the battle against the Hamiltonians and their vision of a commercial and industrial federalist America. The Alien and Sedition Acts, which the Federalists introduced in 1798 in order to gag the propagandists for the French Revolution and Jefferson's Democratic-Republican Party, sealed the fate of radical pastoralism in the United States, and even Jefferson's temporary return to power after the presidential elections of 1800 could not reverse this trend. Significantly, when Count Volney – renowned French traveller, geographer, political theorist, historian, orientalist, and radical thinker – met his old friend Jefferson during his tour of America in 1798, the Frenchman discovered to his great disappointment that the momentum for a French–American strategic alliance was already over. Disappointed and shocked by the strong anti-revolutionary, xenophic mood that had set in in America, Volney could observe only that the Americans were really rather prejudiced and narrow-minded, 'the character and principles of their leaders ... deplorably degenerated', and that they owed the success of their Revolution 'more to their remote and disconnected situation, to their distance from powerful neighbours and the theatre of war, to a lucky and fortuitous concurrence of events, than to the wholesome vigour of their laws, or the wisdom and discretion of their governors'.[37]

To the radical traveller (as Thomas Paine was to discover upon his return to the United States in 1802), America was no longer a congenial destination, nor was the travel narrative any longer the medium of radicalism that it had been in the early 1790s. Commercialism in the book trade had reduced radical thought to just another commodity – a development that is perhaps most ironically illustrated by the fact that the third edition of the *Topographical Description*, a motley miscellany on America which appeared in London in 1797 and which Imlay almost certainly had no hand in, reprints Letter III of Thomas Cooper's book, in which he argues *against* Kentucky and in favour of the Susquehanna, sandwiched between Imlay's Letters VII and VIII, in which the latter offers diametrically opposed arguments. Not that Imlay would by then have minded – or cared: he was too busy trying to stay out of reach of the London courts at that point in time, and besides, he would probably have sold the Revolution to the highest bidder anyway, had there still been a market for it. Similarly, it is unlikely that Cooper would have minded: he was fast on his way to becoming a respected pillar of society – a Pennsylvania land commissioner, and later one of the founding presidents of South Carolina College, Columbia, a man whom President Adams referred to in his old age as 'a learned, ingenious, scientific, and talented madcap'. Cooper thus never quite made it to his utopia on Loyalsock Creek, after all, while Imlay died in virtual obscurity far away from Kentucky, on the isle of Jersey. A shrewd entrepreneur in the guise of naive backwoodsman trying to sell Kentucky to British farmers and French revolutionaries, and an agrarian idealist in the guise of radical trying to sell Pennsylvania to Pantisocrats and the 'friends of liberty': two pedlars of land, dreams, and revolutions overtaken by time.

Notes

1 For a discussion of the popularity of the American Golden Age in the Romantic period and its influence on the history of Romantic primitivism in

general, and on Romantic literature in particular, see Robert Bechtold Heilman, *America in English Fiction, 1760–1800* (Baton Rouge, 1937), notably ch. 9, 'Evolution of the Golden Age'.

2 W. Matthews, *Historical Review of North America – by a gentleman immediately returned from a tour of that continent*, 2 vols (Dublin, 1789), Preface, 1: xiv.

3 Jedidiah Morse, *The American Geography; or, A view of the Present Situation of the United States of America* (Elizabethtown, 1789), Preface, v.

4 Quoted in Howard C. Rice, introduction, *Travels in North America in the Years 1780, 1781, and 1782*, by the Marquis de Chastellux, revised translation (1786; Chapel Hill, 1963), 38.

5 Generally speaking, accounts of America by English travellers published before the first decade of the nineteenth century were not very reliable sources for factual information about the country – some erring (or distorting) on the negative side (notably during and immediately following the Revolution), others on the positive side (notably in radical circles in the 1790s). It is only from the beginning of the nineteenth century onwards that, in the words of Jane Louise Mesick, 'a change becomes quite apparent to the reader of travel literature. One has an increasing sense of treading upon the firmer ground of fact rather than upon the quagmire of imagination and prejudice' (*The English Traveller in America, 1785–1835* (New York, 1922), 344).

6 See Rev. David Jones, *A Journal of Two Visits Made to some Nations of Indians on the West Side of the River Ohio, in the Years 1772 and 1773* (1774; Fairfield, 1973).

7 See Heilman, *America in English Fiction*, 38.

8 In the Preface to his travel novel *The Emigrants*, for instance, Imlay states explicitly that it is his aim 'to prompt many readers to turn their thoughts towards the important political questions now agitated throughout Europe; for upon the fate of which, doubtless, materially depends the happiness of mankind' (*The Emigrants, &c.; or, The History of an Expatriated Family, Being a Delineation of English Manners, Written in America*, ed. and intro. W. M. Verhoeven and Amanda Gilroy (1793; Harmondsworth, 1998), 10.

9 Emigration to America was part of the spirit of the age, becoming increasingly popular in the early 1790s among a wide range of disprivileged and disenfranchised British citizens, not just among radicals. In its issue for May 1793 the *Gentlemen's Magazine* reported, 'Several of our periodical publications have of late abounded with essays written to prove the superior felicity of American farmers, and to recommend our husbandmen to quit their native plains, and seek for happiness and plenty in the Transatlantic desarts' (*Gentlemen's Magazine* 63 (1793), 401). The same periodicals, however, frequently carried essays warning against the dubious activities of British and American land-jobbers, who were trying to tempt potential emigrants to settle in the New World, and sell them land to which they held the rights. Thus, in September 1793 the *Gentlemen's Magazine* published a review abstract of *Letters on Emigration, By a Gentleman Lately Returned from America*, which, according to the reviewer, 'contain[s] much good admonition to the several classes of men who

are disposed to emigrate'. Commenting on the large numbers of emigrants that returned to Britain destitute and disillusioned, the reviewer can conclude only that 'this land of universal promise is the land of general disappointment' (*Gentlemen's Magazine* 65 (1793), 760). The travelling gentleman himself ends his *Letters* on an equally dismissive note: 'But, it may be asked, ought no description of persons to emigrate? The reply is obvious – The guilty *must*, and the very unfortunate *will*, though the prejudices of the natives are too apt to confound the latter with the former' (*Letters on Emigration* (London, 1794), 76). For a detailed analysis of pre-Revolutionary emigration to British North America, see Bernard Bailyn, *The Peopling of British North America: An Introduction* (New York, 1986) and *Voyagers to the West: A Passage in the People of America on the Eve of the Revolution* (New York, 1986).

10 For an introductory study of the influence of these writers on Pantisocracy, see Stuart Andrews, 'Fellow Pantisocrats: Brissot, Cooper and Imlay', *Symbiosis* 1: 1 (April 1997), 35–47.

11 Charles Pigott, *A Political Dictionary* (London, 1795), 17, 113.

12 See *Gentleman's Magazine* (1794), Supplement, 1171.

13 Joseph Priestley, *Memoirs of Dr. Joseph Priestley, to the year 1795 / written by himself; with a continuation, to the time of his decease, by his son, Joseph Priestley; and observations on his writings, by Thomas Cooper* (Northumberland, 1806), 1: 126.

14 For a detailed description of the background of Cooper's emigration scheme, see Dumas Malone, *The Public Life of Thomas Cooper, 1783–1839* (New Haven, 1926), especially chs 1–3.

15 *The British Critic* 5 (January 1795), 27.

16 *Gentleman's Magazine* (1794), Supplement, 1170.

17 See Richard Holmes, *Coleridge: Early Visions* (New York, 1990), 89. For a fascinating full-scale analysis of the emigration of British radicals to America in the Revolutionary period, see Michael Durey, *Transatlantic Radicals and the Early American Republic* (Lawrence, 1997).

18 Gilbert Imlay, *A Topographical Description of the Western Territory of North America* (London, 1792), iv.

19 *Ibid.*, 1.

20 *Ibid.*, 45.

21 *The Emigrants*, 213.

22 *Topographical Description*, 107–8.

23 Gilbert Imlay, *A Topographical Description of the Western Territory of North America* (1792; 3rd, expanded edn, London, 1797), Introduction, xii.

24 John Seelye, *Beautiful Machine: Rivers and the Republican Plan, 1755–1825* (Oxford and New York, 1991), 156.

25 *The Emigrants*, 25.

26 *Topographical Description*, 108.

27 Frederick Jackson Turner, *The Frontier in American History* (Cambridge, Mass., 1920), 161, 205.

28 J. Hector St John de Crèvecoeur, *Letters from an American Farmer* (1782; Harmondsworth, 1981), 70.

29 *The Emigrants*, 233. The community is situated on the banks of the Ohio near Louisville and constitutes in total an area of about 256 square miles, which is parcelled out to men who served with Arl—ton in the Revolutionary War (presumably because they are most likely to be men of honour and common sense). These men and their families will live in an idyllic, enchanting spot, against the background of the impetuous Ohio River, the gushing fountain that gives the community its name, fertile meadows, whispering breezes and warbling birds. The days follow a regular routine of agricultural cultivation and rural relaxation, including much dancing to rustic music. Bellefont is no doubt the type of insular Arcadia promised by Imlay to prospective emigrants as part of his land-jobbing activities. The society is organised along radical, Godwinian notions of social and political justice; each man owns the section of land that he occupies, and all males over the age of twenty-one are entitled to vote for members of a house of representatives, who, in turn, elect a president. The members are to meet every Sunday throughout the year to discuss issues of agriculture, arts, government and jurisprudence. The subversive, anti-ecclesiastical Sunday meeting as well as the structure of its government confirm that Arl—ton's community is to be a secessionist state, independent of the government of the United States: rooted in a tradition of French physiocratic thought, and turning south (*not* east), towards Lousiana, and beyond, towards Revolutionary France, for guidance and support.

30 Imlay, *A Topographical Description*, 3rd edn, Introduction, xi.

31 *Topographical Description*, 7.

32 Thomas Cooper, *Some Information Respecting America* (London and Dublin, 1794), Preface, iii.

33 *Ibid.*, 24.

34 Having just read Cooper's book in 1794, Coleridge wrote excitedly to Southey, 'By all means read, ponder Cooper, and when I hear your thoughts I will give you the results of my own' (*Collected Letters of Samuel Taylor Coleridge*, ed. E. L. Griggs, 6 vols (Oxford, 1956–71), 1: 93).

35 A second edition of *Some Information Respecting America* appeared in London in 1795; a French translation was published in Paris in the same year.

36 *Some Information Respecting America*, 75, 77, 77–8, 78, 73.

37 C. F. Volney, *A View of the Soil and Climate of the United States of America*, trans. Charles Brockden Brown (1803; Philadelphia, 1804), Preface, xv. Charles Brockden Brown, himself at one time an uncompromising convert to Godwin's school of radical anarchy, lashes out at Volney in his 'Translator's Preface' for denouncing the American Revolution. Commenting on the fact that Volney never completed a projected second volume, Brown writes, 'Fortunately for Volney, circumstances have prevented him from publishing his observations on the government and manners of the people. These are topics, on which his prejudices as a Frenchman, and as a vain and captious

mortal, would have abundant opportunity to show themselves, and in which he would have been in perpetual danger of shocking the prejudices of the people he described' (Translator's Preface, xxii).

Francis Wilford and the colonial construction of Hindu geography, 1799–1822

Nigel Leask

In 1799 the English edition of *Asiatic Researches* (the official journal of the Asiatic Society of Bengal) carried the first in a series of sensational articles on ancient Hindu geography and mythography by one Lt Francis Wilford.[1] Little is known of Wilford's life (1761?–1822) except that he was a Hanoverian by birth, married to an Indian woman, Khanum Bibi Sahib, and, as a serving officer in the Bengal Engineers, acted as assistant to the Surveyor-General 1786–90, being passed over for promotion to the post itself in 1794.[2] Initially involved in the survey of Bihar, Wilford moved to Banares, where he commissioned Mughal Beg to make a survey of southern Punjab and Bawalpur in the late 1790s; retiring from the army in 1794, Wilford was appointed secretary of Jonathan Duncan's newly founded Sanskrit College. An institution funded by the East India Company for the training of pandits in Sanskrit language and literature, the Banares College provides the institutional site for the scholarship discussed in this chapter; many of the anxieties and instabilities evinced by Wilford's orientalism seem to have been endemic to the College itself.[3]

Wilford was a respected associate of the Asiatic Society of Bengal, founded by his friend Sir William Jones in 1784. For some years in the 1790s rumours had circulated in orientalist and antiquarian circles in Bengal and Europe of Wilford's 'discoveries' concerning the relationship between Hindu traditions, the Bible, and ancient British antiquities. Reuben Burrow, in an article on Hindu mathematics published in the previous volume of *Asiatic Researches*, announced Wilford's impending work as 'the first true representation of Scriptural and Hindoo geography'. A hint of the extravagance of things to come is contained in Burrow's confident deduction from Wilford's evidence: 'that the Druids of Britain were Brahmins is beyond the least shadow of doubt'.[4]

Throughout the 1790s Wilford had been laboriously combing Puranic and other Sanskrit sources for geographical material, in collaboration with a pandit (never named) for whom he had secured a post at the Banares Sanskrit College. Because, properly speaking, there was no such thing as ancient Hindu 'geography', Wilford was led to admit that his work was more in the nature of a *construction* than a simple translation of his sources. He described how he had extracted his geographical materials from the 'historical poems' or rather 'legendary tales' of the Hindus collected for him by his pandit. Sanskrit cosmography had been metamorphosed into geography by 'follow[ing] the track, real or imaginary, of [Hindu] deities and heroes; comparing all their legends with such accounts of holy places in the regions of the west ... preserved by the Greek mythologists; and endeavouring to prove the identity of the places by the similarity of names and remarkable circumstances'.[5] By proceeding in this manner, Wilford was in fact simply following the methodology of Sir William Jones and other eighteenth-century orientalists in syncretising Sanskrit with classical and biblical narratives, establishing transcultural correspondences by means of often crude conjectural etymologies. Although Wilford's reputation did not long outlast the 'scientific' respectability of his theories, his work none the less exerted a powerful influence on early nineteenth-century antiquarians and Romantic poets like S. T. Coleridge, Robert Southey, Tom Moore, and Percy Shelley.[6]

In her essay on 'Burke and the Indian Sublime', Sara Suleri has described 'the central representational unavailability that Indian cultures and histories, even its sheer geography ... pos[ed] to the colonizing eye'.[7] In light of this discursive difficulty, we can see Wilford's project as being inspired by a will to assimilate the cultural heterogeneity of India into the metanarratives of European universal history and geography. In this chapter my aim is to show how Wilford's mimetic 'recognition' of Christian and British nationalist traditions in the (putative) texts of Sanskrit antiquity – a *displaced* prioritisation of the Same in the Other – would come to be exposed, in the course of his troubled scholarly career, as a form of colonial *mimicry*. Homi Bhabha has described mimicry as characteristic of the ambivalence of colonial discourse; on the one hand it is 'a complex strategy of reform, regulation and discipline, which "appropriates" the Other as it visualizes power', and on the other it is 'a desire that, through the repetition of *partial presence*, which is the basis of mimicry, articulates those disturbances of cultural, racial, and historical difference that menace the narcissistic demand of colonial authority'.[8] The main body of my essay accordingly examines Wilford's appropriation of the Other in terms of the syncretic and mimetic strategies employed in constructing a 'Hindu geography'. By way of a conclusion, however, I consider the scandal which exposed the assumed authority of this project work as a sham, thereby raising the problematic nature of colonial mimicry.

Egypt and Mount Caucasus

Wilford's first essay of 1799 (nine more were to follow over the next decade or so) was entitled 'On Egypt and other Countries adjacent to the Ca'li river, or Nile of Ethiopia. From the ancient books of the Hindus'. He claimed to have discovered a Sanskrit account of Abyssinia (or 'Cusha-dweepa') and the River Nile which corroborated some of the recent theories of the Scottish traveller James Bruce that the site of the terrestrial paradise was the source of the Nile in the unexplored mountains of Ethiopia.[9] More startlingly, he announced his discovery of a Sanskrit version (from a vague source named as the *Padma-puran*) of the story of Noah or Satyavrayata and his three sons Jyapeti, Charma and Sharma. After the Babylonian dispersion, the sons of Sharma had emigrated to the banks of the Nile or Cali. The Negro sons of Charma, cursed because their father had scoffed at Noah when the latter was drunk on rice-wine, had emigrated to India and thence to Egypt. Wilford found proof of this in the fact that 'the very ancient statues of Gods in India have crisp hair, and the features of Negroes',[10] unlike the modern inhabitants. In Egypt the by now well-established sons of Sharma (the Semites) had expelled the Hasyasilas or sons of Charma into the desert, from whence they had populated the entire African continent.[11] This subordination of Egypt to India in terms of chronological priority is accompanied by a distinctly colonial construction of racial hierarchy in which the inhabitants of contemporary Africa are equated with the aboriginal inhabitants of India, both descended from the proscribed family of Ham, Charma or Hasyasilas ('the laugher').

Wilford's attempt to syncretise Sanskrit and Judaeo-Christian universal history here depended on the still-current ethnology of Genesis which had informed Jones's authoritative treatise *On The Family of Nations*. But Wilford's putative discovery of the Indian origin of Egyptian civilisation seemed to settle a long-standing controversy concerning the relative antiquity of the two civilisations, decisively establishing India as the *Ursprung* (a fact which earned Wilford the plaudits of Friedrich Schlegel in his influential *Essay on the Language and Wisdom of the Indians*, 1808). Wilford's discovery of an indigenous Sanskrit account of the post-diluvian dispersal of the family of Noah unquestionably set out to corroborate the authenticity of the Biblical narrative. In conformity with the practice of Anglican mythographers and divines like Jacob Bryant, Thomas Maurice and George Stanley Faber, Wilford sought to confirm the historicity of revelation and of the ethnology of Genesis from external sources, namely the records of Hindu (or other pagan) religions.

However, Wilford's 'discovery' contained distinctly subversive implications, particularly in the light of attempts by French Jacobin mythographers like J.-S. Bailly, Constantin Volney, and Charles Dupuis to discredit the 'originality' and authenticity of Scripture. In 1776 Bailly's *History of Hindu Astronomy* had claimed that the Hindu astronomical tables obtained by Le Gentil at Pondicherry set the date of the last Hindu yuga at 3102 BC, 650 years before the accepted date of the Flood. Moreover, this date was established by astronomical observation rather than the haphazard genealogical method employed by Bishop Usher and his followers in constructing a Bible-based chronology. The possibility therefore existed that the Pentateuch was simply copied by Moses from an earlier Egyptian (and now *Sanskrit*, if Wilford was to be believed) source. The support of French sceptics (and later German 'higher mythographers') for a Hindu source of Scripture subverted the pious project of British orientalism embodied in the work of the Asiatic Society; having lost their foothold in India, the French could well afford to make havoc with the colonial ideology of their rival.

In this connection it is vital to note that Wilford's essays were published in the midst of a 'war of ideas' between Britain and revolutionary France. His 'On Egypt' essay (as well those which followed it) greatly enhanced the European popularity of *Asiatic Researches*, which went through four editions, all of which sold out immediately. In 1803 the issues of the journal to date were translated into French by Louis Langles with annotations by Cuvier, Lamarck, and the astronomer Delambre which fully exploited the subversive potential of Wilford's essays. As if to rub salt in the wounds of pious British orientalists, in 1806 the *Edinburgh Review* published an article detailing the progress made by French orientalists who were turning the 'discoveries' of Bengal-based British scholars to their own sceptical purposes.[12] The article was most probably written by the Scottish Sanskrit scholar Alexander Hamilton, who had been stranded in Paris after the sudden end of the Treaty of Amiens in 1802, during his return journey from India. Here he had collaborated with Louis Langles on a valuable catalogue of Sanskrit manuscripts in the Bibliothèque Royale (Langles notoriously argued that the Pentateuch was based on Vedic sources) and taught Friedrich Schlegel the elements of Sanskrit.[13]

Disturbed by the possibility of such heterodox interpretations of his work, Wilford had apparently hesitated for several years before publishing in *Asiatic Researches*. This is confirmed by the fact that an afterword by Sir William Jones (who had died in 1794) was appended to the 'On Egypt' essay. As President of the Society, Jones testified in fulsome terms to the authenticity of Wilford's Puranic sources (which he claimed to have personally examined) and even quoted a long passage from the Satyavrayata narrative. This would subsequently cause great embarrassment to Jones's admirers, for reasons which will become apparent below. Jones went on to deny (in an uncharacteristically meandering argument) that the similarity between the narratives of Satyavrayata and Noah could in any way jeopardise the priority of the latter or suggest that 'the divine legislator borrowed any part of his work from the Egyptians'.[14] The only unease betrayed by Jones's 'Remarks' is evident in his scruples regarding Wilford's method of 'conjectural etymology' which, although undeniably 'ingenious' and 'often plausible', Jones felt still required to be 'confirmed by historical proof'.[15]

In the 'On Egypt' essay Wilford had announced his forthcoming magnum opus 'On the Sacred Isles in the West', which purported to identify the Hindu sacred isles 'or the place of religious duty' with Bretashtan or Britain. Having whetted the appetites of his readers (in the assurance that the 'Sacred Isles' essay would also contain a systematic account of Hindu geography), he published a number of preliminary essays in the next few issues of the journal. The most notable of these, published in the sixth volume, was the essay 'On Mount Caucasus', of particular importance for poets like Southey, Coleridge, and Shelley as well as for the mythographers Maurice and Faber. Wilford 'orientalised' the Caucasian *Ursrpung* by placing it in the Hindu Kush (the 'Indian Caucasus' used by Shelley as a setting for Act II of *Prometheus Unbound*). He now located the 'abode of the progenitors of mankind, both before and after the flood in th[e] mountainous tract which extends from Balkh and Candahar to the Ganges'.[16] Citing (unnamed) Sanskrit sources and oral legends communicated to him by a Brahmin traveller called 'Areeswara', he located the terrestrial paradise inhabited by 'Adima' and 'Iva' in Kashmir, beneath Mount Meru, the focal point of the Hindu geography.

After the deluge, Satyavrayata or Noah apparently made fast the Ark to the famous peak of 'C'haisa-ghar' which the Puranas denominated 'Aryavarta, Aryawart or India, an appellation which has no small affinity with the Arrarat of Scripture'. The fact that both Caucasus and Arrarat have two locations, one east and one further west, is explained by Wilford in simple diffusionist terms: 'the appellation of Caucasus, or Coh-Cas, extended from India to the shores of the Mediterranean and Euxine seas; most probably because this extensive range was inhabited by C'hasas'.[17] Readers of Jacob Bryant's *Analysis of Antient Mythology* (1774–76), still in 1799 the standard British mythography, would recognise these 'C'hasas' as the Cushite progeny of Ham who, according to Bryant, colonised much of the gentile world from China to Cornwall after the dispersion from Babylon, and traces of whose language were still contained in the radicals of most ancient and modern tongues. We will see how Wilford would adapt this idea in theorising a diagonal 'Sanskrit' of 'Saca' zone stretching from Iceland to Sumatra in his later 'Sacred Isles' essay. It is worth extrapolating one important point from this link with Bryant. Notwith-standing Wilford's claims that his 'discoveries' were based on novel ethnographic information informed by Sanskrit scholarship (such as really did inform Jones's hypothesis of a proto-Indo-European *ursprache*), it is evident that he was still basically dependent on Bryant's 'Cushites', and beyond him to the 'universal histories' of the seventeenth century, for his fundamental thesis.

Developing the claims of his 'Egypt and India' essay, Wilford now produced Hindu versions of the Biblical narratives of Adam and Eve and Cain and Abel as well as of the family of Noah. Wilford claimed that Noah himself, 'an emanation of Vishnu', is also named by the Hindus 'Mach'ho-dar-Nath', or the sovereign prince in the belly of the fish' and that his mummified body still survived in a vaulted tomb at Naulakhi near Kabul. Descending from the Ark on the summit of Ararat/Kashgar, Noah's family inhabited the caves in the region around the city of Bamiyan, the city founded by his son, the patriarch Shem. Wilford cites the fruit trees and vines which apparently abounded in the region between Bamiyan and the source of the Ganges as further evidence that the region was the patriarchal paradise; 'when we are told in Scripture of Noah cultivating the Vine, we may be sure, that it was in its native country, or at least very near it'.[18]

Moving now on to the terrain of Greek mythology, Wilford sought to add evidence from Ptolemy's *Geography* and Nonnus's *Dionysiaca* to the Puranic and biblical medley. By means of an etymological tour de force, Wilford identified the Greek Mount Parnassus with Meru/Kashgar/Ararat, and Dionysus or 'Deva-Nahusha', with Noah the cultivator of vines. In the same region at the foot of Meru, Dionysus founded the city of Deva-Nahusha-nagaris (or Dionysiopolis in Greek), shortened to Nyasa. Although Puranic tradition apparently had Dionysus himself conquering all the land to the north-west of India, including the British Isles, Wilford preferred to argue that the worship of Dionysus was carried into Greece from Kashmir by Deucalion, former king of the region.[19]

Deucalion, familiar to readers of Ovid as the Greek 'Noah' who survives the deluge, was also identified by a process of 'mythological doubling' (although it is never clear whether as the son or the father) with the figure of Pramat'hesa or Prometheus.[20] Like Deucalion/Noah/Satyavrayata, Prometheus descended from his mountain peak in the Hindu Kush where he had been confined (either immolated in his tomb-like Ark or chained to the peak by the vengeful Jupiter) to regenerate humankind. This is figured by his habitation of the cave 'which is to be seen to this day near the pass of Sheibar between Ghor-bard and Bamiyan [Nyasa?]' in the vicinity of Kabul.[21] However extravagant Wilford's account may seem, we can find in it many of the ingredients of Shelley's 'orientalised' lyrical drama *Prometheus Unbound*, which appears in this light as a retelling of the story of Noah and the post-diluvial regeneration of humankind in the light of (an albeit spurious) 'Hindu' mythology rather than biblical tradition. Jones's fears about the sceptical potential of Wilford's 'discoveries' are fully borne out by Shelley's interpretation. In his poetical version of the myth, Prometheus/Noah has to be reunited with the allegorical (geopolitical) female figure of Asia before his full human potential as liberator of mankind can be realised. Shelley's point is that only by correlating the biblical narrative with its classical and oriental sources can it be freed from the dogmatic strait-jacket of organised Christianity. The example of Shelley suggests that French mythographers were not alone in turning Wilford's defence of the historicity of scripture into an *estrangement* of biblical tradition.

The Sacred Isles in the West

Wilford's tour de force, the 'Sacred Isles in the West' essays, took up almost six hundred pages in the eighth to eleventh volumes (1805–10) of *Asiatic Researches*. Despite the fact that the work was prepared with the assistance of the highly respectable Sanskrit scholar Henry Colebrooke,[22] 'The Sacred Isles' took the speculative extravagance of Romantic mythography to a new extreme, in presenting two exorbitant theses deriving from Wilford's putative Sanskrit sources. In the first thesis (outlined in the fourth and fifth essays on 'Vicramaditya and Salivahana' and 'The Origin and Decline of the Christian Religion in India') Wilford claimed to have discovered a Sanskrit version of the birth, life, and crucifixion of Christ, called *Salivahana*. Salivahana was 'the son of a virgin and … the great Tacshaca, carpenter or artist', hunted by the devil-worshipping tyrant Vicramaditya, because it has been prophesied by Cali-devi that the latter's thousand-year-old dynasty will be overthrown by a 'divine child'.[23] Breathing life into an army of clay warriors (both the Qur'an and the Greek apocryphal gospels apparently described the Christ-child 'making figures of clay'), Salivahana defeats Vicrama and cuts off his head. He then retreats into the desert and becomes a Muni or mystic, later to be crucified on a Y-shaped plough.[24] Wilford's Salivahana is a syncretic version of the Gospel life of Jesus and the myth of Prometheus and Jupiter. It also builds on elements of the story of Krishna, whose life had been compared to that of Christ by Sir William Jones.[25] The Anglican mythographer Thomas Maurice had dedicated a third part of the second volume of his *History of Hindostan* (1795–98) to refuting Volney's claim that the Gospels were distorted copies of the Krishna narrative, 'a subject of too deep importance to Britons, both individually and nationally, to be slightly or rapidly passed over'.[26]

Aware of the polemical tightrope he was treading, Wilford qualified his antiquarian enthusiasm by admitting that the Salivahana story 'is a most crude and undigested mass of heterogeneous legends, taken from the apocryphal gospel of the infancy of Christ, the tales of the Rabbis and Talmudists concerning Solomon, with some particulars about Muhammed ... jumbled together with ... the history of the Persian kings of the Sassanian dynasty'.[27] Given that Christianity had been established in India by AD 189, Wilford admitted that certain features of the Christian story had permeated Hindu and Buddhist records and become interpolated into indigenous religious traditions. For all his protestations, however, the subversive implication of Wilford's discovery remained, as the angry reaction of Anglican divines and mythographers to the *Sacred Isles* essays would attest.

Wilford's second exorbitant claim in these essays leads my argument back to the question of the colonial construction of Hindu *geography*, to which Wilford's mythographical speculations about Satyavarata and Salivahana were really only an addendum. In the eighth volume of *Asiatic Researches*, Wilford finally got round to publishing his systematic survey of Hindu geography, drawing upon Major Rennell's recent cartography of the Indian subcontinent in order to 'decode' his classical Sanskrit sources, otherwise more poetic than factual. Wilford began by professing the magnitude of his elucidatory task, given that the Hindus

> seem to view the globe through a prism, as if adorned with the liveliest colours. Mountains are of solid gold, bright with 10,000 suns; and others are of precious gems ... There are rivers and seas of liquid amber, clarified butter, milk, curds, and intoxicating liquors. Geographical truth is sacrificed to a symmetrical arrangement of countries, mountains, lakes and rivers, with which they are highly delighted.[28]

Wilford's impatience with the metaphors and hyperboles characteristic of Hindu cosmography was linked to his obdurate insistence on discovering an underlying 'scientific' truth, in the interest of a thesis every bit as extravagant as these mountains of gems and seas of curd. Incredibly, he sought to prove that the fabled 'Sacred Isles in the West' (the principal of which is 'Sweta-dwipa' or the White Island), source of 'all the fundamental and mysterious transactions of [the Hindu] religion' were none other than the British Isles. The origin of Indian religion and culture now turns out to be located not in the terrestrial paradises of Abyssinia or the Hindu Kush but in the remote northern islands of the colonial motherland itself. Exceeding the claims of a tradition of patriotic antiquarians from William Stukeley to Charles Vallancey and Edward Davies, who had asserted the oriental origins of the ancient Britons, Irish, or Welsh, Wilford now discovered the Indo-Sanskrit *Ursprung* itself to derive from an anterior, British source. In the annals of British colonial discourse it would be hard to find a more transparent case of cultural narcissism.

Detaching the Sanskrit language from the geopolitical entity of India, Wilford postulated the existence of a 'Sanskrit belt' '40 degrees broad, across the old continent, in a SE and NW direction, from the eastern shores of the Malay peninsula to the western extremity of the British isles'.[29] It is surely not fortuitous that this geographical belt – from the British Isles through the Mediterranean and Greek islands, the Near East, Persia, and 'Hindustan' to the Malay peninsula and Java – loosely corresponded with the zone of British political influence or aspiration during the decades which C. A. Bayly has described as Britain's 'Imperial Meridian'.[30] Wilford attributed to his Puranic sources the lotus-like division of the old continent into seven 'dwipas' or climates centred on Mount Meru, from whence four rivers flowed to the cardinal points of the earth. Moving in a north-westerly direction from *Jambu* (India), the six dwipas were as follows: *Cusa* (the country between the Persian Gulf, the Caspian Sea and the western boundary of India); *Placsha* (Asia Minor, Armenia, etc.); *Salmali* (Eastern Europe, bounded on the west by the Baltic and Adriatic Seas); *Crauncha* (Germany, France, and the northern parts of Italy); *Sacam* – alternatively *Swetam*, the 'white islands' (the British Isles, surrounded by the 'sea of milk'); and *Pushcara* (Iceland).[31]

In the 1810 instalment of his essay in *Asiatic Researches*, Wilford appended a map of north-western Europe, including the islands of Sacam, which he claimed to have derived from the Puranas. Following the syncretic procedure of his earlier essays, Wilford identified the British Isles with Atlantis, Crete, and the Aeolian isles of the ancients as well as with the Sanskrit Sacam. The 'aborigines of Britain', he continued, 'call it to this day Inis-wen, or the white island; the Inis-huna or Inis-Uina of Caledonian bards ... or the Al-Fionn, [which] in Galic, answers literally to Sweta-Saila, in Sanskrit, and to the Leucas-petra of Homer, or the White cliffs' [of Dover]. Modern Brahmins (Wilford added in a risible scrap of ethnographical detail attesting to the sanctity of Dover chalk) 'never use any but real British chalk, as they pretend, to mark their foreheads with: and this is carried by merchants all over India'.[32] One can see behind Wilford's method here the same loose transcultural etymologies employed in contemporary antiquarian works like Colonel Vallancey's *Ancient History of Ireland shown from Sanskrit Sources* or Edward Davies's *Celtic Researches*. It is no surprise to find Davies writing approvingly in 1807 that 'the idea of a mutual intercourse, between the sages of the east and the west, is countenanced by Mr Wilford's incomparable dissertation, upon Egypt and the Nile'.[33]

Wilford's identification of the fabular Hindu 'White Isles' with the geographical British Isles leads him to claim that 'in the Puranas, and in the Vedas also, as I am informed, the coming of a saviour from the West is often foretold'. This messianic myth of return is something of a commonplace in the annals of European imperialism, perhaps most famously exemplified by Hernan Cortes's claim to be the white-skinned, bearded Toltec god Queztalcoatl returning from exile in the East. But Wilford lends this venerable redemptive myth a more contemporary dimension. He asserted that Brahmins to this day proclaim that 'every man after death must go to Tri-cuta and Sweta ... there to stand trial before the king of justice, the Dharma-raja'; as such, the British Isles are 'the beginning and end of their worldly pilgrimage'. The Puranas also declare the White Isles to be the home of Vishnu, from whence Krishna (like Noah and Dionysus, apparently originally a British national!) brought the Vedas. Vyasa, the first who presumed to write the Vedas down in a book, resided so long in the White Isles that he was nicknamed Dwaipayana, 'he who resided in the islands'. Connected to this is Wilford's assertion that 'the light of revelation came from the west, and that the Vedas reside in the White Islands in human shape', because 'they are not written, but orally delivered'. In line with their transcendent status, the White Islands are moreover apparently 'incapable of decay, and [are] never involved in the destruction and ruin, which happens at each renovation of the world'.[34]

Wilford's *mimesis* is perhaps here at its most transparent, revealing an *orientalised* (in Edward Said's sense of the word) version of British national and imperial ideology. In the guise of Hindu 'scripture', we have representations of the following national myths: Britain as bearer of the civilising mission to corrupt Asiatic states, and above all the bringer of justice to its colonial subjects, long overshadowed by Asiatic despotism; British national identity defined by an unwritten ('orally delivered') constitution in contrast to, say, Napoleonic France; an account of the immutability of British political institutions ('este perpetua'), resisting the Polybian cycle of birth, maturity, and decay.

Going even further, on the authority of a legend from the 'Bhavishya-puran', Wilford claimed that 'there is a tribe of Brahmins in India to this day, actually descended from a sacerdotal tribe residing originally in the white isles'.[35] (Although Wilford does not have much to say about Druids, this is clearly the source of Reuben Burrow's remark, cited above, about the Druids being Brahmins.) Sacam, one of the names of the White Isles, is named after the Sacas, a heretical tribe who had originally emigrated from India about 2000 BC, at the time of Krishna, and conquered Britain. Significantly the German Wilford chose Sacas (or *Saxons*) as the founding race establishing the British/Indian connection, his adaptation of Bryant's Cushite theory; the Irish Vallancey preferred the Irish, the Welsh Davies the ancient Druids of Anglesey, and so on. Anyway, the sun-worshipping Sacas became renowned in the ancient world for the purity of their religion and, according to a Hindu legend, Krishna travelled to Britain in order to exhort their priests to return to India to restore the true faith. Eighteen families of Saca Brahmins obeyed Krishna's plea by returning to India, bringing with them the Vedic law later transcribed by Vyasa. When their mission was accomplished, however, Garuda refused them permission to go home, and they were forced to settle in India, where their descendants remain to this day.[36]

All Brahmins, Wilford emphasises, will acknowledge that they are not originally native to India (which is not, of course – *pace* Wilford's impeccable logic – the same as to say that they were natives of ancient Britain!). Despite the 'Anglicist' and missionary attacks on Brahmins which were becoming increasingly current by 1810 (in part deriving strength from Wilford's essays, as we shall see in a moment), the selectivity of Wilford's Brahmin genealogy participates in the privileging of Brahminical power by the orientalist institutions of the East India Company, particularly the Banares Sanskrit College, in the late eighteenth and early nineteenth centuries. As C. A. Bayly has written of this orientalist 'mummification' of Indian culture, 'hierarchy and the Brahmin interpretation of Hindu society which was theoretical rather than actual as late as 1750 was firmly ensconced a century later' owing to the colonial promotion of Brahmin influence.[37]

Brahminical fraud detected: Wilford's (unnamed) pandit

I now turn by way of a conclusion to the scandal surrounding Wilford's work, a scandal which highlighted the exorbitant nature, as it compromised the scholarly authority, of the 'Hindu Geography' which we have surveyed. The fact that Wilford's essays turned out to be based on forged sources is in a sense their most interesting feature for the critic, inasmuch as it gives them a literary value quite independent of the question of their geographical or mythographic veracity. The forgery scandal puts 'The Sacred Isles in the West' in the same company as Ireland's forged Shakespeare plays, or Macpherson's *Ossian*, or Chatterton's *Rowley Poems*, although the literary problem of forgery is significantly inflected by the colonial context in which the essays emerged.

When Wilford delivered a précis of his 'Sacred Isles' thesis to the Asiatic Society in 1804, the paper seems to have had a considerable impact and was received, like his earlier essays, as reputable scholarship. But the publication of the complete work in instalments in the *Asiatic Researches* between 1805 and 1810 had a very different effect upon the journal's readers, given Wilford's embarrassed acknowledgement of his forged sources in his introduction to the first essay in the eighth volume, in 1805.[38] Despite his insistence here that the published text had been purged of any details resting on dubious authority, considering the exorbitant nature of the essays' argument it is incredible that Wilford dared publish at all, unless as a sort of orientalist caprice closer in spirit to epic poetry than sober scholarship. How were his readers to take this strange sixty-page hybrid of truth and fiction, fact and fable, which admitted the instability of its evidence at the same time as it paraded its claim to represent truthfully the British origin of the ancient Hindus?

Let us examine Wilford's account of his deception in the 'Introduction' in the hope of casting some light on the matter. The real scandal of the 'Sacred Isles' appears here, appropriately enough, at the moment in which we become aware of Wilford's work as an early form of *ethnography*; that is, precisely at the moment in which his pandit (in the role of 'native informant') assumes an uncanny visibility. To explain the fact of his deception, Wilford needs to break the smooth surface of orientalist discourse and reveal, as it were, the material mode of production of his text. In the 'Introduction' (in contrast to the main text), we are made aware of a practical difference between the old universal histories and mythographies of the seventeenth and eighteenth centuries and the *modern* epistemological project of learned bodies like the Asiatic Society of Bengal. The latter (in contrast to the former) are already partaking in a form of anthropological enquiry, in a recognisably nineteenth- and twentieth-century sense of the term. As James Clifford has written in *The Predicament of Culture*, the authority of the classic Western anthropological text has been historically dependent upon the 'filtering out' of the actuality of discursive situations and individual interlocutors. 'Informants – along with field notes', Clifford writes, 'are crucial intermediaries, typically excluded from authoritative ethnography. The dialogical, situational aspects of ethnographic interpretation tend to be banished from the final representation.'[39] This exclusion is significantly waived in Wilford's 'Introduction', with its embarrassed qualification of the text's authority.

As was the common practice, Wilford always worked in collaboration with a learned Brahmin to whom he paid a generous fee to comb the 'Puranas and other books relative to my enquiries ... and arrange them under proper heads'. Wilford would then, it seems, set about translating these excerpts or 'vouchers' gleaned by his pandit. However, on account of his interest in syncretising European and Hindu traditions, Wilford obviously had had to let the pandit know what sort of game he was chasing: to this end he describes how he had 'amused [him]self with unfolding to him our [i.e. European] ancient mythology, history and geography'. The pandit in question was

> blunt and rough [in manner], and his arguing with me on several religious points with coolness, and steadiness, a thing very uncommon amongst natives ... raised him in my esteem. I affected to consider him my guru, or spiritual teacher; and at certain festivals, in return for his discoveries and communications, handsome presents were made to him and his family.[40]

Wilford relates how he had also given the pandit a generous grant to employ research assistants, as well as promoting his career at the Company-sponsored Banares Sanskrit College.

The crunch came, however, in late 1804 or early 1805. Resting on the laurels of his well-received articles in the Society's journal, Wilford was collating his pandit's excerpts with some of the original manuscripts prior to publishing 'The Sacred Isles'. He suddenly noticed a series of disconcerting irregularities in the text:

> I soon perceived, that whenever the word S'wetam or S'weta-dwipa the name of the principal of the Sacred Isles ... was introduced, the writing was somewhat different, and that the paper was of a different colour, as if stained. Surprised at this strange appearance, I held the page to the light, and perceived immediately that there was an erasure, and that some fize had been applied.

Wilford's subsequent discovery that not only 'The Sacred Isles', but also the 'On Egypt' essay (in particular the Satyavrayata/Noah story), all the Prometheus material, and much of the essay on Semiramis were extensively 'stained', 'brought on such paroxysms as threatened the most serious consequences, in my then infirm state of health'.[41] What made things even worse was that Sir William Jones himself had examined and approved the forged manuscripts upon which the 'On Egypt' essay was based, so that Wilford was guilty of having dragged the good name of the Asiatic Society and its late illustrious founder into the mud along with his own.

In the course of his anxious investigations Wilford discovered that the traditional Hindu 'sources' upon which his essays were based were largely the products of his pandit's syncretic (and *mimetic*) imagination. Wilford's account here slips into the discourse of the colonial stereotype, as it lays the whole blame upon the sly and ungrateful indolence of the native character. Having simply pocketed the money granted him to hire assistants, and 'in order to avoid the trouble of consulting books, [the pandit] conceived the idea of framing legends from what he recollected from the Puranas, and from what he had picked up in conversation [concerning European and Biblical legends] with me'.[42] 'Forging' individual names, altering traditional narratives or simply inventing myths (a practice usually described as 'mythopoeia' when encountered in the work of English poets like Blake, Shelley, and Keats), the mendacious Brahmin had 'disfigured' and 'adulterated' manuscripts in the possession of Wilford and of the library of the Banares Sanskrit College. Wilford suspected him of having forged no fewer than 12,000 lines of Puranic legend, often substituting two or three pages at a time in the loose-leaf Indian books of the period.

Even Wilford's assurance (in the 'Introduction') that he had deposited the vouchers upon which the 'clean' text of 'The Sacred Isles' was based in the hands of various Calcutta libraries and in the possession of reputable scholars like Henry Colebrooke – where they could be examined by sceptics – cannot have offered much reassurance to readers about to weigh through the six-hundred-odd pages which followed. Even the most sanguine must have suspected that the articles might share the qualities of the curate's egg, despite Wilford's remonstrances. A public outcry was initiated by pious reviewers and continued with the appearance of every new instalment of the *Asiatic Researches*, with the consequence that Wilford's essays were increasingly received as tissues of Brahminical mendacity rather than serious oriental scholarship. For obvious reasons the Biblical analogues were regarded as being more offensive than the geographical ones. For example, in an embarrassed recantation of his earlier enthusiasm for Wilford's work, Thomas Maurice published in 1812 a treatise entitled *Brahminical Fraud*. Wilford's revelation of the 'ethnographic' source of his essays in the introduction here became Maurice's warrant for ignoring the fact of Wilford's authorship and laying the whole blame upon his Brahmin informants. Maurice discovered a subversive collusion between the 'French' sceptical interpretation of Wilford's work and Brahminical mendacity. The well-connected Wilford (had not Sir William Jones and Henry Colebrooke 'authorised' his texts?) was cast as an innocent dupe, victim of 'attacks, secret and avowed, from the Asiatic quarter of the world, aided by European [i.e. French] ingenuity'.[43] Like most contemporary reviewers, Maurice did not swallow Wilford's special pleading for 'The Sacred Isles', which he regarded as every bit as much of a forgery as the other essays.

The sanctimonious tone of Maurice's 'indignation at the fraudful baseness of the sacerdotal tribe of India' exemplifies the twilight of orientalist mythography as a support for Christian revelation in Britain. Had not the repeated impositions of the Brahmins, Maurice insisted, 'shaken to the foundations ... all dependence on their vaunted books'?[44] If such was the reaction of the 'orientalist' Maurice, follower of Bryant and Jones and former admirer of Wilford's work, one can only imagine the effect of the Wilford scandal upon more sceptical indologists like Sir James Mackintosh and William Erskine of the Scottish-dominated, Whiggish-minded Bombay Literary Society. In 1805 (that is, in the immediate wake of Wilford's forgery disclosure) Mackintosh had affirmed that the Bombay Society's programme should henceforth exclude all 'antiquarian research as well as uncertain or merely curious disquisitions' in favour of political arithmetic, mineralogy and natural history.[45] Javed Majeed has recently suggested that the Wilford affair was a decisive negative influence upon another Scottish Indologist, James Mill, whose damning indictment of both Hindu tradition and British orientalist scholarship set the tone of his influential *History of British India* published in 1817.[46] In May 1820 the *Edinburgh Review* observed that 'the field of Indian Antiquities have been of late less diligently cultivated' in the context of a review of Franz Bopp's comparative Sanskrit grammar.[47] It is significant that Bopp's grammar was one of the only works on Sanskrit or related Indological subjects to be reviewed by the *Edinburgh* in the 1815–25 period, and that Bopp was profoundly hostile to the method of conjectural etymology employed by Wilford and other orientalists associated with the Asiatic Society. After Wilford, students of Indian language and religion were not going to make fools of themselves; arguably nineteenth-century British Indology never really recovered from the Wilford affair, combined with the hostility of influential commentators like Mill and Macaulay to all things relating to the subject.

It is possible that a postcolonial reading offers a more productive framework for interpreting the Wilford scandal. What if we take Maurice's polemic seriously and read the pandit's mendacity as a form of resistance against colonial authority? It is an especially tempting supposition in the light of Wilford's admission that his pandit had formerly been employed by a Maratha chieftain, that is, a representative of the major source of indigenous resistance to the consolidation of British power in India in this period. It is also noteworthy that the pandit's deception is politicised by its *collective* nature; upon being dismissed by Wilford, he 'brought ten Brahmins, not only as Compurgators, but also to swear, by what is most sacred in their religion, to the genuineness of these extracts'.[48] The abashed Wilford dismissed them all.

On the other hand, such an interpretation may be excessive in terms of the absence in early nineteenth-century India of a nationalist ideology which could focus indigenous resistance to British power, as it would a century later. Moreover, if the 'resistance theory' is to hold, the question remains as to why the pandit should have been forging texts so flattering to British imperial prestige. After all, was he not mimicking biblical narrative and anglocentric myths of origin in an indigenous Sanskrit idiom? A more historically rewarding approach might be to ask whether the pandit's notions of authenticity and 'scriptural' tradition can fairly be considered as equivalent to Wilford's at all. In giving Wilford what he wanted to find, the pandit was simply taking the fantasy of syncretist scholarship at its word, creatively mingling parts of European and Indian traditional narratives. The discrepancy lies between Wilford's notion of his pandit as a 'pure' channel for the transmission of timeless 'scriptural' truth, and the pandit's subaltern position within the apparatus of British colonial power. The pandit's mimicry undermines the essentialist ideology of nation and culture upon which Wilford's text depended. How differently Wilford's redemptive imperialist myth of origins reads when we know that it is based upon the creative misprision of his native informant – upon his *dialogic* involvement in constructing orientalist discourse – rather than upon any 'authoritative' Puranic text.

Regarded in this light, Wilford's real 'discovery' can be seen not as a lost Hindu version of Genesis or a Sanskrit account of Britain as source of Eastern religious mysteries, but rather as the exposure of the colonial power-relations which all along informed his, and the Asiatic Society's, scholarly programme. In Wilford's discovery of his pandit's forgery, what Johannes Fabian has described as anthropology's 'denial of coevalness' becomes suddenly evident, as the crisis-ridden historical moment of European colonialism erupts into the timeless antiquarianism of orientalist discourse.[49] Although it did little for his personal reputation (or that of Indological studies in early nineteenth-century Britain), perhaps after all Wilford did do the right thing by publishing the whole six hundred pages of 'The Sacred Isles'. The veracity of his project crippled by the disclosure of its hybrid provenance, it is paradoxical that this 'inauthentic' piece of Romantic scholarship perhaps offers a *more* authentic picture of the ambivalence of colonial discourse than any other comparable work of the period.

Nigel Leask

Notes

1 Francis Wilford, 'On Egypt and other countries adjacent to the Ca'li River, or Nile of Ethiopia', *Asiatic Researches* 3 (1799), 295–468.

2 Matthew Edny, *Mapping an Empire: The Geographical Construction of British India, 1765–1843* (Chicago, 1997), 137.

3 C. A. Bayly, 'Orientalists, Informants and Critics in Banaras, 1790–1860', unpublished paper presented at Reciprocal Perceptions of Different Cultures in South Asia Conference, Bonn, 15–19 December 1996; C. A. Bayly, *Empire and Information: Intelligence Gathering and Social Communication in India, 1780–1870* (Cambridge and New York, 1996), 91, 130. See 294 for a discussion of the tension in the Banares College between European orientalists like Wilford and the pandits.

4 Reuben Burrow, 'A Proof that the Hindoos had the Binomial Theory', *Asiatic Researches* 2 (1799), 488.

5 'On Egypt', *Asiatic Researches* 3 (1799), 4.

6 Given the habit of mythographers of the Jones school like Thomas Maurice and G. S. Faber of endorsing (with lengthy quotations) each other's theories in each other's books, as well as the massive circulation of *Asiatic Researches*, it is often hard to be exact on the question of transmission of ideas and influence. If one had read Maurice or Faber, or *Asiatic Reasearches*, or any of the many reviews of these works, one would probably be familiar with the theories of Wilford as well as of Jones and other orientalists. We have 'hard' evidence that Southey and Moore read Wilford's essays in *Asiatic Researches* because they cite them, often at considerable length, in the footnotes to their poems. See Robert Southey, *Curse of Kehama*, in *Poetical Works* (London, 1876), 566, 577, 585, 595, 621–2; and Thomas Moore, *Lalla Rookh*, in *Poetical Works* (London and Edinburgh, 1875), 117, 119. Stuart Curran has argued at some length for Wilford's influence on Shelley's *Prometheus Unbound* (*Shelley's Annus Mirabilis* (San Marino, 1975), 60–7). See also Joseph Raban, 'Shelley's *Prometheus Unbound*: Why the Indian Caucasus?', *Keats–Shelley Journal* 12 (1963), 95–106; and John Drew, *India and the Romantic Imagination* (Delhi, 1987), 221–35, 272. For possible links between Coleridge's *Kubla Khan* and Kashmir (the contemporary importance of which was largely influenced by Wilford's work on Hindu geography), see Drew, 203–6; and Elinor Shaffer, *Kubla Khan and the Fall of Jerusalem: The Mythological School in Biblical Criticism and Secular Literature 1770–1880* (Cambridge, 1975), ch. 3 ('The Oriental Idyll').

7 Sara Suleri, *The Rhetoric of English India* (London and Chicago, 1992), 27.

8 Homi K. Bhabha, *The Location of Culture* (London and New York, 1994), 86, 88.

9 *Asiatic Researches* 3 (1799), 298. It is noteworthy that Wilford's account of Hindu cosmography in this essay was quoted at length by Southey in a footnote to *The Curse of Kehama* (1810).

10 *Ibid.*, 355.

220

11 *Ibid.*

12 *Edinburgh Review* 9 (October 1806), 92–4.

13 Jane Rendall, 'Scottish Orientalism: From Roberston to James Mill', *The Historical Journal* 25: 1 (1982), 53–4.

14 *Asiatic Researches* 3 (1799), 466.

15 *Ibid.*, 467.

16 'On Mount Caucasus', *Asiatic Researches* 6 (1799), 485.

17 *Ibid.*, 523, 456.

18 *Ibid.*, 479, 494.

19 *Ibid.*, 500–1, 503.

20 For a sophisticated account of 'mythological doubling', see Shaffer, *Kubla Khan*, 183–6.

21 *Asiatic Researches* 6 (1799), 495.

22 In all fairness to Colebrooke, he does not seem to have been at all impressed by Wilford's 'discovery', as he writes to his father in 1804: 'Captain Wilford ... will soon publish his lucubrations ... You will find in his treatises on those subjects very curious matter, but very little conviction' (quoted in O. P. Kejariwal, *The Asiatic Society of Bengal and the Discovery of India's Past* (Delhi, 1988), 101.

23 *Asiatic Researches* 9 (1807), 118.

24 *Ibid.*

25 *Asiatic Researches* 10 (1808), 34.

26 Thomas Maurice, *The History of Hindostan, its Arts and Sciences, as connected with the History of the other great Empires of Asia, during the most ancient periods of the world*, 2 vols (London, 1795–8), 2: vii.

27 *Asiatic Researches* 9 (1808), 118.

28 *Asiatic Researches* 8 (1805), 271.

29 *Ibid.*, 264.

30 See C. A. Bayly, *Imperial Meridian: The British Empire and the World 1780–1830* (London, 1989).

31 *Asiatic Researches* 8 (1805), 286.

32 *Asiatic Researches* 11 (1810), 34, 87.

33 Edward Davies, *Celtic Researches, or the Origin, Traditions and Language, of the Ancient Britons, with some introductory sketches of Primitive Society* (London, 1804), 197.

34 *Asiatic Researches* 11 (1810), 89, 48, 53, 80, 69, 74, 4.

35 *Ibid.*, 69.

36 *Ibid.*, 70–82.

37 C. A. Bayly, *Indian Society and the Making of the British Empire* (Cambridge, 1988), 158. See also my *British Romantic Writers and the East: Anxieties of Empire* (Cambridge, 1992), 91–103.

38 *Asiatic Researches* 8 (1805), 247–63.

39 James Clifford, *The Predicament of Culture: Twentieth-Century Ethnography, Literature and Art* (Cambridge, Mass., 1988), 40.

40 *Asiatic Researches* 8 (1805), 250.

41   *Ibid.*, 248.
42   *Ibid.*, 251.
43   Thomas Maurice, *Brahminical Fraud; or the Attempts of the Sacerdotal Tribe of India to invest their Fabulous Deities and Heroes with the Honours and Attributes of the Christian Messiah, Examined, Exposed, and Defeated, in a series of letters to the Episcopal Bench* (London, 1812), 25.
44   *Ibid.*, 59.
45   Jane Rendall, 'Scottish Orientalism', 49.
46   Javed Majeed, *Ungoverned Imaginings: James Mill's 'The History of British India' and Orientalism* (Oxford, 1992), 128.
47   *Edinburgh Review* 33 (May 1820), 440.
48   *Asiatic Researches* 8 (1805), 251, 253.
49   Johannes Fabian, *Time and the Other: How Anthropology Makes Its Object* (New York, 1983).

Byron's digressive journey

Jane Stabler

One of the best-known accounts of the reception of *Childe Harold's Pilgrimage* is Byron's recollection that he 'awoke one morning and found [him]self famous'.[1] The poem was phenomenally popular throughout the nineteenth century and, as James Buzard has shown, Byron remained 'a presence in British culture through his particular influence on the habits of tourists'.[2] This chapter will explore some of the more contentious aspects of the poem's reception with a view to showing how Byron's art of digression in the first two Cantos of *Childe Harold's Pilgrimage* is generated by conflicting discourses of travel.

In August 1812 the *Anti-Jacobin* protested that Byron had deliberately misled his audience by subtitling the first two Cantos of *Childe Harold's Pilgrimage* 'A Romaunt': '"A Romaunt," without interesting incidents, daring enterprizes, or heroic achievements; and, above all, without a hero, endowed with a soul and spirit, capable of great actions, and ardent to engage in them, is a perfect anomaly in the annals of chivalry, or in the history of romance.'[3] A more appropriate title for the publication, the reviewer added, would have been, '"Sketches of scenery in Spain, Portugal, Epirus, Acarnia, and Greece"' which he said, might better account for a hero 'wandering over the world, without any fixed object'.[4]

Writing in June 1812 for the *British Review* William Roberts also queried the invocation of the genre of romance and identified *Childe Harold's Pilgrimage* as travelogue:

> our puzzle is now to account for those portentous titles of a poem, the subject of which is certainly neither chastity, nor valour, nor truth; nor fairies, nor damsels, nor deliverers; nor heroes baptized, or infidel, but the narrative of a modern tourist, passing from place to place, with little or no incident, but with local descriptions most poetically dressed, and reflections which might occur to a mind like Lord Byron's without the pain or peril of travel.[5]

The identification of Byron as an aristocratic male traveller was an important factor in the reception of the poem, and one which disrupted attempted categorisations of its genre. First, Byron's peerage was incongruous with *Childe Harold* (according to the *British Review*) because the Childe 'is no child of chivalry'.[6] The *Anti-Jacobin* also noted his lack of chivalry: 'nor does even the fair sex escape the keen venom of his scandalous tongue', though it was clear that this deficiency could be attributed to both the Childe and the narrator: 'the laugh at *honour* ... as the deliberate reflection of a noble English mind ... staggers credibility, for it resembles the rant of democracy in its wildest form'.[7]

The 'puzzle' about the genre of the poem was not helped by Byron's Preface, where he emphasised that the poem was written 'for the most part, amidst the scenes which it attempts to describe', and indicated that the poem's reception would determine whether the author might 'venture to conduct his readers to the capital of the East, through Ionia and Phrygia'.[8] These comments employed the conventional register of travel writing whereas Byron's apology for his choice of metre referred the reader back to the authority of the romance writers Ariosto, Spenser, Thomson, and Beattie. Byron cited these authors to justify what he called 'variations' after the style of Beattie who had adopted the Spenserian stanza ' "to give full scope to [his] inclination, and be either droll or pathetic, descriptive or sentimental, tender or satirical, as the humour strikes [him]" '.[9]

The reviewers' problem with Byron's variations was that he seemed to depart *wilfully* from Beattie's model. William Roberts found that reflections ascribed to the Childe persistently interrupted the narrative descriptions of the tour in the first two Cantos: 'We deem the introduction of the character altogether reprehensible ... the mischief lies in foisting him where he has no business, and can only invest the scenes of the poem with the sickly hues of his own morbid disposition.' The same reviewer used the metaphor of a difficult journey when he suggested that '[Byron's] subject has put some impediments in his way which it was not easy to overcome'.[10] The *Anti-Jacobin* also responded to the poem as an ill-advised expedition when it cautioned, 'we should intreat him for his own sake, and for that of the younger part of his public, who are most likely to be misled by his sophistry, to change the course of his studies'.[11] For the contemporary reviewers, therefore, we can see that not only was *Childe Harold's Pilgrimage* not a Romaunt, it was also not a descriptive tour: instead of 'adventures', the *Anti-Jacobin* complained, there are merely 'excursions' and (according to the *Eclectic Review*) the Childe sometimes 'deviates into a species of pleasantry' which the reviewer considered to be both 'very flippant' and 'very unworthy'.[12]

The complaints about 'excursion' and 'deviation' suggest that reviewers were responding to an early form of Byronic digression. Digression has been understood predominantly in spatial terms as a journey away from the norm, the rule, the subject.[13] The transgressive sense of digression co-existed with its meaning as an ill-advised rhetorical flourish in the seventeenth century, but in the eighteenth century digression acquired a new significance in sentimental literature.[14] The changing roles of paren-thetical digression have been analysed in John Lennard's study *But I Digress: The Exploitation of Parentheses in English Printed Verse.* Concentrating on the form of digression which is enclosed by round brackets (or *lunulae*), Lennard shows that although parentheses were regarded as stylistic flaws well into the middle of the eighteenth century, the developing literature of sentiment located a new and particular value in reflective asides. Joseph Warton exemplifies the sentimental appreciation of digression in *An Essay on the Genius and Writings of Pope* when he finds himself 'imperceptibly led' into digressions on the merits of other writers. Warton's defence of pathetic reflection involves a comparison with the delights of picturesque excursion: 'The unexpected insertion of such reflections, imparts to us the same pleasure that we feel, when in wandering through a wilderness or grove, we suddenly behold in the turning of the walk, a statue of some VIRTUE or MUSE.'[15] Byron's 'unexpected intrusions' were criticised for displaying waywardness, indulgence, inconsistency, and for marring the spirit of poetry. These objections suggest an affront to both aesthetic and political discourses of travel: in the late eighteenth and early nineteenth centuries digression and tourism represent two forms of travel which, for Englishmen, were expected to uphold English cultural authority.

Richard Terry has examined theories of transition and digression in the eighteenth-century long poem. He argues that model eighteenth-century digressions offered the pleasure of surprise discovered by occult connection or the pleasure of being 'imperceptibly led' by gentle gradation from one subject to another. In each case, digression was a figure 'presanitized by requirements of propriety' contributing to an overall sense of coherence. It was important, therefore, that in the long poem the figure 'had never to devolve to mere waywardness'.[16] Byron was seen to be deviating from this measure of coherence but, although complaints about the 'waywardness' of the poem derived from his disruption of aesthetic conventions, they were also strongly inflected with political disapproval. Byron was con-demned for destabilising two genres, romance and travelogue, which had both been associated with the consolidation of English nationalism.[17]

In 1809, when Byron set off on what he called his 'Eastern Pilgrimage', he followed a standard route round the Grand Tour during the Napoleonic Wars – Portugal, Spain, Gibraltar, Malta, Albania, Greece.[18] Throughout the eighteenth century, the tour abroad had provided an opportunity to reflect on the advantages of being English and this attitude was intensified by the wars with France. In order to appreciate why Byron's digressive asides were received as 'flippant' and 'unworthy' it helps to consider the attitude to home which was displayed by some of Byron's contemporary travel writers. An ardent belief that England was the only power capable of '[checking] the torrent of French ambition' in the early nineteenth century meant that literary tours were often structured around reference points in the wars against Napoleon or with a view to extending lucrative trade routes.[19] Annesley's *Voyages and Travels to India, Ceylon, the Red Sea, Abyssinia, and Egypt* contained a reflective aside calling for the restoration of independence to Abyssinia:

> That the connection with England may tend to tranquillize Abyssinia, and restore it to its former independence, is the wish nearest my heart ... The communication being once opened, I trust that it will never be closed by the baneful spirit of monopoly, and that the interests of individuals will not be permitted to interfere with the truly British objectives of greatly increasing our foreign trade, and at the same time benefitting [*sic*], in every point of view, an amiable, oppressed, and, what ought to have still greater weight, a Christian country.[20]

Annesley's work was dedicated to the Marquis Wellesley, Late Governor-General of the British possessions and Captain-General of the British Forces serving in the East Indies, 'by whose great political talents, promptitude and decision, the extensive and important Empire of India has been preserved from the secret machinations of traitors, combined with the open hostility of an implacable enemy'.[21] In a similar vein, William Gell (or 'rapid Gell' as Byron called him because of the speed with which he produced his travel writing) dedicated his *The Geography and Antiquities of Ithaca* to George III, advertising his wish that a description of the probable locations for scenes in Homer's *Odyssey* 'may not be entirely uninteresting to a Monarch, who, by success of His arms and the wisdom of His counsels, has extended the influence of Britain to every quarter of the globe'.[22] British researches in international geography were far from disinterested and the continuance of the national interest appeared in much the same form whether the writers were supporters of the party of government or not.

Accompanying Byron was the liberal Whig John Cam Hobhouse whose prose *Journey Through Albania* affords an example of reflective concern for the nation: 'Properly speaking, the word comfort could not be applied to any thing I ever saw out of England, which any one in my place, who was not afraid of being charged with a foolish nationality, would be ready to confess.'[23] Like other English travel writers, Hobhouse allowed himself digressions which kept in sight the values and institutions of English society. These reflective passages were common in both verse and prose travelogues from the late eighteenth and early nineteenth centuries. In the middle of the third *Eastern Eclogue* (1779) by Eyles Irwin, for example, the reader's attention is caught by a dense footnote sparked by the mention of the activities of 'the insidious Hollander' throughout India. Part of the footnote reads:

> every lover of his country must consider with pleasure the conduct and success of the English in this quarter. Acquired at first by self defence against the attacks of native and foreign enemies, a commercial company continues to support an extensive and remote empire, as much by the exercise of moderation and justice as by the terror of her arms.[24]

Irwin's extensive travels were conducted in the service of the East India Company. Together with the diplomatic service, this imperial institution may be said to have funded most of the travel which led to 'Researches', 'Descriptive Tours', and 'Letters from Abroad' published before *Childe Harold's Pilgrimage*.[25] Indeed, Byron and Hobhouse were dependent upon the same vehicles of British imperial rule for hospitality and transport. Hobhouse opens his narrative with an interesting indication of how the apparent randomness and freedom of their journey was in fact shaped by British foreign policy:

> My friend and myself, after a stay of three weeks at Malta, and after many hesitations whether we should bend our steps towards Smyrna or some part of European Turkey, were at last determined in favour of the latter, by one of those accidents which often, in spite of preconcerted schemes, decide the conduct of travellers. – A brig of war was ordered to convey about fifty sail of small merchantmen to Patrass, the chief port on the Western side of the Morea, and to Prevesa, a town on the coast of Albania. The Governor of Malta was so obliging as to provide us with a passage in this ship to the latter place, whence we resolved to commence our Tour.[26]

Hobhouse follows the models of eighteenth-century travelogue when he describes the wretched accommodation, the rain, and the savage appearance of the local inhabitants of Prevesa in terms of a tour around the British Isles: 'The reader will fancy himself deep in the distresses of some Scottish tourist, if he is entertained much longer at this rate.'[27] For Hobhouse, the difficulty and danger of travel abroad becomes a reinscription of the centre of civilised life and value in England. Hobhouse was not a supporter of the Tory government at home in 1809, but his travel writing exemplifies the way in which digressive asides in early nineteenth-century travelogue continue to fulfil the role of footnotes and appendices in Irwin's *Eastern Eclogues*. In each case, the writer steps aside from his description of another country to locate the scene in relation to British commercial or political interest. Byron's approach to the tour is, for its time, noticeably more free in the way comparisons are made with 'home'. This is not to suggest that *Childe Harold's Pilgrimage* stands outside the prevailing discourses of empire and enlightenment; its sense of identity is complex and contradictory and it is, for example, an anti-war poem written by someone who enjoyed the convenience of transport on a British brig of war. I think that initial responses to the poem, however, show that Byron's mixture of travel discourses creates a literary texture which enables the reader to question some of the antecedents and assumptions of that literature.

Sir John Carr was one of the writers with whose work Byron became familiar as he made the first draft of *Childe Harold's Pilgrimage*. Carr coincided with part of Byron's route and with that of *Childe Harold's Pilgrimage* but the different political emphasis of each journey is instructive and helps us to see why the reviewers were disturbed by Byron's design for his material. Carr's *Descriptive Travels in the Southern and Eastern parts of Spain and the Balearic Isles* was published the year before *Childe Harold's Pilgrimage* and dedicated to Lord Holland. In his Preface, Carr helpfully outlined his criteria for the selection of scenes: 'every inch of ground which yet remains free from French contamination cannot but be dear and interesting to Englishmen'. Sardinia, for Carr, was worthy of remark as 'it affords some field for the commercial enterprize of Englishmen' and 'its harbour has been eulogized by the immortal Nelson'. Sardinia was also interesting in an anti-French sort of way: 'particularly the abortive attempts of the French to extend their usurpation over it, have added some charms of novelty to the familiar attractions of that favoured island'. Throughout Carr's account, scenes of interest are defined in terms of the presence of the English or the absence of the French: 'the hatred which all classes in Cadiz seemed to bear to the French, was in proportion to their love and admiration of the English'.[28]

Carr's catalogues of English commercial and military achievement allow us to see what the *Anti-Jacobin* thought was missing from *Childe Harold's Pilgrimage* when its reviewer condemned 'the indiscriminate abuse lavished on the troops, without any distinction as to the *cause* which they are respectively engaged to support'.[29] Whereas Carr found on passing Trafalgar that his mind 'could not but dwell upon the fate of the illustrious Nelson',[30] Harold is unmoved by the memories of any battle:

Oft did he mark the scenes of vanish'd war,
Actium, Lepanto, fatal Trafalgar;
Mark them unmov'd, for he would not delight
(Born beneath some remote inglorious star)
In themes of bloody fray, or gallant fight,
But loath'd the bravo's trade, and laugh'd at martial wight.[31]

Instead of pointing out the remissness of his hero in a footnote, Byron is equally dismissive. As his ship passed the site of the battle, Carr dwelt on the noble thoughts occasioned by pieces of driftwood: 'Even at this day, several pieces of wrecks are to be found upon the beach, as proud, though melancholy, memorials of that great battle, in which the joyous sensations excited by glory were qualified by a pensive sympathy for the loss of one of the greatest of our heroes.'[32] By contrast, Byron signals a note to Trafalgar to which we turn in order to be told that 'Trafalgar needs no further mention'. We are, however, informed that the Battle of Lepanto was where the author of *Don Quixote* lost his left hand. The *Critical Review* detected a violation of propriety in the scant attention paid by the Childe to the English naval victory: 'how strange is the absurdity of painting him as brooding over the convention of Cintra, and marking unmoved the scene of "fatal Trafalgar"?'.[33]

This foregrounding of the literary over national or political interest may be contrasted with Hobhouse's account of the Gulf of Lepanto with its picturesque prospect of Patrass: 'Nothing could be more inviting than the appearance of this place ... clothed with gardens, groves of orange and lemon trees, and currant-grounds, which, when seen at a distance, remind one of the bright green of an English meadow.'[34] Hobhouse, as might be expected, invests the scene with tints of homesickness. His was the conventional perspective but we can see that other perspectives and tones were available, for example in the subversive humour of John Galt, whose *Letters from the Levant* was published a year after *Childe Harold's Pilgrimage*. Like Byron, Galt is mocking the traditions of travel writing and he uses the occasion of passing the site of Lepanto to signal his independence as a traveller:

By the way of letting you know, however, what advantage it is to the world that travellers should not write in their journals until they have leisure to rummage as many books as possible, I confess, that all the time of my passage to Patrass, I quite forgot that somewhere in the same waters Cervantes lost his hand. The circumstance stands in my mind so much alone, that I scarcely remember any thing more about the famous battle of Lepanto than what relates to the author of Don Quixote.[35]

Galt here displays a tone similar to the note in *Childe Harold's Pilgrimage*, but, as this tone is consistent throughout the *Letters from the Levant*, Galt's flippancy is less unsettling than Byron's. Galt's (Scottish) sceptical view of the English was also less of a shock to reviewers than Lord Byron's. In the first two Cantos of *Childe Harold's Pilgrimage* Byron uses first-person plural pronouns when talking about the English but he rejects the absolute and systematic alignment of sympathy with English interests which had conditioned the work of the majority his predecessors and contemporaries on the same tour. Byron's reservations about English policy at home and abroad are markedly different from the tone of Carr's travel writing but not unique in this period. John Galt, for example, undercuts Carr's faith in the high moral regard which the English (as opposed to the French) command abroad. He reports a conversation with an Albanian whose father was in the service of Bonaparte but who liked the English better because '"they are richer, and pay better"'.[36] Clearly Byron was not the first the writer to question English foreign or domestic policy. What I want to suggest is that, beyond its political content, the form of Byron's poem offers the possibility of a radical critique of early nineteenth-century travel literature.

Two polarised readings of *Childe Harold's Pilgrimage* are familiar to us today. The first was put forward by Jerome McGann in the 1960s when in his study *Fiery Dust* he advanced the view that it was a personal travelogue dramatised into revolutionary romantic confessional poem. In the 1980s McGann shifted towards a belief that the whole of the first two Cantos make up 'a commentary on Greece and Europe's relation to Greece's political condition under Turkish rule'.[37] The earlier reading depends on an analysis of Byron's textual revisions, and the later view relies mainly on the paratextual matter of notes and appendices, and on contextual material. McGann's later reading is a revisionary one, and because of this he has no space for a consideration of how one reading might inflect the other. I would like to suggest that the prose notes to *Childe Harold's Pilgrimage* offer an early instance of Byron's 'turn for satire' which interrogates not only the early nineteenth-century rhetoric of British imperialism but also the rhetoric of the self and the system of the Romantic revolutionary poet.

Reviews of the first two Cantos of *Childe Harold's Pilgrimage* indicate that the notes were regarded as a significant part of the volume. There was, however, no consistent method as to how to approach them: they were read in parallel with the poem by some of the reviewers and treated separately at the end of the review of the poetry by others. When quoting from the poem, the *Gentleman's Magazine* inserted the notes to each stanza where they occurred as footnotes. The reviewer for the *Eclectic* stated that he would not comment on the notes 'for we know not how, upon that subject, anything could be said, with truth, which would not qualify the praise we have felt ourselves compelled to bestow upon the other parts of Lord Byron's publication'. The review went far enough to link the verse parody on Cintra with what it called Byron's 'caustic animadversions' on Lady Morgan in the prose notes.[38] In this reading both satirical verse stanzas and prose note function as an interruption which qualifies, perverts, or mars the spirit of poetry.

In the *British Review*, William Roberts struggled to account for the difference in tone between the prose notes and the pleasingly melancholy verses, concluding that 'the notes ... appear however to have been put together in haste; and in a style and tone which we cannot wholly admire'.[39] The *Edinburgh Review* recorded the difference of tone which Byron exercised in the notes which, it found,

> are written in a flippant, lively, *trenchant* and unassuming style – neither very deep nor very witty; though rather entertaining, and containing some curious information as to the character and qualifications of the modern Greeks; of whom, as well as of the Portuguese, Lord Byron seems inclined to speak much more favourably in prose than verse.[40]

The *Quarterly* also registered some disquiet about the tone of the notes, claiming that, 'on the subject of the notes, which are always lively and amusing and sometimes convey much curious information, we should have had no comments to make, if Lord Byron had not occasionally amused himself with provoking controversy'.[41]

Once again, it is the idea of 'wanton' satire which is considered intrusive. The suggestion that the notes had been composed separately and in haste has some truth in it. Byron did indeed 'sweat notes' to augment the poem when he was back in England, but prose notes were also present in the earliest manuscript of *Childe Harold's Pilgrimage*.[42] In the manuscript of Canto II, Byron interrupts the stanza which begins: 'This be the wittol Pict's ignoble boast / To rive what Goth, and Turk, and Time hath spar'd.' Following these two lines, the page is divided with a single stroke of ink after which Byron plunges into prose: 'At this moment (January 3, 1809), besides what has been already stolen and deposited in [Piccadilly] London, an Hydroit vessel is in the Piraeus to receive every portable relic ...'. In this case, the prose note counters the archaic language of the Spenserian stanza and makes the satire insultingly clear.[43] This note survived the process of revision although it was moved to the end of the poem rather than appearing as a footnote as it does in the manuscript draft. Like several of the satirical stanzas, some of the more overtly critical notes were suppressed at the insistence of Robert Charles Dallas.[44] Dallas was not the only figure to worry about Byron's obtrusive suggestions. John Murray, the publisher of *Childe Harold's Pilgrimage*, expressed concern that:

> There are some expressions concerning Spain and Portugal which, however just at the time they were conceived, yet, as they do not harmonise with the now prevalent feeling, I am persuaded would so greatly interfere with the popularity which the poem is, in other respects, certainly calculated to excite ... I hope your goodness will induce you to remove them; and with them perhaps some religious sentiments which may deprive me of some customers amongst the Orthodox.[45]

Murray locates disruption in the poem ('expressions ... which ... do not harmonise') and projects this form of interruption into an effect on the sale of the poem ('would so greatly interfere with the popularity').

In response to the requests from his agent (who like his publisher inclined to a Tory political standpoint), Byron removed satirical stanzas about Cintra and the author of *Vathek*. The note to stanza 73 of Canto II on Athens and on the fallen state of the Greeks was, however, retained and published as a separate paper at the end of the poem. This note was singled out for particular criticism by the *British Review*, the *Anti-Jacobin* and the *Satirist*. William Roberts made the nature of his complaint specific:

> We do not, however, think he is at all warranted in comparing their [the Greek] condition either to that of the Jews or the Irish catholics. His lordship's sentiments, as well as those of the wisest of the persons whose sentiments he adopts, may one day change altogether on the subject of the Catholic claims. In the mean time we will venture to suggest to him, that he greatly disparages the cause he so decisively assumes to be right, by indulging in comparisons which his excellent sense must feel to be unfounded, and which are too preposterously violent for declamation, or even poetry to adopt.[46]

As Terence Spencer has shown, travel poetry which discussed the condition of the Greeks under Turkish rule was a commonplace before the publication of *Childe Harold's Pilgrimage*.[47] Most of these writers, however, assumed Britain to be the model deliverer and paradigm of liberty. Charles Kelsall's poem 'A Letter from Athens' published in 1812 meditates on various scenes in Athens and calls on Britain to liberate the Greeks:

> Rise, Britain, rise! (for to thy sons is giv'n
> That high prerogative of fav'ring Heav'n,
> To rescue nations from the tyrant's lust,
> To scourge the guilty, and avenge the just,)
> Pour forth thy dauntless legions, and release
> The fetter'd Hellespont – ah! rescue Greece! – [48]

This stirring stuff was followed by William Haygarth's poem 'Greece' (1814), which also draws on England's 'virtuous name' for freedom:

> And O my country! let thy voice be heard
> Amidst the din of battle, like the cry
> Of the wild eagle in the tempest's roar;
> When Hellas rises to assert her rights,
> Be not far from her: let thy chieftains sage
> Direct the onset, and thy hardy sons
> Be foremost in the fight which Britons love,
> The fight for liberty. [49]

With these representative examples in mind, it is easy to see why Byron's note was at odds with audience expectations. Looking at the source of the note in the poem at Canto II, stanza 73, the line 'Fair Greece! sad relic of departed worth' is entirely in keeping with contemporary addresses to Greece which defined the country in terms of the absence or lack of its glorious past. In Byron's poem, however, this perspective is undercut (sooner or later, depending on when the reader consults the notes) by Byron's scathing prose observation on travellers 'turning periods in their eulogy, and publishing very curious speculations grafted on their [the Greeks'] former state, which can have no more effect on their present lot, than the existence of the Incas on the future fortunes of Peru'. [50] Byron's note therefore disturbs the conventional pattern of reflection as well as the lyrical genesis of *Childe Harold's Pilgrimage*. [51]

The apostrophe to Greece in stanza 73 sets up a familiar run of questions:

> Who now shall lead thy scatter'd children forth,
> And long accustom'd bondage uncreate?
> Not such thy sons who whilome did await,
> The hopeless warriors of a willing doom,
> In bleak Thermopylae's sepulchral strait -
> Oh! who that gallant spirit shall resume,
> Leap from Eurotas' banks, and call thee from the tomb?

This offers the familiar rhetoric of literary philhellenism – Byron's own scrawled answer on the manuscript was 'Byron', but most of the poem's audience in 1812 would have been happy to settle for 'England' until they reached the notes. Here Byron begins with a conventional meditation on oppression abroad, but the serene gaze of an Englishman surveying less happier lands is interrupted when the note turns home: 'The English have at last compassionated their Negroes, and under a less bigoted government may probably one day release their Catholic bretheren [*sic*].'[52] In an 'Additional note on the Turks', Byron refined this point, remarking that as 'a kind of Eastern Irish papists' the Greeks were allowed a college at Haivii, but, though the Turks tolerate this:

> they will not suffer the Greeks to participate in their privileges: no, let them fight their battles, and pay their haratch (taxes), be drubbed in this world, and damned in the next. And shall we then emancipate our Irish helots? Mahomet forbid! We should then be bad Musselmans, and worse Christians; at present we unite the best of both – jesuitical faith, and something not much inferior to Turkish toleration.[53]

Byron's coining of the phrase 'Irish Helots' challenges contemporary discourses of travel, turning poetic commonplace into satirical critique. Not only the content of the 'Additional note' but, crucially, its tone works to complicate the single-minded sweep of stanza 73. The challenging qualification or afterthought of Byron's prose afterword anticipates the digressive technique of *Beppo* (1818), where in stanza 47, for example, Byron turns William Cowper's lyrical reflection on England in *The Task* to satire:

> 'England! with all thy faults I love thee still,'
> I said at Calais, and have not forgot it;
> I like to speak, and lucubrate my fill;
> I like the government (but that is not it);
> I like the freedom of the press and quill;
> I like the Habeas Corpus (when we've got it);
> I like a parliamentary debate,
> Particularly when 'tis not too late.

The parenthetical asides in *Beppo* work to produce an oppositional voice which interrupts and undercuts lyrical reflection. The first two Cantos of *Childe Harold's Pilgrimage* may be seen to anticipate this destabilising play of *ottava rima* through sudden changes of tone in the verse and in the way that uncompromisingly detailed factual observation in the prose notes punctuates and interrogates the verse.

We can hear a *Beppo*-like qualifying movement in the earlier poem in Byron's view of Cintra (Canto I, stanzas 24–6). The caricature and pointed satire of these lines is obvious: in place of Haygarth's 'chieftains sage', Byron jeers, 'For chiefs like ours in vain may laurels bloom'. Appropriately using a metaphor of digressive travel, the *Satirist* expressed its disapproval: 'we do not see why Lord Byron should have gone out of his way, and with apparent complacency too, to dwell on an event which ... he conceives to have been disgraceful to his country'.[54] Byron's note to the Cintra stanza is, however, tonally more complex than the verse. It begins as a source of tourist information, (wrongly) giving the name of the palace where Byron believed the notorious convention to have been signed. There then follows an observation on Wellington which begins by sounding laudatory: 'The late exploits of Lord Wellington have effaced the follies of Cintra. He has, indeed, done wonders: he has perhaps changed the character of a nation, reconciled rival superstitions, and baffled an enemy who never retreated before his predecessors.'[55] In the course of the note, Byron undercuts the certainties of Murray's 'customers amongst the Orthodox' – his 'rival superstitions' refer to the Catholic and Protestant faiths, and the sly suggestion that Wellington's success was highlighted by the abject failure of his predecessors denied these same readers the pleasure of unequivocal assent. By changing the subject of both romance and travelogue, Byron enraged the *Anti-Jacobin*:

> The loose sneers, and sarcastic remarks, which an author, who suffers no restraint from principle, may introduce in the course of a poetical narrative, where they appear to be merely *incidental,* are calculated to do more mischief, because the ordinary reader is not on his guard against them; than laboured treatises, composed for the avowed purpose of attacking the settled order of things in any state or government.[56]

For the benefit of the unguarded 'ordinary reader', therefore, when quoting from both the poem and the notes, the *Anti-Jacobin* italicised all the incidental remarks which it considered to be unobtrusive but 'calculated to do more mischief'. Unwittingly this italicisation replicates exactly what the *Anti-Jacobin* perceived to be most dangerous in Byron's work. The juxtaposition of the two typefaces emphasises that mixture of discourse which is the generating moment of Byron's art of digression.

For new-historicist critics in the 1980s the contents of Byron's prose notes to *Childe Harold's Pilgrimage* and the Oriental tales supplied what Thomas Moore called 'a mode of turning dull poetry to account, and as horses too heavy for the saddle may yet serve well enough to draw lumber, so poems of this kind make excellent beasts of burden, and will bear notes, though they may not bear reading'.[57] In their own time, however, we can see that they anticipated a new-historicist critique of Romantic ideology. Byron's digressive notes to *Childe Harold's Pilgrimage* were unlike any other interruptions to prose or verse travelogue. They offered neither consistent antiquarian annotation nor reassuring commentaries on recent political history. Carr's prefaces, by way of contrast, had advertised the way the author had 'advanced nothing which can have the remotest tendency to inflame the public mind'. [58] The satirical specificity of Byron's prose notes questions the rhetoric of sentimental journey *and* British colonial expansion, or 'plunder' as Byron referred to it in the notes.[59]

The hybrid form of *Childe Harold's Pilgrimage* may be said to combine the modes of digression employed by two eighteenth-century writers of radically different temperaments, Jonathan Swift and Laurence Sterne, anticipating the disruptive effects of *Don Juan* (the work Byron called his 'poetical T[ristram] Shandy').[60] We can catch the inflection of Sterne in *Childe Harold's Pilgrimage* in the way that subjective, whimsical digression interrupts and diverts the linear purpose of a pilgrimage. There is, however, an element of Swiftian critique in the poem which emerges in the way that prose notes qualify the subjective world of the Childe, insisting on the social and political circumstances which underwrite his peregrinations. The unsettling intermittence of tone and voice in the first two Cantos of *Childe Harold's Pilgrimage* and the reviewers' unfavourable responses to 'so much invective' explain why Byron's prose notes were often cut from nineteenth-century selections of his poetry or relegated to the back of the volume after Canto IV as in the present Clarendon edition.

Byron's publications after *Childe Harold's Pilgrimage* Cantos I and II suggest that he rode, albeit uneasily, with Scott, Southey, Wordsworth, Moore, and Campbell 'upon a wrong revolutionary poetical system' until the Pope/Bowles controversy in 1820–21.[61] In his 'Letter to John Murray Esqre' (1821) Byron accused the English 'poetical populace' of the day of needing to subject Pope in order to advance their own '*invariable* principles'.[62] Byron returned to his memories of being a tourist on an Eastern pilgrimage in order to counter Bowles's claims. Referring to contemporary English poets, he adopted the familiar British register of criticism of the Turks in Greece:

> They have raised a Mosque by the side of a Grecian temple of the purest Architecture – and more barbarous than the Barbarians from whose practice I have borrowed the figure – they are not contented with their own grotesque edifice – unless they destroy the prior and purely beautiful fabric which preceded, and which shames them & theirs forever and ever.[63]

In the same letter, however, Byron was referring to England as 'your Country'.

Notes

1 *Works of Lord Byron*, ed. Thomas Moore, 17 vols (London, 1832–3), 7: vi.
2 James Buzard, *The Beaten Track: European Tourism, Literature, and the Ways to 'Culture' 1800–1918* (Oxford, 1993), 115.
3 *The Anti-Jacobin Review* 42 (August 1812), 344.
4 *Ibid.*
5 *The British Review* 3 (June 1812), 278.
6 *Ibid.*, 280.
7 *The Anti-Jacobin Review* 42 (August 1812), 345, 352.
8 Lord Byron, *Childe Harold's Pilgrimage*, in Jerome J. McGann, ed., *The Complete Poetical Works*, 7 vols (Oxford, 1980–93), 2: 3.
9 *Ibid.*, 2: 4–5.
10 *The British Review* 3 (June 1812), 285–6, 278.
11 *The Anti-Jacobin Review* 42 (August 1812), 346.
12 *The Eclectic Review* 8: 1 (December 1811–June 1812), 632.
13 See *OED*, definitions 1–3.
14 For an analysis of positive appraisals of stylistic digression in the eighteenth century, see Joel Dana Black, 'The Second Fall: The Laws of Digression in Romantic Narrative and Their Impact on Contemporary Encyclopaedic Literature' (diss., Stanford University, 1979).
15 Joseph Warton, *An Essay on the Genius and Writings of Pope*, 2 vols, 2nd edn (London, 1762–82), 1: 264, 1: 31.
16 Richard Terry, 'Transitions and Digressions in the Eighteenth-century Long Poem', *Studies in English Literature* 32 (1992), 502–3.
17 For the relationship between the culture of picturesque ruins and cultural identity, see Anne Janowitz, *England's Ruins: Poetic Purpose and the National Landscape* (Oxford, 1990); Stuart Curran, *Poetic Form and British Romanticism* (Oxford, 1986); David Duff, *Romance and Revolution: Shelley and the Politics of a Genre* (Cambridge, 1994).
18 It is possible to trace a 'wayward' progress in the physical journey prefiguring the erring nature of the poem. Byron and Hobhouse were deflected more than once by chance circumstances. For a full account of their haphazard plans and travels, see William A. Borst, *Lord Byron's First Pilgrimage* (New Haven, 1948).
19 William Martin Leake, *Researches in Greece: With Remarks on the Modern Languages* (London, 1814), iii.
20 Annesley, *Voyages and Travels to India, Ceylon, the Red Sea, Abyssinia, and Egypt in the Years 1802, 1803, 1804, 1805, and 1806*, 3 vols (London, 1811), 3: 268–9.
21 *Ibid.*, from the dedication on the title-page.

22 William Gell, *The Geography and Antiquities of Ithaca* (London, 1807), un-
    paginated title-page.
23 John Cam Hobhouse, *A Journey Through Albania and other provinces of Turkey
    in Europe, and Asia to Constantinople, during the years 1809 and 1810*, 2 vols,
    2nd edn (London, 1813), 1: 40.
24 Eyles Irwin, *Eastern Eclogues: Written During a Tour through Arabia, Egypt,
    and Other Parts of Asia and Africa* (London, 1779), note to l. 73.
25 For details of contemporary attitudes to British colonial settlement, see Nigel
    Leask, *British Romantic Writers and the East: Anxieties of Empire* (Cambridge,
    1992), especially ch. 2.
26 *Journey Through Albania*, 1: 1.
27 *Ibid.*, 13.
28 Sir John Carr, *Descriptive Travels in the Southern and Eastern parts of Spain
    and the Balearic Isles in the Year 1809* (London, 1811), 3, 2–3, 3, 39.
29 *The Anti-Jacobin Review* 42 (August 1812), 351.
30 *Descriptive Travels*, 114.
31 *Childe Harold's Pilgrimage*, Canto II, ll. 355–60.
32 *Descriptive Travels*, 114.
33 *The Romantics Reviewed: Contemporary Reviews of British Romantic Writers*, ed.
    Donald H. Reiman, part B, 'Byron and Regency Society Poets', 5 vols (New
    York, 1972), 2: 613.
34 *Journey Through Albania*, 1: 3.
35 John Galt, *Letters from the Levant; containing views of the state of society,
    manners, opinions, and commerce, in Greece, and several of the principal islands
    of the Archipelago* (London, 1813), 65–6.
36 *Ibid.*, 12–13.
37 Jerome J. McGann, *Fiery Dust: Byron's Poetic Development* (Chicago, 1968);
    The Beauty of Inflections: Literary Investigations in Historical Method and Theory
    (Oxford, 1985), 283n.
38 *The Eclectic Review* 8: 1 (December 1811–June 1812), 641, 639.
39 *The British Review* 3 (June 1812), 299.
40 *The Romantics Reviewed*, 2: 841.
41 *Ibid.*, 5: 1994.
42 See *Byron's Letters and Journals*, ed. Leslie A. Marchand, 13 vols (London,
    1973–94), 2: 99, 106, 130.
43 I acknowledge with gratitude the permission of John Murray to consult the
    MS of *Childe Harold's Pilgrimage* in the Murray Archive and am particularly
    grateful to Virginia Murray for her kindness in helping to arrange access and
    her permission to describe the appearance of the MS.
44 For a stimulating discussion of the importance of the omitted stanzas and the
    way that Byron's juxtapositions transfer 'the problem of accommodating the
    discord' to the audience, see Philip W. Martin, *Byron: A Poet Before his Public*
    (Cambridge, 1982), 9–29.
45 Samuel Smiles, *A Publisher and His Friends: Memoir and Correspondence of*

the Late John Murray, with an Account of the Origin and Progress of the House, *1768–1843*, 2 vols (London, 1891), 1: 208.

46   *The British Review* 3 (June 1812), 299.

47   Terence Spencer, *Fair Greece, Sad Relic: Literary Philhellenism from Shakespeare to Byron* (London, 1954).

48   *Ibid.*, 280–1.

49   *Ibid.*, 284–5.

50   *Childe Harold's Pilgrimage*, 203.

51   Jacques Derrida offers a model for footnotes as 'textual grafts' in *Acts of Literature*, ed. Derek Attridge (London and New York, 1992), 153. Byron discusses the existence of the Incas indirectly in Canto I, stanza 89, when he refers to the 'wrongs that Quito's sons sustain'd'.

52   *Childe Harold's Pilgrimage*, 202.

53   *Ibid.*, 211.

54   *The Romantics Reviewed*, 5: 2112.

55   *Childe Harold's Pilgrimage*, 188.

56   *The Anti-Jacobin Review* 42 (August 1812), 348–9.

57   Thomas Moore, *Corruption, and Intolerance: Two Poems Addressed to an Englishman by an Irishman* (London, 1808), unpaginated preface.

58   Sir John Carr, *The Stranger in Ireland or a Tour in the Southern and Western Parts of that Country in the Year 1805* (London, 1806), preface, i.

59   *Childe Harold's Pilgrimage*, 191.

60   *Letters and Journals*, 10: 150.

61   *Ibid.*, 5: 265.

62   Lord Byron, *The Complete Miscellaneous Prose*, ed. Andrew Nicholson (Oxford, 1991), 148–50.

63   *Ibid.*, 148.

Shelley's *Alastor*: travel beyond the limit

Saree Samir Makdisi

Following hard on the tracks of its Visionary, *Alastor* takes us on a journey deep into the vast expanses of what Byron in *Giaour* called the 'boundless East'. Like *Childe Harold* II, *Alastor* faces the dilemma of having to create its own object, that which it wants simultaneously to describe and to 'represent'. It does so at a crucial historical juncture, in which the multiple conditions of that rapidly developing 'object', the East – its location, its figurative and material possibilities, its value, its history, its peoples, its usefulness, its rule, and above all its relation to 'the West' and to Europe – were undergoing momentous changes. *Alastor*'s map of the East has no real referent: it does not and cannot simply 'represent the Orient', a region and a space that did not and does not exist as such, but that had to be endlessly reinvented by its symbiotically related opposite term, 'the West', during the long and bloody history of imperialism. Inhabiting the form of a travel narrative, Shelley's poem is in large measure informed by the shock of (imaginary) encounter on the imperial frontier, a region in which, as Mary Louise Pratt has observed, 'Europeans confront not only unfamiliar others, but unfamiliar selves'.[1] Torn by the anxieties of colonialism and of oppression, *Alastor* is a profoundly disturbed meditation on empire.

'The philosophical traveller, sailing to the ends of the earth, is in fact travelling in time; he is exploring the past; every step he makes is the passage of an age.'[2] Joseph-Marie Degérando's observation, made in 1800 following his excursion from Europe into lands inhabited by 'savages', provides a strangely appropriate description for *Alastor*'s Visionary. In the prime of his youth, the Visionary – just such a philosophical traveller – leaves 'his cold fireside and alienated home / To seek strange truths in undiscovered lands'.[3] His thirst for knowledge is at first satiated by what he can grasp through intercourse with Nature and the magnificence of 'the external world'. But the charms and intellectual treasures of a sweet and domestic Nature are quickly exhausted, and the Visionary takes his search into lands 'undiscovered' not by people but specifically by Europeans. He pushes away from the tranquil scenes of domestic Wordsworthian Nature, and towards the (Byronic and Southeyan) realm of the foreign and distinctly non-European: 'Many a wild waste and tangled wilderness / Has lured his fearless steps; and he has bought / With his sweet voice and eyes, from savage men, / His rest and food.' Having pursued like her shadow 'Nature's most secret steps', the Visionary leaves behind the familiar world of squirrels and deer and begins his fantastic adventure back in time, not only to Eden, but to what came long before. At the end of the poem, once he has reached the very heart of the East, the so-called 'cradle' of (Western) civilisation, and still in pursuit of the phantasmatic and elusive 'veilèd maid' of his dreams, the pitch and velocity of his journey accelerate 'beyond all human speed'. A tiny boat carries him on to his destiny at the very origins of time: 'Nature's ... cradle, and his sepulchre'.[4] This cyclical inversion of time, in which a cradle is also a sepulchre, in which the beginning is also the end (oddly reminiscent of Wordsworth's 'the child is the father of the man'), is accomplished precisely through the translation of a forward movement in space into a backward movement in time. For, propelled by a supernatural whirlpool, the quasi-magical boat is indeed a time-machine of sorts, taking the Visionary *up* the cavern of a river which pours *down* into the Caspian Sea:

> Seized by the sway of the *ascending stream*,
> With dizzy swiftness, round, and round, and round,
> Ridge after ridge *the straining boat arose*,
> Till on the verge of the extremest curve,
> Where, through an opening of the rocky bank,
> The waters overflow, and a smooth spot
> Of glassy quiet mid those battling tides
> Is left, the boat paused shuddering.[5]

Having reversed and rewound time, having defied the laws of gravity and of physics, the Visionary's boat arrives at the source of space and time (to which I shall return a little later). This dizzying upward and backwards journey bears a synecdochical relationship to the entire poem's spatial–temporal flow, especially that of the section preceding this mystical last stage of his journey. For even before this apotheosis, each of the Visionary's steps towards the East is signalled as a troubled step 'back in time'. The passage recounting his travel to and arrival in *Alastor*'s Orient is worth quoting at length:

> His wandering step
> Obedient to high thoughts, has visited
> The awful ruins of the days of old:
> Athens, and Tyre, and Balbec, and the waste

Where stood Jerusalem, the fallen towers
Of Babylon, the eternal pyramids,
Memphis and Thebes, and whatosoe'er of strange
Sculptured on alabaster obelisk,
Or jasper tomb, or mutilated sphynx,
Dark Æthiopia in her desert hills
Conceals. Among the ruined temples there,
Stupendous columns, and wild images
Of more than man, where marble daemons watch
The Zodiac's brazen mystery, and dead men
Hang their mute thoughts on the mute walls around,
He lingered, poring on memorials
Of the world's youth, through the long burning day
Gazed on those speechless shapes, nor, when the moon
Filled the mysterious halls with floating shades
Suspended he that task, but ever gazed
And gazed, till meaning on his vacant mind
Flashed like strong inspiration, and he saw
The thrilling secrets of the birth of time.[6]

These passages, 'set' in the Levant and north-eastern Africa, are of course only the beginnings, the westernmost leading edges, of *Alastor*'s map of the East, for the Visionary will penetrate deeper still, beyond Arabie and Persia, beyond Kashmir, beyond the Caucasus, beyond the Caspian and Aral Seas. This eastward movement (the opposite of Keats's 'westering') involves a complex and subtle temporal play. On the one hand, the Visionary has arrived in the space of Oriental and hellenic antiquity, intact and laden with its tombs and palaces, its memorials and sphinxes, its columns and its halls. On the other hand, he has not quite gone back to the *time* of antiquity; or, rather – paradoxically – he has *and* he has not. Time has stopped: nothing has changed in this mythic Orient, nothing has altered the Roman temples of Baalbeck, the Phoenician palaces of Tyre, the temples of Athens, the towers of Babylon. The 'eternal' pyramids are as they were when Cheops was entombed; Tyre has neither grown nor changed since Alexander's siege; Jerusalem's temples remain as they were left by the city's last pillagers or pilgrims; the Parthenon stands silently awaiting its sacrificial trains; Memphis, once the united capital of Upper and Lower Egypt, is frozen, its palace of Apis remaining as it was – though all of these places are desolate and depopulated, at once preserved and emptied out. And yet, of course, time has moved on: these are ruined temples, open wastes, fallen towers, mutilated monuments.[7] In other words, these 'awful ruins of the days of old', these 'memorials to the world's youth', have somehow been frozen in time – as though nothing has changed and no one has lived here since some vanished moment of antiquity – and yet they have also been inscribed by the movement of time and the passage of the ages: they are ruins, they are memorials. *Alastor's* map undermines and contradicts itself. If this *is* a move back in time, why are these temples and palaces not alive, rather than being dead? And if this is *not* a move back in time, then where are the living people of the present? How can great and living cities – Athens, Tyre, Jerusalem – be reduced to ruination and to waste, to the eternal silence of death? The difference between this vision of the Levant and that of *Childe Harold* II is striking, for this is ostensibly the same landscape in which Harold finds both the same ruins *and* the civilisation that has developed in the Levant since the temples and palaces were destroyed. Where Harold sees the ruins of paradise mingled with the signs and peoples of the contemporary East, however, the Visionary sees only ruins – not only because the narrator has effectively obliterated the people of the present from the Visionary's field of vision, but *because this is indeed not the Orient toured by Childe Harold.* Having been reinvented, it is an altogether different space, one that cannot be reconciled with the latter, but that can only take its place – for these visions and versions of the East are mutually exclusive and all-demanding.

Thus, while Byron and Childe Harold retrospectively mourn the passage of time from their inescapable standpoint in the present, viewing the Levantine ruins as the traces of premodern and bygone times, Shelley's East is always already in ruins, the flow of history – impossibly and paradoxically – having inexorably moved on to the future, in order to leave behind ruins, and at the same moment having ground to a halt in some fixed and immutable space of the past. 'The waste where stood Jerusalem' presents the exalted city itself as at once preserved as a trace, and simultaneously cancelled and blasted out of existence, its inhabitants written over and hidden away, vanished refugees banished from their land. 'The eternal pyramids' are eternal, living for ever before and after, and yet at the same time they are consigned to the oblivion of the past. Such ruins are in one sense the 'concretisation' of history, bearing in their very materiality the inscriptions of the passage of time, that is, the movements and flows of historical events. Temples, castles, memorials, columns, statues, tombs stand as place-markers on imaginary maps, the signposts of spots of time which open up from present and future moments to past ones – each is a space that has been temporalised. The spots of time in *Alastor's* map of the East are, however, fleeting and illusory, sometimes reactivating and reanimating the glories of the past – so that the Visionary can literally 'see' the birth of time – and sometimes falling short and yielding nothing but mute and non-signifying memorials, piles of barren and silent rocks. While each of the signposts on the map ('Tyre', 'Memphis', 'Babylon', 'Jerusalem') might open to a different temporal level, none allows for the reactivation of events, so that they finally succeed one another as a series of flashes which flatten out into a more or less uniform time and space of a 'past' seemingly without history. There is a certain order of succession, however, for they form a series that describes a gradual curve, an inverted 'fertile crescent', first towards the south-east (Athens–Tyre–Baalbeck–Jerusalem–Babylon) and then towards the south (Babylon–Giza–Memphis–Thebes[8]–Ethiopia). At a more abstract level this series also describes a temporal trend, with every shift south or east marking a corresponding move 'back' in history, that is, roughly from ancient Greece to Phoenicia to Sumer to ancient Egypt. Yet this temporal hierarchy breaks down and dissolves, not least because each of these civilisations had (spatially) moved out of its area of origin and (temporally and historically) mingled with the others. Again, *Alastor*'s map is undecided and unclear, and what we are left with is a more or less haphazard spatial identification of the Orient with the past. There is a will to render it past, despite the awareness that Athens and Tyre and Jerusalem live on into the poem's own historical present, the one in which Childe Harold encounters them. Shelley's vision of the East is ruthlessly violent, for he symbolically depopulates a space in order to establish the possibility (or even inevitability) of its reclamation as part of some suddenly invented 'Western' heritage. For *if* this journey to the Orient is a journey back in time, its condition of possibility is the annihilation of the present Orient, which is necessarily reduced to desolation and ruin, not to life and 'living history' but to spatialised and ossified, 'dead' history – or rather to a place altogether without history (i.e., outside the diachronic and universal history of modernity and Europe).

Emptied of their peoples, the living cities of the Orient are rendered as tombs of the dead, frozen museum-piece images, icons of antiquity – as if Tyre and Athens and Jerusalem exist not for the sake of their own peoples and cultures but for the sake of the European explorer who 'discovers' them, indeed as if they would not exist at all without this explorer and discoverer who, even if he does not actually bring them into being, at least confirms their existence (as 'dead civilisations', as more than one contemporary critic has put it). These cities, in other words, exist as signs to be read and suddenly understood, like statues or columns or paintings, by the European explorer, the 'philosophical traveller:' marks upon a suddenly aestheticised landscape.

Alastor, however, again undermines itself, for the Visionary does indeed encounter one inhabitant of the present Orient on his eastward journey:

> Meanwhile an Arab maiden brought his food,
> Her daily portion, from her father's tent,
> And spread her matting for his couch, and stole
> From duties and repose to tend his steps: -
> Enamoured, yet not daring for deep awe
> To speak her love: – and watched his nightly sleep,
> Sleepless herself, to gaze upon his lips
> Parted in slumber, whence the regular breath
> Of innocent dreams arose: then, when red morn
> Made paler the pale moon, to her cold home
> Wildered, and wan, and panting, she returned.[9]

But the Arab maiden is (paradoxically) out of place in this Orient, a disruptive eruption, interfering with the Visionary (who resolutely ignores her as if she were not there at all), just as the phantasmic Arab horseman intrudes on Wordsworth's dream of the East in *The Prelude*. The maiden is not part of the (dead) past, she shares the present with the Visionary. Or does she? She can see him; but does he see her, does he recognise her presence? For their encounter is non-synchronous, not as if they were in separate spatial compartments, but on the contrary as if they 'share' or overlap in the same space but at different times, and hence as if they do not share it at all. She is like a ghost from the past who remains unseen and whose presence goes unrecognised in the present; she is there and yet not there; she is in the Visionary's time and yet not in it, she is simultaneously absence *and* presence, a kink, a distortion in an impossibly convulsed and twisted imaginary map. The maiden is like one of Byron's voluptuous Eastern women, but where Byron's Eastern poems are tales of encounter with the other, *Alastor* is a narrative of non-encounter. While the maiden, hence, cannot be accommodated or reconciled with the map, and remains an intrusion on its surface, *Alastor* is nevertheless uneasy in its treatment of the peoples of the East, principally their representative, this maiden who falls in love with the Visionary and who tends him, feeds him, clothes him only to be mutely and carelessly unacknowledged as he moves on in search of his ideal and phantasmic love – a gesture of which the Narrator is highly critical.

The ruins of the East are silent and deserted, places where dead men hang their *mute* thoughts on the *mute* walls around. Byron's Childe Harold, in Greece, mourns for the fact that 'these proud pillars', which to him are laden with all the meaning of hellenic antiquity, 'claim no passing sigh; / Unmoved the Moslem sits, the light Greek carols by'.[10] In *Alastor*, though, Orientals are not just unmoved – they are altogether absent from the stupendous ruins of the days of old, where the 'speechless shapes' of the

East are finally unveiled, unlocked, understood by the silent gaze of the European, upon whom alone inspiration can flash and to whom alone visual and graphic meanings can be transmitted from these memorials of the past. *This* Orient, in other words, is a vacancy and an absence to be filled in (a 'land without a people', to cite the planners of a later episode in the region's colonial history) to be brought to life by the European, who alone can fulfil its hidden potential and make this symbolic desert 'bloom'. Unlocking this Orient's potential wealth, both material and figurative, in other words, fundamentally requires the intervention of Europe, without which this wealth would go unappreciated and hence unexploited.

In his 1820 essay 'A Philosophical View of Reform', which is often taken to be the poet's greatest political statement (though indeed its explicitly imperialist orientation usually passes unnoticed), Shelley argues that 'the Turkish Empire is in its last stage of ruin, and it cannot be doubted but that the time is approaching when the deserts of Asia Minor and of Greece will be colonised by the overflowing populations of countries less enslaved and debased, and that the climate and the scenery which was the birthplace of all that is wise and beautiful will not remain forever the spoil of wild beasts and unlettered Tartars.'[11] This view of Britain's and indeed Europe's colonial project (one which prefigures later developments in colonialism, not least in its evocation of Zionism), contributes also to the shaping of *Alastor*'s map of the East, though in the poem it is to a certain extent qualified and undermined. In either case, the appreciation of the Orient's monuments comes to stand for the awareness and productive exploitation of its *other* resources, so that what European intervention accomplishes is not the *creation* of wealth, but its actualisation and realisation, its redemption. In his 'Philosophical View of Reform', Shelley goes on to argue that the introduction of 'enlightened' European institutions, literatures and arts into Egypt 'is *beginning* that change which Time, the great innovator, will *accomplish* in that degraded country; and by the same means its sublime and enduring monuments may excite lofty emotions in the hearts of the posterity of those who now contemplate them without admiration'.[12] Without this European impetus, time would not be able to accomplish anything; or, rather, it is the arrival of Europe in the Orient that activates 'History' and allows time to begin moving and accomplishing 'historical' and modernising change there – *the very change from which Byron, for his part, had turned to the Orient as a refuge in* Childe Harold *II*.

Alastor's map of the East emplots the creation of an altogether new Orient through the arrival there of European influence and empire. This is at once a spatial creation, in so far as a new oriental space has been 'discovered', and a temporal one, in so far as this new Orient is determined by the beginning of a new temporal structure: not the time – or timelessness – of the old Orient toured by Childe Harold, but the time of the 'new' Europe (which would not include places like the Scottish Highlands, Ireland, Sicily, etc.), or in other words the time of modernity from which Harold and Byron had fled. Shelley's poem charts out a polymorphous and multidimensional Orient, only one 'layer' of which is occupied by its Visionary. It constructs a spatialised map of time that effectively opens a fourth dimension, which for want of some more appropriate language I find myself forced to describe three-dimensionally as the 'layers' and 'levels' of an imaginary map. The Visionary's push into the East involves the penetration into and literally the discovery of a previously hidden – *because not yet invented* – layer of the Orient, a layer that *Alastor* 'peels' away from other versions and visions of 'the' Orient. What the poem maps out is thus a new space-time of the Orient, 'outside' or 'underneath' of which other Orients (that is, the Orients inhabited, lived and experienced by others and by European tourists in search of an Orient of difference) still manage to 'exist', though they are inaccessible to the Visionary, just as *his* Orient is spatially and temporally forbidden to these others. The Arab maiden is a troubling and even transgressive figure who undermines and threatens the coherence of this structure: she is a refugee, a vagrant in space-time who floats in between the different dimensions of *Alastor*'s East, coming to 'haunt' the poem in his own private Oriental space, only to finally give up and return to her father's tent, or in other words, to her 'proper' space, that Orient where she 'belongs'.

Alastor concerns itself with and limits itself to the Orient that its Visionary has discovered, explored, appreciated and above all understood. The 'living' Orient of the poem's own present, as opposed to the 'dead' Orient of ruined temples and palaces, is not seen (just as the Visionary does not really see the Arab maiden). Thus when the Visionary explores the 'waste where stood Jerusalem', or the deserted and dust-blown ruins of Tyre or Athens or Memphis or Thebes, it is *his* own Jerusalem, his own Tyre, Athens, Memphis and Thebes, that he sees – oriental spaces upon which he meditates and ruminates. There are other visions and versions of these places, inhabited (though apparently not appreciated) by others. *Alastor*, a travel narrative of sorts, commemorates a certain type of tourism in which the tourist is 'free' to consume the objects of his contemplation in his own private way, though unlike Childe Harold's tourism, which involves a private voyeuristic consumption of the otherness of the (contemporary) Orient. On its own terms, *Alastor*'s vision or re-vision of the East is *the* East, which is being 'faithfully' re-presented to its Western readers. In other words, *Alastor* makes a claim about the universality and the truth of its vision and re-presentation of the Orient. Its Orient is the Orient; there is no other. Or: the Orient which *Alastor* discovers – that is, invents – is not just cut off, isolated and placed in radical opposition to other versions of the Orient: it is linked to, and placed in continuity with, a larger vision of the world which lies to the west. *Alastor*'s East does *not* exist in isolation from some putative West; if it dives underneath other layers of the Orient, it does so partly in order to establish connections and continuities between *its* Orient and what lies to the west of this Orient, as though this (equally invented) West had seeped or pushed eastwards along with *Alastor* to claim this other Oriental space as its own, as part and parcel of the space that it had left 'behind' – as an extension, or better yet, a colonial possession, of the West and of Europe.

In this sense, *Alastor* maps out a temporal colonisation coinciding, complementing, and constituting European spatial and material colonisations of the Orient in the late eighteenth and early nineteenth centuries. On the one hand, this involved the process that Johannes Fabian has identified as the simultaneous secularisation and universalisation of time.[13] On the other hand it involved a colonial reclamation and appropriation through the invention and spatial production of a certain version of the Orient as Europe's source of origin ('the birthplace of all that is wise and beautiful'). Not merely the 'cradle of civilization', but the site, the scene, of Europe's heritage, this space suddenly needed to be understood and explained in terms of a (fabricated) historical and cultural 'continuity' with modern Europe. It was gradually appropriated by the universalising European claims that time and history are uniform natural 'essences' that point to modernity and to Europe.

What *Alastor* does, then, is to re-orient the East in terms of this newly developed universal essence of time. I say re-orient, because the other Orients (or older visions and versions of the Orient), including that of *Childe Harold*, cannot be accommodated in this newly produced configuration of the East. Indeed, this Orient – *Alastor*'s East – has to be fundamentally reinvented in a recuperative gesture that removes it from the claims of the other Orient. One can posit a temporal divide separating these Orients from each other, as I have already suggested, the dimension of the East which the Visionary discovers and explores being neatly cut off from and made inaccessible to Orientals themselves, so that the Visionary is free to appreciate and understand it on his own. What I am arguing involves the production of an analogue to Frantz Fanon's great dictum that 'the colonial world is a world cut in two'.[14] For Fanon, the profound dividing line is spatial, as expressed in the violent division of the colonial city (of which French-occupied Algiers is his prime example):

The zone where the natives live is not complementary to the zone inhabited by the settlers. The two zones are opposed, but not in the service of a higher unity. Obedient to the rules of pure Aristotelian logic, they both follow the principles of reciprocal exclusivity. No conciliation is possible, for of the two terms, one is superfluous. The settlers' town is a strongly built town, all made of stone and steel. It is a brightly lit town; the streets are covered with asphalt, and the garbage cans swallow all the leavings, unseen, unknown and hardly thought about ... The settler's town is a well-fed town, an easygoing town; its belly is always full of good things. The settlers' town is a town of white people, of foreigners.

The town belonging to the colonized people, or at least the native town, the Negro village, the medina, the reservation, is a place of ill fame, peopled by men of ill repute. They are born there, it matters little where or how; they die there, it matters not where, nor how. It is a world without spaciousness; men live on top of each other, and their huts are built one on top of the other. The native town is a hungry town, starved of bread, of meat, of shoes, of coal, of light, a town on its knees, a town wallowing in the mire. It is a town of niggers and dirty Arabs.[15]

Alastor's map of the East is not only an intervention in the Orient and hence (which is to say the same thing) in the imaginary terrain produced by orientalism; it produces a new version of oriental space-time that must be placed in radical opposition to previous European conceptions, versions, productions, of this space, not least that of *Childe Harold*. Its logic of separation and division is not solely spatial, but simultaneously spatial and temporal. The natives, the Orientals themselves, are consigned to their own version, their own space, their own time – none of which concern *Alastor* or its Visionary, as they are displaced beyond the poem's rigorously self-imposed limits and remain ghosts hovering on the edges of the poem, haunting it. They exist on the multiple other sides of this interdimensional frontier: in the Orients of Beckford's *Vathek*, of Southey's *Thalaba* and *Kehama*, of Byron's *Corsair*, of De Quincey's opium-induced Asiatic nightmares, in the worlds of European penetrations and visits to the Orient of the other, as opposed to this newly invented 'European' Orient. And yet, of course, both these Orients are produced, and policed, by Europeans – by the orientalists, the colonial administrators, the armies of occupation. This amounts to something more than what Fabian terms the 'denial of coevalness', through which Europeans distinguished themselves from their colonial interlocutors according to their supposed relative positions on the stream of evolutionary time, so that European ventures into the colonial realm were seen as voyages 'back' to the time of the other.[16] Thus the clash of cultures on the imperial frontier is also a clash of temporalities: this newly invented Orient, and hence this whole new set of relations between Orientals and Europeans (which is what the Orient and Orientalism always imply and delineate, as Said argues), could thus be opposed to older versions, older and now-subsumed 'layers' of this imaginary map of the imperial domain.

In the meantime, this new Orient could be excavated and explored, could be recuperated, redeemed, put to good use, saved from itself and from degradation and waste. And indeed its inhabitants could and even had to be reinvented as well. They had to be re-orientalised.[17] Europe's colonial project could change to a benevolent mission of salvation, by which the Orientals could be given aid and allowed, through 'catching' what Shelley called a 'contagion of good', to break out of the prison of their old space and hence into 'our' world, 'our' world history, and the stream of evolutionary time which is warily patrolled by 'our' gunboats. While this vision of the colonial mission anticipates the Victorian conception of empire, in Shelley it is still premature, as if the terrain on which its great drama will eventually unfold has only just been captured, and hence is still composed of ruins and deserts in urgent need of repopulation and reconstruction. In a long and careless, though impassioned, paragraph of his 1820 essay, Shelley writes:

> Revolutions in the political and religious state of the Indian peninsula seem to be accomplishing, and it cannot be doubted but the zeal of the missionaries of what is called the Christian faith will produce beneficial innovation there, even by the application of dogmas and forms of what is here an outworn incumbrance. The Indians have been enslaved and cramped in the most severe and paralysing forms which were ever devised by man; some of this new enthusiasm ought to be kindled among them to consume it and leave them free, and even if the doctrines of Jesus do not penetrate through the darkness of that which those who profess to be his followers call Christianity, there will yet be a number of social forms modelled upon those European feelings from which it has taken its colour substituted to those according to which they are at present cramped, and from which, when the time for complete emancipation shall arrive, their disengagement may be less difficult, and under which their progress to it may be the less imperceptibly slow. Many native Indians have acquired, it is said, a competent knowledge in the arts and philosophy of Europe, and Locke and Hume and Rousseau are familiarly talked of in Brahminical society. But the thing to be sought is that they

should, as they would do if they were free, attain to a system of arts and literature of their own.[18]

The arrival of Europe in the Orient thus suddenly and even violently wrenches the latter into 'the' stream of history. Not only does it begin the process of freeing the Orientals literally from themselves (from their culture, their social institutions and organisations), but it begins their gradual and total re-development, through which they have to begin from nought, leaving behind the cultural products of their past only to hope for the vague possibility of some day developing 'their own' arts and literature. What has been used up and rendered outmoded in Europe, including for instance Christianity, thus has some usefulness and applicability to this region which can now aspire to cultural, philosophical, economic and political handouts, aid and encouragement from Europe. Whereas Byron turned to the East, in *Childe Harold* and his Tales, as a space towards which to escape – and from which to critique and contest – modernity and its claim on the space of Europe, this newly produced Eastern terrain is effectively an extension of Europe, no longer an opposite but a space which Europe could colonise and thus use to reproduce itself. In other words, the supposedly specific, cyclical and even centripetal time and history of the East can now be opened up and channeled into the uniformationist, unilinear, and universal time and history of modernisation and development. I have already said, however, that *Alastor* is not quite so straightforward as this later summary of the dubious benefits of colonisation. If the latter is reminiscent of a retrospective history of contact on the imperial frontier, *Alastor* represents a first glimpse at a new space that would be elaborated in later visions of the East, including Shelley's 1820 Essay.

These possibilities of the new East exist not merely for the Orientals themselves (if at all) but for the Europeans who have captured this terrain by the act of having defined it. Greece, in particular, becomes a site which had to be cut off from its oriental affiliations and completely redeemed as a part of Europe, thus pushing the imaginary frontier between East and West further east, towards Turkey. In a now often-quoted claim, Shelley argues in the preface to *Hellas* (1821):

> The apathy of the rulers of the civilised world to the astonishing circumstance of the descendants of that nation to which they owe their civilisation rising as it were from the ashes of their ruin is something perfectly inexplicable to a mere spectator of the shews of this mortal scene. We are all Greeks – our laws, our literature, our religion, our arts have their root in Greece. But for Greece, Rome, the instructor, the conqueror, or the metropolis of our ancestors,

would have spread no illumination with her arms, and we might still have been savages, and idolaters; or, what is worse, might have arrived at such a stagnant and miserable state of social institution as China and Japan possess.[19]

And yet, when he was writing those words, in 1821, Greece was still a part of the Ottoman Empire, and hence merely one of the many parts of the Orient which Europeans were gradually beginning to claim for themselves. As he announces in *Hellas*, the modern Greeks ('descendants of those glorious beings whom the imagination almost refuses to figure to itself as belonging to our kind'), through their revolution against the Turks, are somehow reinventing themselves, rising as reincarnated Europeans from the ashes of Oriental despotism: 'Greece which was dead is arisen!' And yet in this reinvention lay opportunity not only for the Greeks but for the other Europeans, who could now establish their claims to an 'authentically' Greek (as opposed to Egyptian, Persian, or Arab) heritage. Indeed, this reclamation and recuperation of 'our' heritage establishes, on this Romantic hellenophilic (or, rather, hellenomaniac) view, not only a claim to some past but the basis for security for the future, almost a renewal, or rather re-beginning of time and of history: 'The world's great age begins anew, / The golden years return, / The earth doth like a snake renew / Her winter weeds outworn.'[20] This is precisely the standpoint on Greek renewal and rebirth – a reawakening of hellenism – denied and rejected by Byron in *Childe Harold* II and its notes, which instead insist on the final death of Greece, albeit as one that ought to be commemorated.[21]

Elsewhere in the East, Europeans were laying their claims to have derived their heritage from certain 'pure' strains of Indic civilisation, leading ultimately to the construction of an 'Indo-European' language family, civilisation, and race, supposedly distinct from the taints and impurities of Africa or the rest of Asia. This newly discovered Orient, however had first to be separated from the old Orient (that is, other 'layers' of the imaginary map), and purged of its influence, whether through the fires of revolution (as in Greece) or through the discipline of archaeological or philological research (as in India). Thus, as Martin Bernal has suggested, in the late eighteenth and especially the early nineteenth centuries, Europeans began to fundamentally re-cast their relations with and to the Orient, selectively claiming heritage from this or that corner of the East, while separating these putative heritages from less convenient or desirable cultural, historical, and political attachments and associations (for example, the enormous influence of Egypt on classical Greek culture, or the interpenetration of Indian cultures with Arabic, Persian, and Chinese civilisations).[22] Indeed, the Orient itself, as a space of material, discursive, and figurative opportunity, had to be entirely reinvented and rediscovered. It had to be altogether re-produced, and Orientals, born 'anew', had to begin their 'progress' from scratch, the cultural productions and achievements of their previous incarnation being not merely devalued but, in the course of their new development, inappropriate, as the outworn remnants of a bygone age. As Shelley puts it in his essay, they could now only 'aspire' to arts and literature 'of their own', like good pupils who have plenty of potential and yet have not actually produced anything to show for themselves. For (as I have already said) in Shelley's terms, the arrival of European influence 'begins' the change that time 'will accomplish'. Until then, time was unable to accomplish anything: not only had the Orient 'stopped developing' but time itself had stopped there, and had thickened and congealed into endless and everlasting ruin and decay without or outside of history. Yet even if it opens up into the 'new' Orient, *Alastor* marks a transition between orientalist structures and paradigms, and the supposedly displaced other returns in the form of the Arab maiden, a haunting presence who is recognised by the Narrator and not by the Visionary – as though the Narrator could see the 'old' Orient inhabited by this other, whereas the Visionary can see only the ruins and temples of the 'new' Orient which are there for him to understand, to know, and to map on his journey and his quest into the Orient.

Perhaps for obvious reasons, I have not been concerned in this reading of *Alastor* with an examination of this quest itself, or in other words with an examination of the poem's narrative. Instead my analysis has been restricted to the terrain on which the narrative takes place, a terrain that has more or less been taken for granted by recent critics, whose readings uncritically reproduce Shelley's vision of the East as a tantalising imaginary space, which serves – for them as well as for the poet – merely as a necessarily silent surface for (Western) inscriptions and interventions. For insufficient critical attention has been given to the imaginary terrain on which the Visionary's (I use Earl Wasserman's terminology to avoid confusion [23]) quest unfolds. Instead, critics have focused on the nature of the quest. Thus, while Earl Wasserman's reading of the poem has become one of the central landmarks on the terrain of these critical debates, and if more recent critics try either to support, to attack, to refine, or to develop Wasserman's careful and nuanced reading of the quest, the poem's historical ground – and, again, the terrain on which the quest is written – recedes farther and farther from view. That is to say, this 'critical' terrain supplants the imaginary oriental terrain produced in the poem as a basis for readings and rereadings of *Alastor*. The main issue at stake in the critical discussion of the poem has recently shifted towards a debate over whether *Alastor's* narrator and the Visionary are two different characters (which is what Wasserman proposes), one character struggling with himself, two different versions of the same persona (as Christopher Heppner argues), or indeterminate identities (the position taken by Martyn Crucefix and Frederick Kirchhoff).[24] For all the critics' disagreements about the similarities or differences between the Narrator and the Visionary, they seem to be virtually unanimous in their view of *Alastor*'s representation of the Orient, almost entirely taking for granted the poem's assumptions about Asia and the peoples and civilisations that happen to be there – whose existence and history make it difficult, in my view, to take Shelley so easily and uncritically at his word. Harold Bloom, for instance, writes simply that the Visionary 'moves on to the foothills of the Caucasus, retracing in reverse the march of civilization',[25] a march that in this view 'obviously' took a westward course, reaching its height in Europe and America, so that the Visionary, going back in time, goes back to the cradle of (ultimately a Western) civilisation. Heppner writes that the Visionary tours the ruins of 'Nature and past culture'; Strickland says that the voyage is to 'dead civilizations ... away from civilization altogether;' while John Reider, offering his reading as 'a politicizing supplement to other interpretations', has little differences with other critics on this point.[26] In the poem's own terms, of course, these critics' claims have truth-content; but it seems to me that one must question and interrogate not merely the poem's narrative but its very terms and conditions of possibility. My own reading of *Alastor* proposes that the quest and the terrain on which it unfolds are not coincidental to each other and must be read together; a detailed reading of the quest, which lies outside the scope of this chapter, must be informed by a reading of the terrain, by placing both in a historical and historicised perspective.

The Narrator's reappearance and intervention in the text of the poem highlights the Visionary's death and the total failure of his quest. Up to that moment, however, the Narrator's involvement complements the Visionary's voyage. It is the Narrator who translates the spatial production of the East undertaken in the poem into visual terms, and hence it is structurally and formally through the device of the Narrator that the Visionary is placed on *Alastor*'s map of the East. Until that final moment, therefore, the Narrator and the poem both enable and participate in the Visionary's quest through and across the space of the Orient. The Narrator's 'reversal' of position – even if it had been anticipated and prepared for in the Preface and the opening lines of the poem itself – retroactively and retrospectively unravels and condemns the Visionary's quest. *Alastor* produces an imaginary map of the space of the East and then consumes it. It puts it forward and then withdraws it and cancels it out. Put in slightly different terms, the quest that takes place – a quest for a self-projected and self-confirming other (in other words, a version of the self *itself*) – is enabled and sustained by the terrain on which it takes place, that is, the particular version of the space of the East that the poem itself produces. In simultaneously producing this terrain and narrating the quest that it finally condemns, the poem rewrites and destroys itself.

Alastor produces a version of the Orient in which otherness has been all but obliterated (save for its traces and vestigial hauntings, for example, the Arab maiden), and in which a search can take place for images and reflections of Europe; this new Orient is thus no longer a refuge offering and containing the other, it is a cleaned-out slate ready for European colonisation and inscription – even if these processes are condemned by *Alastor's* Narrator. In *Childe Harold* II, Byron produces a spatial version of the Orient as a refuge from modernity; he and his alter ego venture into that space in search of otherness, and precisely in search of the sort of exchange and reciprocity with otherness that the Narrator of *Alastor* affirms. Against *Childe Harold's* dreams of an immortal, everlasting and immutably different East, Shelley's poem puts forward a vision of the East as a space for European redemption in evolution and in progress, in the development and improvement of others who turn out to be merely inferior versions of 'ourselves'.

Notes

A slightly different version of this chapter appears in Saree Makdisi, *Romantic Imperialism: Universal Empire and the Culture of Modernity* (Cambridge, 1998).

1   Mary Louise Pratt, 'Scratches on the Face of the Country; or, What Mr. Barrow Saw in the Land of the Bushmen,' in *'Race', Writing, and Difference*, ed. Henry Gates Jr (Chicago, 1986), 140.

2   Joseph-Marie Degérando, *The Observation of Savage Peoples* (1800). Quoted in Johannes Fabian, *Time and the Other: How Anthropology Makes Its Object* (New York, 1986), 7.

3   Percy Bysshe Shelley, *Alastor*, in *Shelley's Poetry and Prose*, eds Donald H. Reiman and Sharon B. Powers (New York and London, 1977), ll. 76–7.

4   *Ibid.*, ll. 78–81, 81, 429–30.

5   *Ibid.*, ll. 387–93 (emphasis added).

6   *Ibid.*, ll. 107–28.

7   The sphinx was damaged by Napoleon's artillery in 1798.

8   Not the Thebes in Greece, but the Thebes in Upper (that is, southern) Egypt, which was the Greek name for the capital of Upper Egypt, Luxor.

9   *Alastor*, ll. 129–39.

10 Lord Byron, *Childe Harold's Pilgrimage*, in Jerome J. McGann, ed., *The Complete Poetical Works*, 7 vols (Oxford, 1980–1993), 2: Canto II, st. 10.

11 Percy Bysshe Shelley, 'A Philosophical View of Reform', in *The Prose Works of Percy Bysshe Shelley*, ed. E. B. Murray, 2 vols (Oxford, 1993), 2: 225.

12 *Ibid.*, 226 (emphasis added).

13 See *Time and the Other*, 1–35.

14 Frantz Fanon, *The Wretched of the Earth*, trans. Constance Farrington (Harmondsworth, 1983), 38.

15 *Ibid.*, 38–9.

16 *Time and the Other*, 30.

17 To use one of Said's terms. See Edward Said, *Orientalism* (London and New York, 1978), 49–72.

18 'Philosophical View', 225–6.

19 Percy Bysshe Shelley, *Hellas*, in *Shelley's Poetry and Prose*, Preface, 408–9.

20 *Ibid.*, l. 1059, ll. 1060–3.

21 As my distinction between Byron and Shelley suggests, the relationship between different versions of philhellenism and imperialism needs to be examined much more closely. On the one hand, I am uneasy with Jerome McGann's proposition that Shelley's ideals, as expressed in his proclamation that 'we' are all Greeks, are 'typical philhellenist illusions, and, as such, were open to political exploitation by Europe's imperialist powers, as well as to poetical exploitation by writers like Shelley and Byron'. On the other hand, I have grave disagreements with Mark Kipperman's reductive assertion that, in the context of the eastern Mediterranean in the 1820s, 'philhellenism could be seen as nothing less than a challenge to the global order of empires negotiated in 1815'. Kipperman goes on to say that, 'Within its own forms and the real historical context it evokes, Shelley's idealism in *Hellas* does reflect the constitutionalist, nationalist, and essentially anti-imperialist progressivism of his time'. I believe that Shelley represents a much more aggressive form of colonialism than Byron, precisely because his imperial world view is fired by progressivism, whereas Byron's is sustained by some sort of respect in the inalterable otherness of other cultures, a respect that, at least in his 1812 *Childe Harold*, tempered his philhellenism. But the point is not that Shelley was imperialist and Byron was anti-imperialist; as I have tried to suggest, their different approaches to and versions of philhellenism and orientalism correspond to different moments or phases of imperial development. See Jerome McGann, *The Romantic Ideology* (Chicago, 1983), 125; and Mark Kipperman, 'Macropolitics of Utopia: Shelley's *Hellas* in Context,' in *The Macropolitics of Nineteenth-century Literature*, ed. Jonathan Arac (Philadelphia, 1991), 92.

22 See Martin Bernal, *Black Athena: The Afroasiatic Roots of Classical Civilization* (New Brunswick, 1985), 189–245.

23 See Earl Wasserman, *Shelley: A Critical Reading* (Baltimore, 1971), 3–46.

24 See Martyn Crucefix, 'Wordsworth, Superstition, and Shelley's *Alastor*', *Essays in Criticism* 33 (April 1983), 126–47; Christopher Heppner, '*Alastor*: The Poet and the Narrator Reconsidered,' *Keats–Shelley Journal* 37 (1988), 91–109; Frederick Kirchhoff, 'Shelley's *Alastor*: The Poet Who Refuses to Write Language', *Keats–Shelley Journal* 32 (1983), 108–22.

25 Harold Bloom, *The Visionary Company: A Reading of English Romantic Poetry* (Ithaca, 1971), 289.
26 Heppner, '*Alastor*: The Poet', 97; Edward Strickland, 'Transfigured Night: The Visionary Inversions of *Alastor*', *Keats–Shelley Journal* 33 (1984), 148–60 (152); John Rieder, 'Description of a Struggle: Shelley's Radicalism on Wordsworth's Terrain', *Boundary* 2, 13: 2–3 (1985), 267–87 (273).

Index

Note: literary works are listed under authors' names; page numbers in italic refer to illustrations; 'n' after a page reference indicates a note number on that page.

Index